D0603208

CONTEMPORARY *WEDDING CAKES*

CONTEMPORARY *WEDDING CAKES*

NADENE HURST
JULIE SPRINGALL

Contents

Authors' dedications

My contribution to this book is dedicated to my husband, Bruce, who is my constant source of love, help and support. My grateful thanks to Kathleen for her help with the flowers. NH

Dedicated to my husband, Mikey, thanks for your love, encouragement, constructive criticism and for reworking my templates; also to Chloe, our chocolate cake baker and tester. JS

Introduction

A request for a wedding cake is both special and daunting at the same time. For most people their wedding day is one of the most important days in their life, and the wedding cake is a centrepiece, worthy of careful planning and execution. With the help of these designs, you will be able to create a cake to match almost anyone's dreams and expectations. A variety of styles, mediums and techniques are offered, reflecting the growing trend for something different and unusual, therefore traditional ideas have been updated to respond to this demand. We hope you like our ideas and enjoy making the cakes.

Nadene Hurst

When I first came across sugarpaste I was amazed how versatile it was. I was inspired by the work of Greg and Max and their approach to cake decoration, along with other new decorators, although I now feel wedding cakes got left behind in the cake revolution and need a fresher, modern approach for the millennium. I have gone for bold and dramatic colours, taking inspiration from greetings cards, interior design and artists' works. I have designed a couple of classic cakes but given them a modern look with a quirky touch here and there. I hope we will inspire some of you to create your own works of art.

Julie Springall

Royal-iced wedding cakes

Royal icing is the traditional form of decoration used for wedding cakes and cakes created for special occasions. Its flat surface and delicate finish creates a very versatile style, which is of great beauty and elegance when executed to a good standard. The cakes in this section reflect a variety of the techniques possible with this classical medium, while representing an up-to-date approach to cake design.

Royal icing techniques

Royal icing is extremely versatile: it can be spread to give a flawlessly smooth top coating to fruit cakes, piped into bulbs, loops and scrolls, or thinned down into run icing and used to create any number of decorative shapes.

HOW TO MAKE ROYAL ICING

Making royal icing with an electric mixer

45g (1½oz) albumen powder
315ml (10fl oz/1¼cups) water
1.75kg (3½lb/14cups) icing (confectioners') sugar, sieved

Method

1. Dissolve the albumen powder in the water, strain and measure out 315ml (10fl oz/1¼cups).

2. Place the liquid in a clean, fat-free, mixer bowl with the icing sugar, and stir to combine the ingredients.

3. Using an electric mixer, set to the slowest speed, beat the mixture until the required consistency is reached (see page 11).

Electric mixer

Although not an essential piece of equipment, an electric mixer will save time when making royal icing. Beating times will vary according to the speed of the individual mixer, but are about five minutes to create soft peak icing (used for the first coat and to fill writing tubes [tips]) and seven minutes to create full peak icing (used for piping work, see page 12).

Making royal icing by hand

30g (1oz) albumen powder
60ml (2fl oz/¼cup) water
455g (1lb/4cups) icing (confectioners') sugar, sieved
(Do not attempt to make more than 500g [1lb] at one time)

Method

1. Dissolve the albumen powder in the water, then strain.

2. Place the albumen mixture in a large, clean bowl.

3. Gradually add the icing sugar, one tablespoon at a time, and beat the two together. It will take about 20 minutes to reach soft peak consistency.

Storing

Cover the royal icing with a damp cloth whilst working, to avoid a crust forming. Store in an airtight container, with cling film (plastic wrap) on the surface. It is not necessary to keep the icing refrigerated. Re-beat the icing to its original consistency, preferably in a mixer, at least every two days or the icing will lose aeration and will be difficult to work with.

Albumen (egg white) powder

Powdered egg white is recommended for making royal icing, as it complies with food safety standards and gives consistent results, which can be difficult with fresh egg whites, due to the variation in egg sizes and water content. Being able to accurately measure the ingredients makes royal icing simple to make.

Albumen powders are available either as pure albumen (below right) or as an albumen substitute (below left). Albumen substitutes are cheaper, and can be used for most tasks, particularly coating, as they produce a slightly crumbly icing, which is easier to cut. Pure albumen powder is stronger. Use when working on delicate designs, such as brush embroidery, stringwork, lace and separately piped decorations.

Pure albumen is a deeper colour than the substitute. When mixed with water, the substitute will dissolve, but pure albumen forms a sticky mass, and needs to be soaked for at least one hour to dissolve. Sieve both solutions before use.

❋ ❋ ❋ ❋

Royal icing techniques

Icing (confectioners') sugar

There are different grades of icing sugar available, the most suitable being 'bride cake' icing sugar, which is extra fine and does not require sieving before use.

If possible avoid using icing sugars with cornflour (cornstarch) added. Differing amounts are present, depending on the manufacturer, and these icing sugars often require extra moisture to obtain the correct consistency. Icing made with this type of icing sugar also loses aeration quickly, meaning that you will need to re-beat it more often.

Glycerine

Glycerine is often added to royal icing to prevent it from drying too hard, and making it difficult to cut. Add one teaspoon of glycerine to every 500g (1lb) of royal icing just before use. Never add glycerine to run icing (see page 13) as it will prevent the run-outs from drying thoroughly. Other additions to royal icing, for various reasons, are stated in the instructions for the cakes.

Using royal icing

Covering a cake with royal icing

Three coats of royal icing should be applied to a marzipanned cake, leaving the cake to dry for about eight hours between each layer. Use soft-peak icing for the first coat, then add water to soften the icing slightly for the second coat, then soften again to apply the final coat.

Top coating a round or square cake

Spread a little royal icing over the top of the cake with a palette knife (metal spatula). Hold the knife horizontally and work it backwards and forwards to eliminate any air bubbles in the icing. Spread the icing evenly to the edges of the cake. Take the cake from the turntable, and place it on the work surface, placing the board on a cloth or mat to prevent it from slipping while you are working on it. Draw a clean straightedge over the top of the cake in one continuous movement to create a smooth finish (use a straightedge that is as long as the width of the cake). Leave to dry before coating the sides of the cake.

Side coating a round cake

Place the cake on a turntable and start applying the royal icing to the side of the cake with a palette knife. Hold the knife vertically and position your finger at the back of the blade to apply pressure to the icing and disperse any air bubbles. Rotate the cake and paddle the icing as you work to form an even thickness.

Ensure that the icing covers the cake from top to bottom and that no marzipan can be seen. Use a plain cake smoother, pulling it round the cake in one smooth, even movement. When the scraper has been pulled around the whole cake, pull it off towards yourself to finish.

This will leave a 'take off' mark, which will be removed later in the process. Neaten the top edge of the cake, and the board, with the palette knife before leaving the icing to dry.

Side coating a square cake

Coat the first side of a square cake in the same way as a round cake. Move the scraper along the side, and at the

Icing consistency

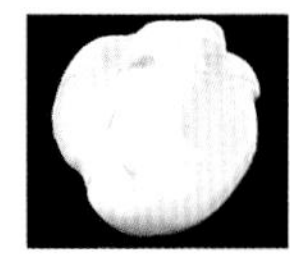

Soft peak is the first consistency reached during beating, and is used for coating the cake and piping with writing tubes (tips). When lifted from the bowl with a spatula, soft peak icing should retain a peak that will hold its shape but not be stiff and over-firm.

Full peak is a stiffer, firmer consistency, leaving a definite peak when lifted from the bowl with a spatula, which will not fall when shaken. Use full peak icing for piping decorative borders that need to retain their shape as soon as they are piped.

end of the side pull the scraper off towards yourself. Start the second side by bringing the 'take off' mark from the previous side round and onto the second side. Repeat this process until all four sides of the cake are coated. Always ensure that all the edges are neat before leaving to dry.

Coating a cake board with royal icing

Coating cake boards can be done in two ways. The easier and quicker method is to leave the board until you have finished coating the final side of the cake then, while the icing is still wet, coat the board with a soft consistency of icing, resembling thick run icing. Smooth the top with a palette knife, without removing any of the icing. Trim any excess icing from the edge of the board, then allow it to settle and dry.

Alternatively, for a better finish, coat the boards separately from the cakes. Smaller sizes of boards can be coated with icing all the way across, while the larger boards should be coated with a 8cm (3in) band of royal icing around the edge.

Coat the cakes on temporary boards, also placing a thin cake card, the same size and shape as the cake, underneath. This thin cake card should be kept under the cake when it is transferred to the final board to avoid any staining on the icing from the fruit cake, and the cake becoming sticky underneath.

The cake can be removed from the temporary cake board by scoring round the base with a scalpel, before gently pulling it off.

Piping royal icing

Piping is the extrusion of royal icing from tubes (tips) to form straight and curved lines, and is used in the designs of most royal-iced cakes. First, select the size of tube that you wish to use. When piping, take care not to overfill the piping bag with icing. It is more comfortable and easier to pipe using a bag that is only about two-thirds full of icing.

Both linework piping and piping borders require accurate control of pressure against speed; however there is a difference in holding the bag. When piping borders, you will be using a greater volume of icing with tubes of a wider aperture; therefore grip the bag firmly in one hand to force the icing through the tube. When piping fine linework using small tubes, hold the bag in one hand but support it with the other, which will stop your hand shaking and will also help create an accurate line.

Take-off marks

The softer icing used for the final coat is much finer, and is easier to handle on the final coat if you scrape off most of the excess icing first, then repeat, pressing harder, for a perfect finish. Take-off marks are reduced by using progressively softer coats of icing. If you are left with an unsightly take-off mark on the final side coating, wait until it is dry, then carefully shave it off with a scalpel, and paint over the whitish mark with a clean, damp paintbrush.

Colouring royal icing

There are a variety of colourings that are suitable for use with royal icing. The advantage of liquid colouring is that it can be measured into the icing with a dropper. Count the necessary number of drops of liquid colouring into each 500g (1lb) of royal icing to

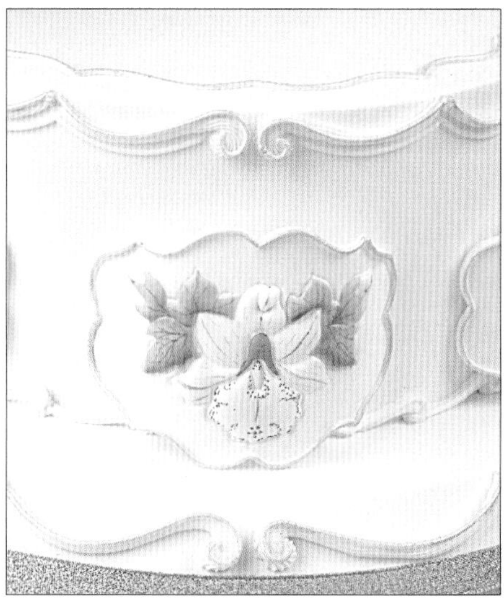

achieve the desired colour. This way an exact colour can be repeated accurately for other batches of icing, as required. Paste colours are not recommended for royal icing, except for small amounts where an accurate repeat of the colour is not required.

Liquid food colourings can be mixed together to produce a desired shade. Blend and experiment with different colours, using spare icing, before starting to decorate the cake.

To paint royal icing, mix the liquid colouring with a little white powder and water on a white plate or tile. Use the paintbrush drier rather than wet, painting the colour in broad strokes with a larger brush to cover the main areas, and smaller strokes with smaller brushes to paint details.

Royal icing techniques

Run icing

Use thinned royal icing to create decorative shapes which, when hard, can be used on the cake. Thin the icing with water until it resembles thick cream. The consistency will vary according to the desired use, but generally, the smaller and narrower

the area to be covered, the thicker the run icing needs to be.

Place the pattern under run-out film. Outline with a piped line of royal icing, using a writing tube. Thin the icing with water and pour into a piping bag without a tube. Cut a small hole in the end, about the size of a no.2 tube, and fill in the outline, covering the outline with run icing. Place the pieces under direct heat, such as an angle poise lamp fitted with a reflector bulb, until a shiny crust has formed, then leave in a warm place to dry. When the pieces are hard transfer them to the cake.

Where no outline is used, for example when creating lettering, the consistency should be thick enough to smooth, but hold its shape well.

Problems and causes with run icing

Air bubbles: *hole too big in piping bag*
Dull finish: *not enough direct heat or slow drying*
Uneven finish: *consistency too thick or insufficient run icing*
Will not dry: *Not enough heat or using poorly aerated icing*
Sinking: *too much water or slow drying*
Streaky: *icing not mixed properly*
Scratches: *water on paintbrush*

HOW TO MAKE PASTILLAGE

The surface of dried pastillage is very similar to a royal-iced coating, and the two mediums combine very well. It is useful for off-pieces, particularly on curves, and for making ornaments as it dries very hard. Pastillage can be purchased ready-made, or can be made using the following recipe.

1½ teaspoons powdered gelatine
60ml (2fl oz/¼cup) water
½ teaspoon gum tragacanth
455g (1lb/4cups) icing (confectioners') sugar

Method

1. Sprinkle the gelatine on the water and leave to sponge.

2. Sieve the gum tragacanth and icing sugar together into a mixing bowl, and warm gently.

3. Dissolve the gelatine mixture slowly over a pan of hot water.

4. Add the gelatine to the icing sugar mixture and beat on a slow speed in an electric mixer for approximately three minutes.

5. Scoop the soft paste into a polythene bag and store in an airtight container in the refrigerator. Leave for 24 hours before use, then knead until smooth, and roll out.

Working with pastillage

Place a piece of thick run-out film on a flat board and tape down at the corners. Dust lightly with icing sugar. Roll out the pastillage to the required thickness on the board. Cut out the pieces, and remove the excess paste, leaving the cut-outs on the board. Press down lightly on the pieces with a smoother and leave to dry (the paste sticks to the film, preventing it from distorting while drying). Remove the cut-outs from the film by sliding a cranked palette knife underneath. This paste skins over very quickly, so keep covered with cling film (plastic wrap) as much as possible when working. (See page 17.)

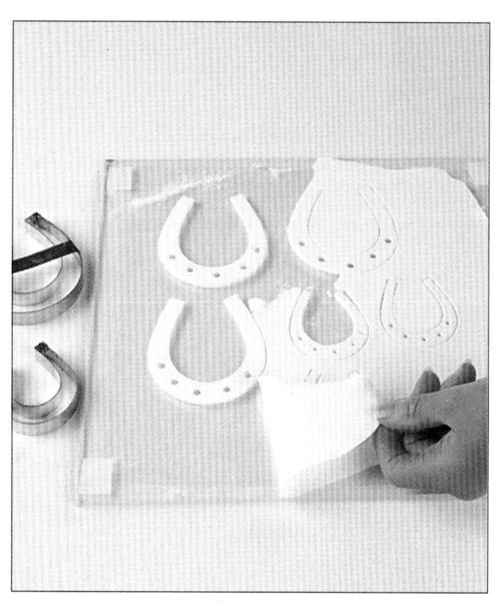

Springtime daisy

Stringwork is a striking technique that could fill a cake decorator with fear. However, if the icing is prepared correctly, then these loops are easy to pipe and dry surprisingly quickly. Once the piping is dry, the cakes can be transported safely and the piping will remain in place.

✳  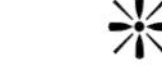

CAKE AND DECORATION

18cm (7in) and 28cm (11in) round fruit cakes
25cm (10in) and 35cm (14in) round cake boards
2.5kg (5lb) marzipan
3kg (6lb) royal icing
Cream liquid food colouring [MF]
Silver dusting powder (petal dust/blossom tint)
Gum tragacanth
Liquid glucose
60g (2oz) flower paste
125g (4oz) pastillage
1cm (1/2in) wide silver ribbon
6mm (1/4in) wide silver ribbon
Small wired arrangement of silk or sugar daisies and leaves
Yellow sugartex [S]

ESSENTIAL EQUIPMENT

Compass
Paper template (see step 2)
Small natural sponge
Cake scraper
Nos.1 and 3 piping tubes (tips)
No.16 large plain piping tube
Tilting turntable
Eight-petalled daisy cutter [TKT]
Ball tool
Large and small horseshoe cutters [TKT]
Cake stand

1 Marzipan the two round cakes (see page 143). Colour the royal icing by adding one drop of cream food colouring to every 500g (1lb) royal icing. Apply three coats of cream-coloured royal icing to the cakes; the boards will only need one coat.

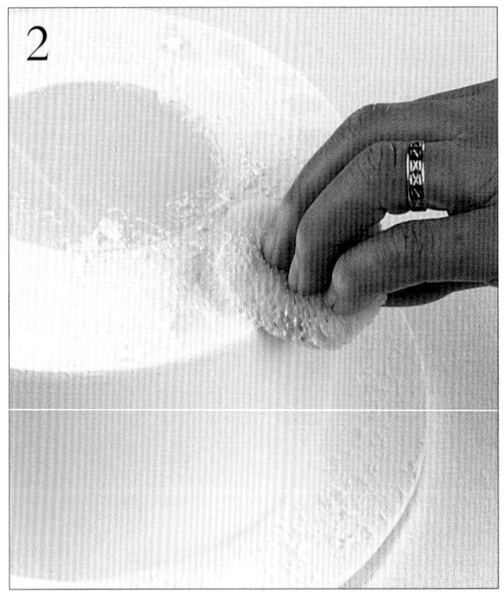
2

2 When dry, use white royal icing to stipple the top of the base tier and both cake boards, using a small, slightly damp sponge. Make a circular paper template measuring 8.5cm (3 1/4in) in diameter and place it on the top tier of the cake. Hold it firmly in place while you stipple around the rest of the area. When dry, dust the cake with silver dusting powder (petal dust/blossom tint).

3 Make two paper templates the same depth and circumference as each cake. Fold the template for the top tier into eight sections and the template for the bottom one into twelve. When folded, cut small notches in the corners, top and bottom, to act as markers. Fasten the templates around the cakes.

4 To prepare the icing for the bulbs and the stringwork, place a little royal icing on a cake scraper and add to it approximately one-eighth of a teaspoon of gum tragacanth and one-quarter of a teaspoon of liquid glucose. Paddle the ingredients together to mix them thoroughly, then place in a piping bag fitted with a no.1 tube (tip).

Helpful Hint

Gum tragacanth makes the icing harden quickly, enabling you to work faster. It also makes the icing stronger, so it is less likely to be damaged when moving the cake. Liquid glucose helps the icing to stretch more easily, which is invaluable when piping several rows of loops.

5 Using the notches in the templates as a guide, pipe tiny bulbs around the base of the larger cake in order to mark out the different sections. Pipe larger bulbs around the top edge of the cake,

5

pulling out each one as you pipe to form a tall bulb. Allow the icing to dry, repeat for the other cake, then carefully remove the templates.

6 Pipe a series of bulbs around the side of the cake – measure the exact position by placing a ruler against the side of the cake and lining it up with the top and base bulbs. Pipe two additional bulbs, in the same way as the top ones (see step 5) and position them at 3cm (1 1/4in) intervals down the side of the cake. As before, repeat for the other cake.

7 Elevate the turntable to eye level and then tilt it towards you. Place the larger cake on the turntable and pipe a row of loops around the top of the cake from bulb to bulb. Make the loops approximately 1cm (1/2in) deep and allow them to hang free of the cake – pause for a moment in between piping each loop so that the icing can set. Pipe two additional rows of loops further down the cake in between every other bulb.

8 When the piping is dry, level the turntable and carefully turn the cake over, so that it is upside down, and replace. (The larger cake will overhang the turntable giving you clear access to the loops.) Using a no.1 tube, pipe suspended loops all around the top edge of the cake. Try to make them as close in size as possible to the first set of loops and of equal distance apart. Repeat the loops around the side of the cakes.

9 Overpipe all the bulbs with another tall bulb of icing. Allow to dry, then pipe a second row of

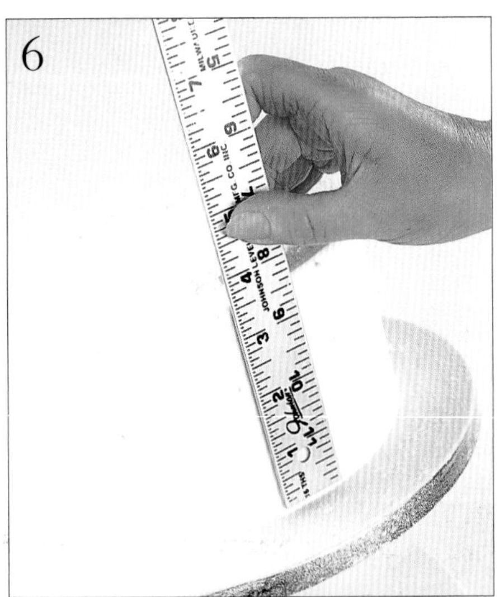

6

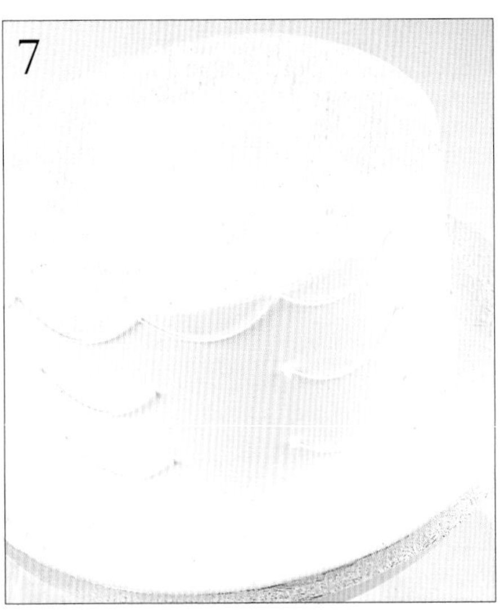

7

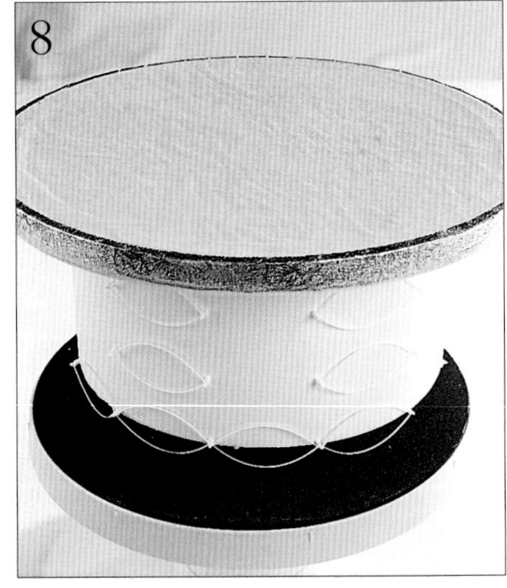

8

✳ ✳ ✳ ✳

Springtime daisy

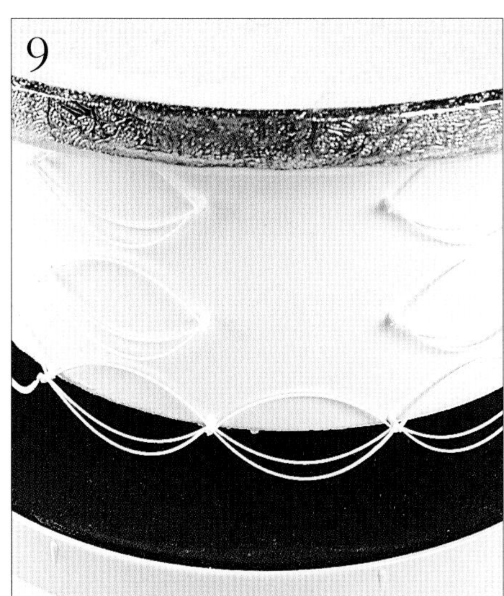

9

loops around the edge of the cake. Use a steady hand to make them hang below each loop on the first row.

10 When the icing is dry, turn the cake the right way up. Tilt the turntable and pipe the second row of loops around the side. Leave to dry, then remove the cake from the turntable.

11 Repeat steps 7 to 10 for the smaller cake, with the turntable straight. At the turning stage support the cake in the centre with a small bowl or cake tin (pan), so that the edge of the cake will hang free.

12 To make the daisies, roll out some flower paste and cut out 60 flowers with an eight-petalled daisy cutter. Place each flower on a firm pad and mark a line down the centre of each petal with a pin. Press a ball tool into the centre for a curved effect. Pipe in a bulb of royal icing and sprinkle it with yellow sugartex before the icing dries. Attach a daisy over the join of each loop.

12

Helpful Hint

To make your own texture powder (sugartex), put a small amount of semolina powder, or ground rice, in a jar with some yellow dusting powder (petal dust/blossom tint). Screw on the lid and shake vigorously.

13 For the top decoration, roll out the pastillage (see page 13) and cut out a 8cm (3in) disc. Then cut a large and small horseshoe using the horseshoe cutters. Use nos.3 and 16 piping tubes to cut out small holes in the horseshoes.

When dry, brush the decoration with silver dusting powder and attach a 6mm (1/4in) silver ribbon to the back of the large horseshoe. Pipe a large bulb of icing onto one side of the pastillage disc and stand both horseshoes on it, supporting them with a piece of sponge foam until the icing is set.

14 Place the decoration on the top. Wire a small spray of silk or sugar daisies and leaves together and arrange in front of the horseshoes.

13

Victorian nostalgia

This cake takes us back to the traditional art of royal icing, employing the skills of past masters. It presents the opportunity to test your piping expertise in the form of double scrolls and intricate decorations, with particular emphasis on frill piping which gives this pretty 'hemmed' effect.

Cake and decoration

Two 23cm (9in) round fruit cakes, 5½cm (2¼in) deep
28cm (11in), 30cm (12in) and 32cm (13in) round cake boards
1.5kg (3lb) marzipan
2kg (4lb) royal icing
Cream liquid food colouring [MF]
24 piped, or silk, miniature roses
1cm (½in) wide gold ribbon
Gum tragacanth
Glycerine

Essential equipment

Templates and patterns (page 147)
Nos.1.5 and 3 piping tubes (tips)
Nos.32, 43 and 44 shell piping tubes
No.52 leaf piping tube
No.57 petal piping tube
No.060 frill piping tube
Nylon piping bag and adaptor
4cm (1¾in) diameter plastic tubing, cut into 10cm (4in) lengths
Run-out film
Double (or single) modelling curves

1 To make a chamfered cake board, stick all the boards together with glue, with the smallest one on top, leaving an even margin all around. Sandwich together the cakes with apricot jam or masking jelly, with a thin layer of marzipan between. Centre the cake on the triple-board.

2 Marzipan the cake (see page 143) and place it on the boards. Colour the royal icing by adding the required number of drops of liquid cream colouring to every 500g (1lb) royal icing. Coat the top of the cake and fill in the gap between the boards to form a gradual slope (see page 12) at the same time. Complete three coats of cream royal icing to the cake and board. Coat the top of the board at the same time as the final side coat.

3 Measure the circumference of the cake, cut out a template the same length, which is also 9cm (3½in) deep. Fold this strip into eight sections, mark, and cut out a shallow semicircle from the top and bottom of each one. Attach this to the side of

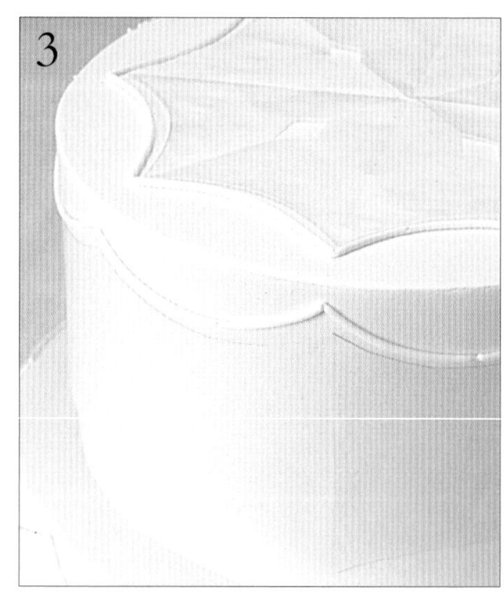

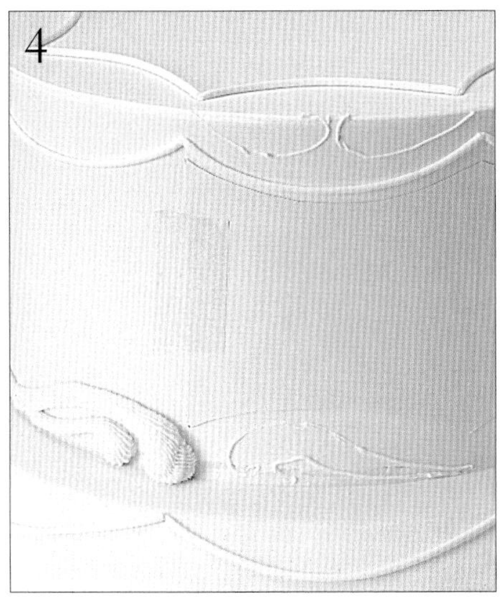

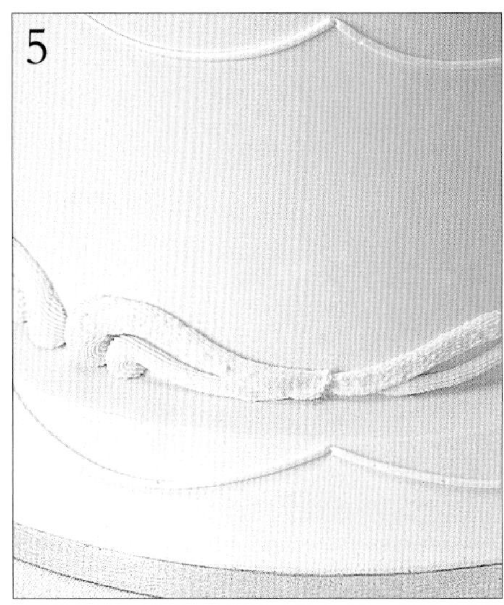

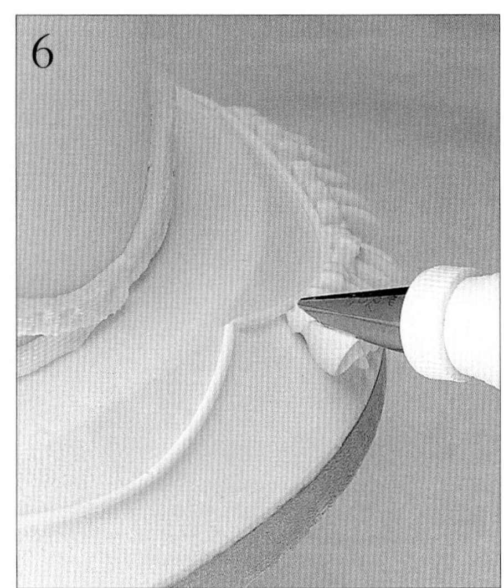

the cake, 1cm (½in) from the top edge. Make the top template by folding a 20cm (8in) circle into eight sections, then cut a semicircle from each one. Place it on the cake and line up with the points on the sides.

Using a no.3 tube (tip), pipe a line of icing around the top template, and above the top edge of the side one. Pipe the semicircles on the slope of the board, lining up the points with those on the cake. Do not drop the line below the halfway point of the slope to allow space for the frill.

Helpful Hint

Adding 1 teaspoon of glycerine to each 500g (1lb) of icing will enable you to easily cut through the coating and decoration.

4 Scratch pipe the shape of the scrolls at the top edge and base of the cake using a no.2 tube; this gives you a line to follow with the scroll tube. Scratch piping is performed freehand, fitting the shape of the scroll into the space available.

5 Using a no.32 tube, pipe the 'S' scrolls around the base, over the scratch piping. This makes it easier to see than a scribed line when you are following with a thicker tube.

6 Using a no.060 tube, pipe the frills below the line on the slope. Lift the tube and push it backwards slightly each time you touch the surface to form the frilled effect. By this method, you will also pipe the top 'hemmed' effect at the same time.

7 Pipe the top edge 'S' scrolls, and the long 'C' scrolls over the edge of the frills using a no.44 tube.

8 Overpipe the no.32 base scrolls with a no.44 tube. It is necessary to work in a sequence when piping, as it allows the scrolls to dry a little in between, making overpiping easier.

9 Remove the templates, pipe another no.3 line inside the top design and below the loops on the side linework. Then overpipe the original lines using the same tube.

10 Overpipe all the no.44 piping with a no.43 tube, and then again with a no.3 tube. Keep the piping along the centre of the scroll or the line beneath.

11 Pipe the miniature roses onto greaseproof (wax baking) paper, using a no.57 petal tube. Before filling the piping bag, add extra cream liquid food colouring to the royal icing to achieve a rich gold colour. Attach the roses by piping three leaves onto the cake with no.52

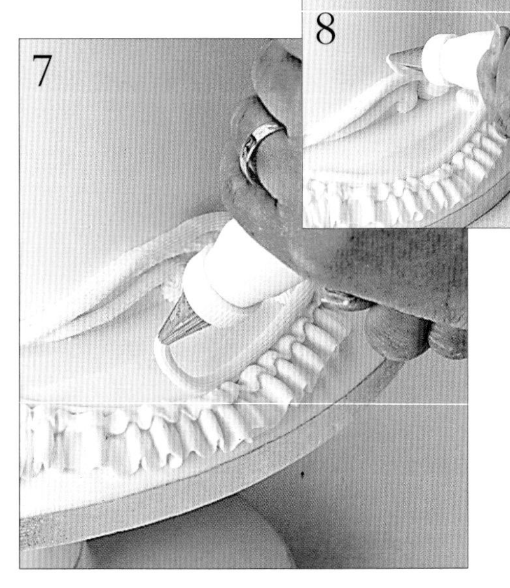

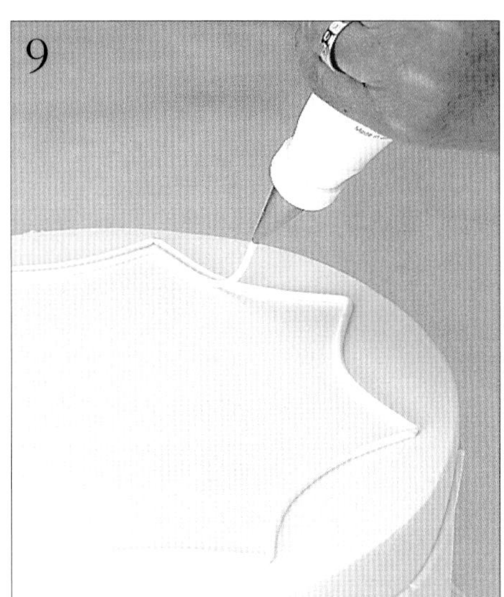

tube, and pressing the flowers into them while still wet. Wiggle the tube as you pipe to vary the finish.

12 To make the top rings, place the pattern (see page 147) around a piece of tubing, cover with run-out film, and secure with the minimum of adhesive tape.

Before placing the icing in the piping bag, add a pinch of gum tragacanth to strengthen the icing, then paddle it to remove as many air bubbles as possible.

Helpful Hint

Do not use icing containing glycerine, or the rings will disintegrate when you try to remove them from the curves.

Pipe the outline and the trellis lines with a no.1.5 tube, adding an extra line in between the ones drawn on the pattern. Then overpipe the outline, and pipe a line down the centre, using a no.3 tube. Repeat this until you have eight rings. When the

piping is dry, cut away the tape, and slide each ring off its tube. Place them upside-down on sponge foam and peel away the film. Pipe a line of icing along the short edges to attach them to the cake.

13 For the side decorations, place the pattern (see page 147)

under run-out film, on a double or single modelling curve. Pipe the trellis and outlines using a no.1.5 tube. Then overpipe the outline and down the centre with a no.3 tube. When the decorations are dry, slide them off the curves and attach each one to the cake with bulbs of royal icing at top and bottom.

14 Trim the edge of the cake board with a length of 1cm (½in) wide gold ribbon.

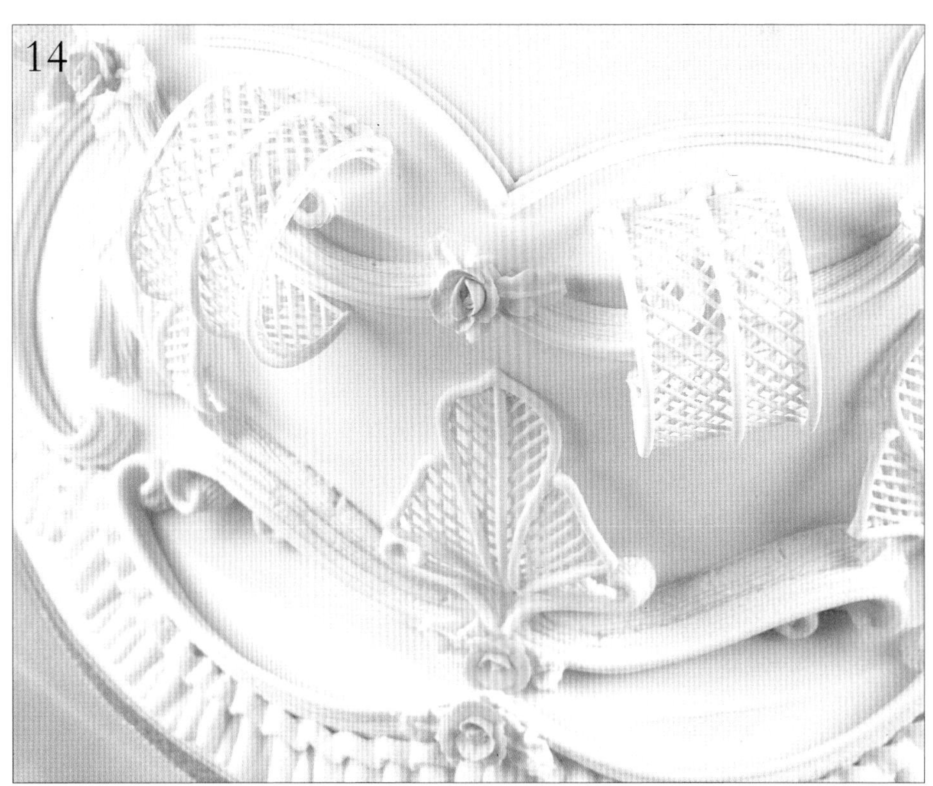

Briar rose

Run-out collar pieces and panels make this cake a sugar jigsaw puzzle. Placing the hexagonal cakes on round boards adds more space for matching decoration, while the addition of delicate briar roses give colour to the design, and the scribed bible provides a personal touch.

CAKE AND DECORATION

18cm (7in) and 25cm (10in) hexagonal fruit cakes
25cm (10in) and 35cm (14in) round cake boards
2.5kg (5lb) marzipan
3kg (6lb) royal icing
Peach and yellow liquid food colourings
30g (1oz) pastillage
60g (2oz) sugarpaste (rolled fondant)
30g (1oz) flower paste
Gold dusting powder (petal dust/blossom tint)
1cm (½in) wide peach ribbon
Sugar, silk or fresh briar roses

ESSENTIAL EQUIPMENT

Templates and patterns (see page 147)
Run-out film
Nos.0 and 1 piping tubes (tips)
No.43 shell piping tube
Impression mat [CC]
Playing card cutter [J]
3cm (1¼in) diameter modelling curves [W]
No.3 paintbrush
Perspex bible stand [SC]
Perspex cake separators

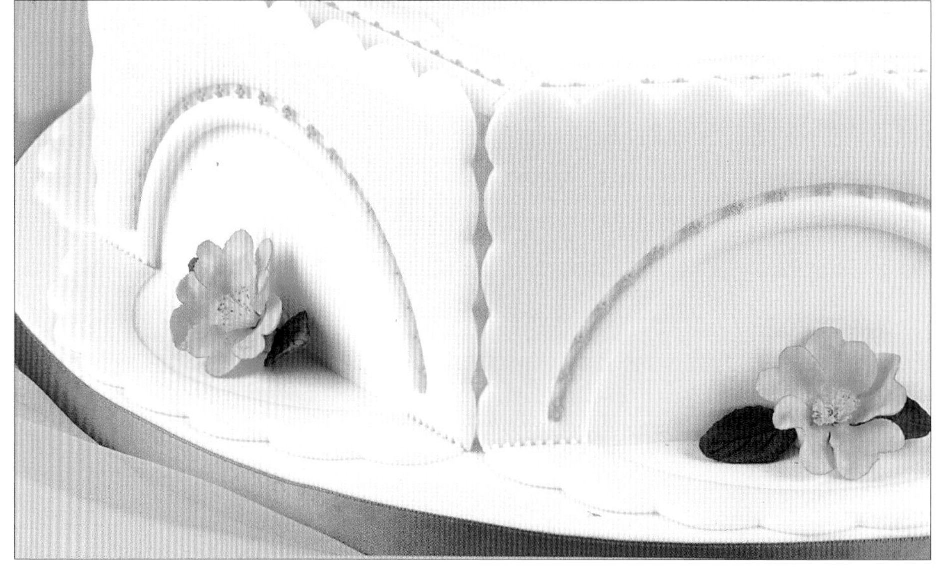

1 Marzipan the two hexagonal cakes (see page 143). Apply three coats of pale-peach royal icing (see page 12), coating the boards at the same time as the final side coat.

HELPFUL HINT

Check that the measurements of the sides of the cakes are equal before marzipanning, and if they are not, adjust accordingly. This is easier than correcting the shape with the coating. It may be necessary to adjust the size of the patterns for the panels.

2 Place all the patterns under run-out film, and outline using a no.1 tube (tip). You will need six of each of the pattern side panels, top collar sections and board run-out pieces. As you pipe the scalloped edges, extend each semicircle into the area of the run icing, then start the next one from the side of this line (see below). This will ensure neat indents when the pieces are finished. (Try outlining with no.0 tube for an even daintier appearance.) When outlining the cut-out sections, extend the outlines

2

ON
14TH
MARCH
2000
JULIE
&
JAMES

Pink orchid

Dried pastillage, with a surface similar to a royal-iced coating, provides a simple way of producing curved panels for this three-tiered cake. The directly piped run-outs work particularly well on this medium, and the linework and 'S' scrolls give a truly regal effect.

CAKE AND DECORATION

15cm (6in), 20cm (8in) and 25cm (10in) round fruit cakes
23cm (9in), 25cm (10in), 28cm (11in), 30cm (12in), 32cm (13in) and 35cm (14in) round cake boards
3kg (6lb) marzipan
3.5kg (7lb) royal icing
500g (1lb) pastillage
Pink and green liquid food colourings
Silver and white dusting powders (petal dusts/blossom tints)
Clear alcohol
Gum tragacanth
1cm (½in) wide silver ribbon
Two sugar, silk or fresh orchids

ESSENTIAL EQUIPMENT

Templates (see page 149)
Plaque cutter [OP]
Small orchid cutter [PC]
Six 11cm (4½in) diameter modelling curves
No.3 paintbrush
No.2 piping tube (tip)
No.44 shell piping tube
Piping bag with adaptor (optional)
Tilting turntable (optional)
Three-tiered cake stand

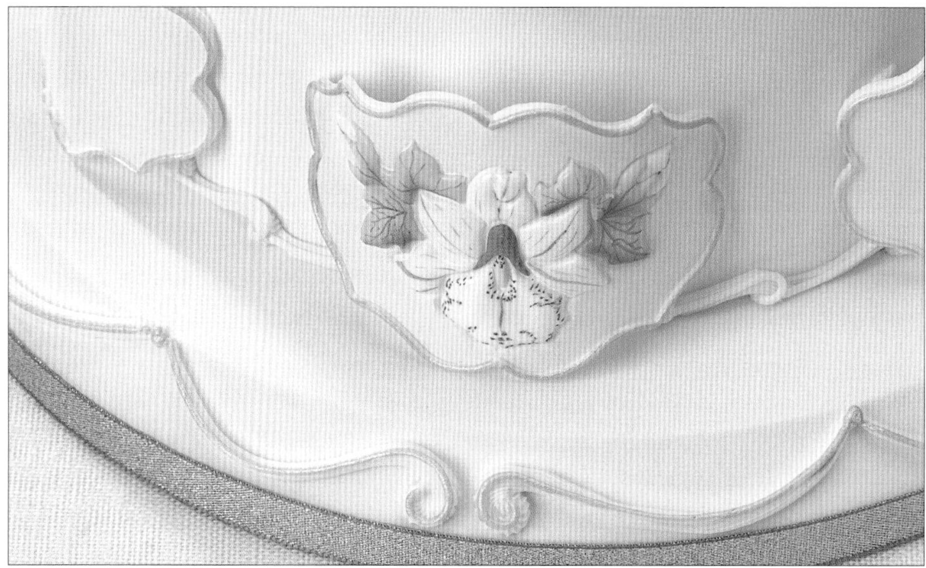

1 Prepare the boards by sticking with glue the 23cm (9in) to the 25cm (10in) board, the 28cm (11in) to the 30cm (12in) board, and the 32cm (13in) to the 35cm (14in) board, making sure the top boards are in the centre of the base ones. Place weights on top and leave the boards to dry. Fill in the gap between each of the joined boards with royal icing, smoothing to a gradual slope.

2 Marzipan the three cakes (see page 143) and place them on the boards. Weigh out 500g (1lb) of royal icing and add, drop by drop, pink liquid food colouring until a pale pink colour is achieved. (This ratio can then be repeated to replicate the colour exactly when matching up the pastillage.) Using the pink royal icing, coat the top and sides of each cake. Apply three coats to each cake, coating the cake board slopes at the same time as the top of the cakes. When applying the final side coat, also coat the top of the boards with a soft consistency icing.

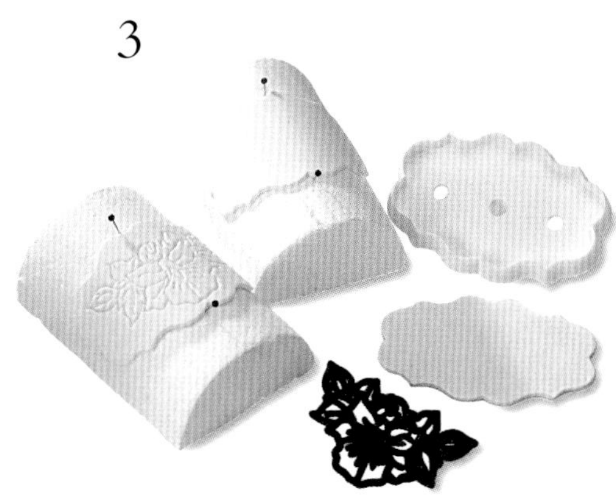

3 To make the side panels, colour the pastillage pale pink to match the cake coating (this should be done using the same ratio as for the royal icing). Make four panels for the top, six for the middle, and eight for the base tier. Thinly roll out a small amount of pastillage at a time, and cut out the side panels with a plaque cutter, impressing half of them with the orchid cutter. Immediately, place each one on a modelling curve to dry. Always work quickly when using pastillage, as it soon 'skins over' and will crack if overhandled.

4 To decorate the panels, use the orchid-cutter impression as an outline and fill in the sections with a thick consistency of coloured run icing (see page 13). Use white for the buds and orchids, with a deep pink centre, and pale green for the leaves. Allow each section to skin over before proceeding to the next. Place under the direct heat of an angle poise lamp to dry to a good shine. It is best to work in sequence when colouring the plaques, so that one section can be skinning over under the lamp while you work on another section of a different plaque.

5 Paint in the shading and details with the pink and green food colourings, using white dusting powder (petal dust/blossom tint) to reduce the strong colours. With a no.2 tube (tip), pipe a line around the edge of each panel, piping the ends of the lines into scrolls at the centre top and bottom of the plain panels. When the piping is dry, paint the line, using a mixture of silver dusting powder and clear alcohol. Use a no.3 paintbrush, only loading the tip of the bristles with the paint.

6 To make the ornament for the top of the cake, use the same cutter as for the side panels. Cut out two panels for the uprights and straighten them out at one end. Place the panels on a modelling curve, securing with pins to keep their shape, and cut out an oval from the centre of each one. Cut out a full plaque for the base and allow it to dry flat. Pipe a no.2 line around all the edges, and paint silver to match the side panels.

Helpful Hint

If the silver dusting powder and clear alcohol mixture is too pale, add a small amount of dark grey dusting powder.

7 To assemble, stand the cut-out sections upright on the base plaque, and secure with a little royal icing. When dry, fix a small ball of pastillage in the centre, and insert the two orchids and silver ribbons.

8 Cut out the linework templates (see page 149) in greaseproof (wax baking) paper and place them

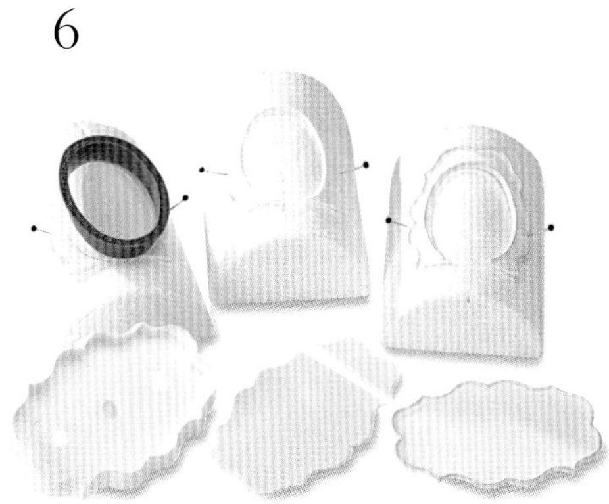

6

on top of the cakes. It can be helpful to place a few coins round the edge of a template to hold it in place. Pipe around the edge of the template with a no.2 tube. Divide the edge of the cakes by piping a small marker bulb in line with each point on the template. Pipe bulbs at the base of the cake, below the marked points, and on the edge of the slope of the board. These can be covered by the heavier piping later.

9 Pipe two 'S' scrolls, using a no.44 tube, between each of the marker bulbs around the top of the cakes, with the tails meeting on the marked points. Overpipe with a no.2 line, and pipe a dropped line below each one. A no.2 bulb will cover the joining of the tails. Pipe small 'S' scrolls around the base of the cakes, and overpipe with a no.2 tube, all in one direction.

Helpful Hint

For convenience, use a fabric piping bag fitted with an adaptor for scroll piping. The bag holds a large quantity of royal icing and the tubes can be changed easily.

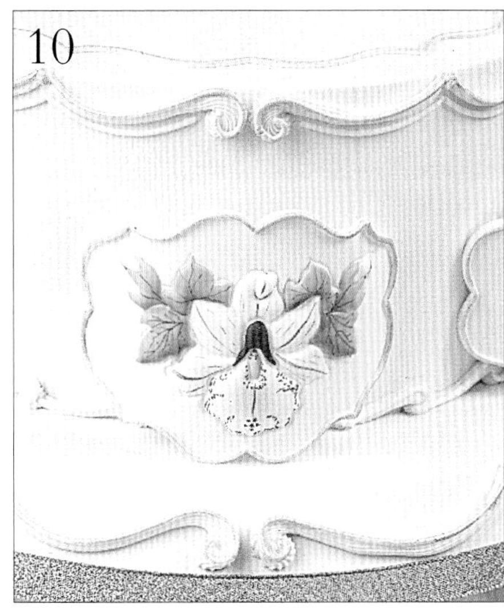

10

10 Pipe 'S' scrolls on the slope of the boards to match the ones on the top edge of the cake, but make them longer so that the tails finish in line with the ones at the top of the cake. Again, overpipe with the no.2 tube. It is helpful to tilt the cake when working on the slope. Paint the top linework on top of the cakes and the overpiping on the top edge and board slopes, with the same silver mixture used in step 5. When dry, attach the side panels with bulbs of royal icing, resting the bottom edges on the cake boards. Keep the centre of each panel in line with the centre of each pair of scrolls.

11 Trim the edges of the boards with 1cm (½in) wide silver ribbon. Assemble the cakes on a three-tiered cake stand but do not attach the top ornament as it will be easier to transport in separate pieces.

Helpful Hint

If the edges of the pastillage plaque are rough when dry, scrape along the edge with your fingernail, or rub with an emery board or fine scrubbing pad.

11

Floral panels

Highly stylized collars and panels, together with opulent two-tone gold give this cake an art nouveau feel. The rounded shape of the cakes is achieved at the baking stage and the smooth expanse of royal icing on the lower tier gives you the chance to practise your coating skills.

CAKE AND DECORATION

25cm (10in) and 18cm (7in) specially shaped fruit cakes
35cm (14in) and 18cm (7in) specially shaped cake boards
2.5kg (5lb) marzipan
3kg (6lb) royal icing
Old gold and marigold liquid food colourings [S]
60g (2oz) flower paste
Gold dusting powder (petal dust/blossom tint)
1cm (½in) wide gold ribbon
Silk flowers and leaves

ESSENTIAL EQUIPMENT

Templates and patterns (see pages 148–9)
Run-out film
Nos.0 and 2 piping tubes (tips)
No.58 petal piping tube
Two 11cm (4½in) plastic modelling curves
No.3 paintbrush
Two-tiered cake stand

HELPFUL HINT

Cake boards can be made to your exact specifications by any good sugarcraft shop, if you supply them with a template.

1 To shape the cakes, line the inside of two square cake tins (pans) with a band of corrugated cardboard, covered in cooking foil. Then line the tin in the usual way with baking parchment paper. Use separate lining paper for the base and sides in the same way as for a round cake.

2 Measure out 500g (1lb) of royal icing and add two drops of old gold and three drops of marigold liquid food colourings to make a gold colour. For the lighter (cream) icing, add an equal amount of white royal icing to the gold. In this way the colours can be accurately repeated.

3 Cut out templates for the shapes of the rounded-corner cake and board shapes and, if necessary, use these to correct the cake shape at the marzipanning stage. Cover the

1

✳ ✳ ✳ ✳

Royal-iced wedding cakes

3

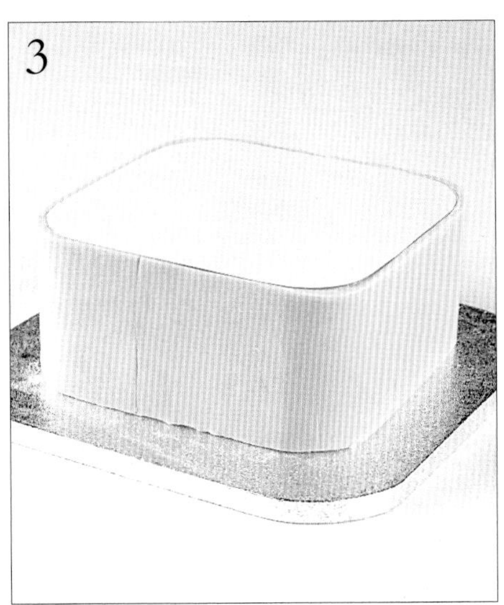

top of the cake with marzipan (see page 143), then compare it with the template, and trim the cake accordingly. When covering the sides, join the marzipan in the centre of the side, rather than on a corner. Leave for at least 24 hours to dry.

4 Apply three coats of gold royal icing to the cake, including one coating on the boards when you apply the final side coat.

5 Trace or photocopy four outlines of each of the top collars, side panels, and board decorations (see pages 148–9). You will need to trace and reverse four board designs, making eight board decorations in total. Place them on flat boards, under run-out film.

Outline all the tiny circles in the design, collar outlines, and top and bottom strips of the side panels, using cream royal icing with a no.0 tube (tip). Using the same colour, fill in the circles and the decorations without an outline, by pressure piping with a thick consistency of run icing (see page 13). This should be done in stages, allowing each section to skin over under the direct heat of an angle poise lamp before piping an adjacent pattern, touching the one before. When the centre decoration is complete, fill in the outlined portions with gold-coloured run icing.

> **Helpful Hint**
>
> Before filling in the outer edge of the collars, overpipe the inner outline with short lines where the decoration touches. This will provide better definition.

6 Outline and fill in the base plaque for the top ornament, using gold royal icing. Place the pattern for the upright panels onto 11cm ($4^1/_2$in) plastic curves (as pictured). Outline the whole of the design using a no.0 tube and fill in with a thick consistency run icing.

6

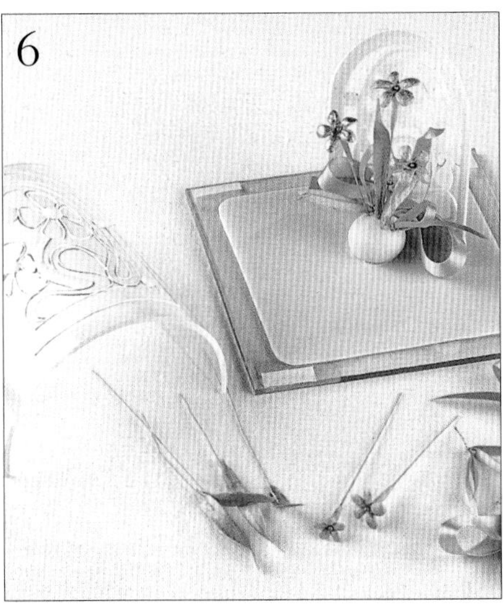

7 Using cream-coloured flower paste, make twelve 'pulled' flowers in varying sizes, and dust with gold dusting powder (petal dust/blossom tint) while they are soft. Insert a

5

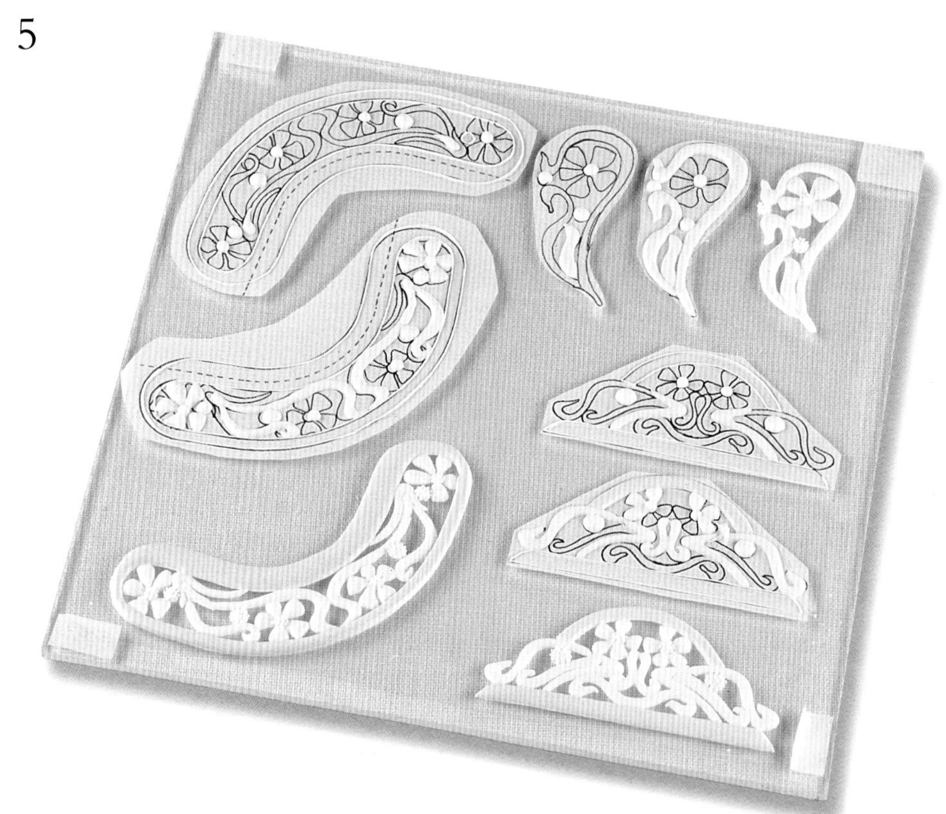

single, gold stamen head into the centre of each flower. Cut out (freehand) about eight long, narrow leaves, slightly varying in length, insert wire through the centre of each one, then twist to give the impression of movement. Dust with gold dusting powder, using a no.3 paintbrush, before leaving to dry.

8 To assemble the top decoration, attach one panel with a line of icing, across a corner of the plaque,

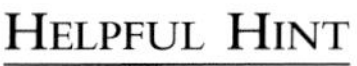

Helpful Hint

If preferred, the top ornament can be assembled directly onto the cake. Use the template for the shape of the top cake and cut out the shape of the plaque from the centre. This can be used to position the ornament.

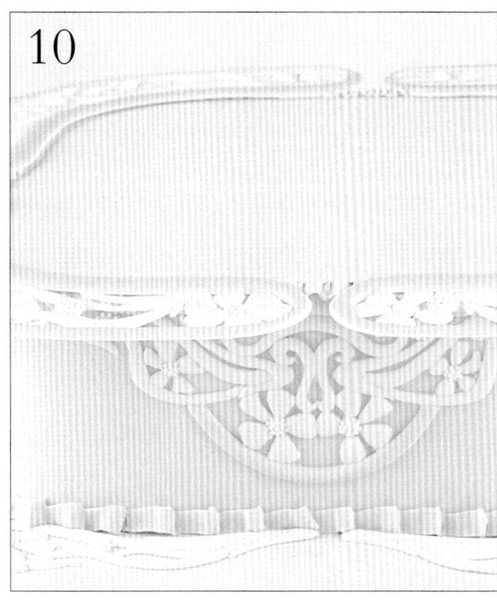

approximately 2cm ($^{3}/_{4}$in) from each side. To secure it, pipe pearls, inside the base line, using a no.2 tube.

Attach a ball of flower paste in front of the panel, and arrange the flowers and leaves in this, filling in the gaps with loops of gold ribbon. Attach the second panel, and pipe bulbs with a no.0 tube along the outside bottom

edge of both. Place the ornament on the cake, and pipe bulbs using a no.0 tube around the edge of the plaque.

9 Remove all the run-outs from the film. Attach the panels to the centre of each side of the cakes, with the flat edge level with the top. A few small bulbs of icing dotted on the back of these will keep them in place.

10 Using a no.58 petal tube, pipe gold icing in a folded ribbon effect around the base of the cakes, keeping the edge of the tube flat against the cake. As you proceed, keep pushing back into the icing to create the folds with the same movement as when piping shells.

Attach the board decorations in the position shown, and pipe a no.2 bulb between them on the corners of the board. Pipe the same border around the tops of the cakes, and attach the collars while the piping is still wet.

11 Finally, trim the edge of the cake boards with the 1cm ($^{1}/_{2}$in) wide gold ribbon.

Embroidery blossom

Expertise in brush embroidery follows a natural progression to create the design on this impressive free-standing cake display. The traditional use of three cakes of different sizes has been replaced by two of equal size and one smaller – this provides extra cake pieces if catering for a large party.

CAKE AND DECORATION

18cm (7in) square fruit cake
Two 25 x 18cm (10 x 7in) oblong fruit cakes
25cm (10in) square cake board
Two 35 x 28cm (14 x 11in) oblong cake boards
Spare cake boards
3kg (6lb) marzipan
3.5kg (7lb) royal icing
Pink and green liquid food colourings
Silver dusting powder (petal dust/blossom tint)
Clear alcohol
Gum tragacanth
1cm (½in) wide silver ribbon

ESSENTIAL EQUIPMENT

Templates and patterns (see page 146)
Run-out film
Nos.0, 1, 1.5 and 2 piping tubes (tips)
No.3 sable paintbrush
Sponge foam
Three tilting cake stands

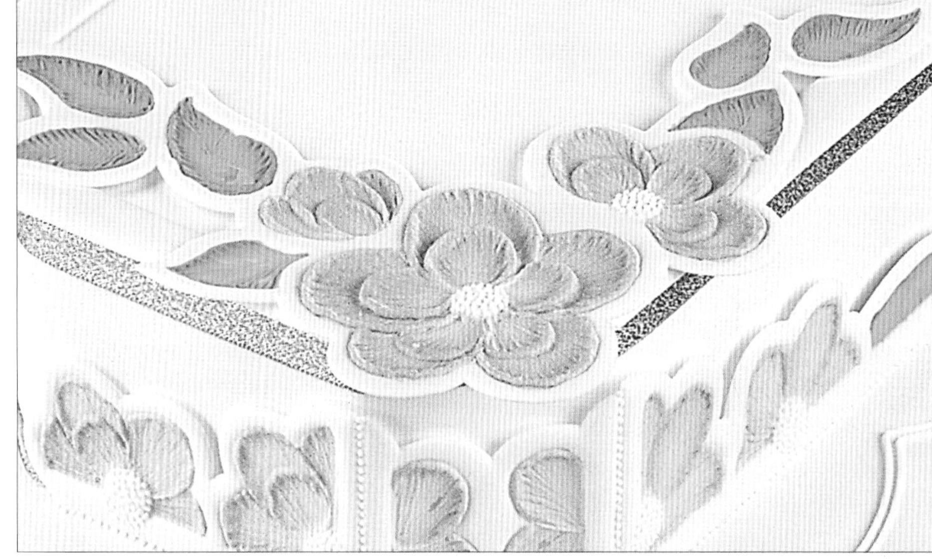

1 To produce fruit cakes in this shape, pre-shaped cake tins (pans) are available, although it is easy to cut the shapes from square and oblong cakes. Simply measure 4cm (1½in) along each side of the cakes from the corners and cut off diagonally. To adapt the boards, measure 8cm (3in) along each side of the oblong boards and 6cm (2½in) along each side of the square board and cut diagonally. If preferred, specially shaped boards may be purchased by special order (check with your local sugarcraft shop).

HELPFUL HINT

Because of the delicate brush embroidery pieces, it is advisable to make the icing with pure albumen powder.

2 Marzipan the cakes (see page 143). Put them on the boards, and apply three coats of white royal icing. Coat the boards at the same time as the final side coat.

3 To make the top edge full collars, place the patterns (see page 146) under run-out film on flat boards. Outline with a no.1 piping tube (tip) and fill in with run icing (see page 13). Dry them under an angle.poise lamp to achieve a shiny surface.

4 For the side panels, remember to reverse the pattern for half of the side panels in each size. You will need six corner sections, four long side sections, and eight short side sections. Place them on a flat board, and cover with run-out film.

Our
Wedding Day

5 Using a no.1 tube, outline the flower petals, then the rest of the panels with white icing. To fill in the petals and leaves, prepare pink and green icing (see page 12), adding a pinch of gum tragacanth to both mixtures. This will strengthen the brush embroidery, but means work must be carried out fairly quickly before the icing dries.

6 Pressure pipe with a no.2 tube a line of pink royal icing around the inside of the white outline, making it thicker at the top of the petal. Using a slightly damp no.3 paintbrush, flatten the bristles, and brush the icing from the side of the line, down towards the base of the petal. If the petal is large, a second line can be piped in freehand, inside the first, creating another layer of smaller petals. This will enable you to brush the icing all the way to the centre of the flower. Where only part of the petal is shown against a straightedge, pipe a thin line along this edge, as well as a thick one at the top, and brush towards the centre.

6

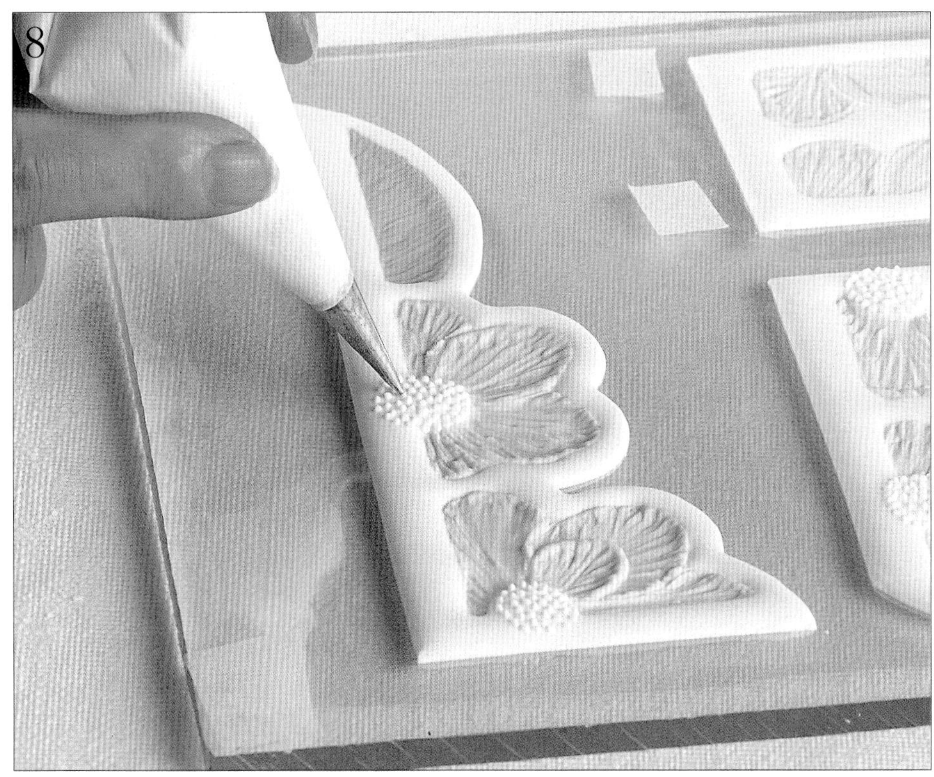
8

Helpful Hint

This type of brush embroidery needs to be thicker than that which is worked directly onto the cake, and over the whole surface. Otherwise there is a danger of it all collapsing when the paper is removed.

7 Where only half a leaf is showing, pipe a green line using a no.3 tube around the curved edge, increasing the pressure at the widest point in the middle. Brush at an angle towards the straight edge to give the impression of leaf veins.

For a full leaf, pipe down both sides of the shape, again increasing the pressure at the widest point. Brush the icing towards the centre of the leaf, like veins, until the two sides meet. Pipe an extra bulb of icing inside the point at the top, and brush this down the centre to the base.

8 To finish off the side panels, fill in the surrounding outlined areas with white run icing (see page 12). Dry in the same way as the collars (see step 3). When dry, pipe tiny white bulbs, using a no.0 tube, over the centres of the flowers. Extend the outlines with the bulb piping onto the panel frame, to form complete circles.

9 For the top floral collars, you will need four large and one smaller one (this should be made at 85 per cent of the size of the large collar pattern). Work these in the same way as the side panels.

10 Attach a length of 1cm (½in) wide silver ribbon to the top and bottom edge of the sides of each

cake, using a line of royal icing to secure it. Remove the full top collars from the run-out film and attach them to the top of each cake.

Remove the corner panels from the run-out film. Pipe a line of icing on the inside of the bottom section of each one, and attach them to the lower ribbon on each corner, allowing an equal overhang on each side. This will make the panels stand slightly away from the side of the cake. Support with pieces of sponge foam until firm.

To attach the side panels, pipe a line of icing down the side edges of the corner panels, and along the board, close to the base of the cake. Put the edges of the panels together, and push the bottom edge against the line on the board, this will attach it without the icing squeezing under the base. Support with sponge foam and leave to dry.

11 Pipe a line of bulbs, with a no.0 tube, down the joins of the side panels, and along the bottom edges, to disguise the joins.

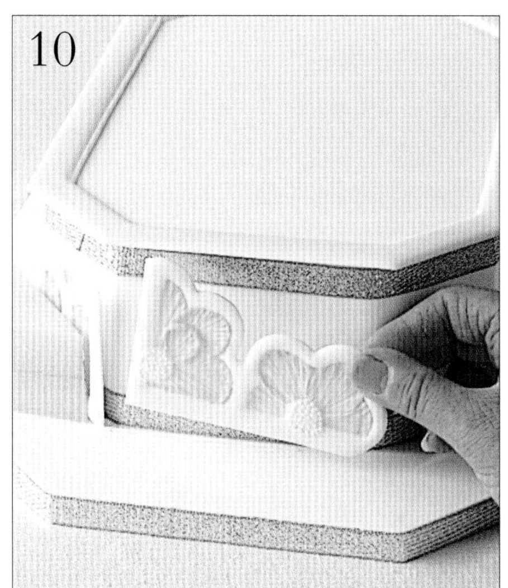

12 Make the board linework templates (you only need one of each as you can move them around as you work). Place the corner section up to the base of the panel, and the side sections in line with it. Pipe two parallel lines with a no.2 tube around the outside of the templates, joining between the sections.

13 To attach the top flower decorations, pipe some royal icing on the corner of the top collars, above the corner panels. Remove the top flower panels from the run-out film, and position as shown below.

14 Before attaching the top collar, trace on the lettering and overpipe with white icing using a no.1.5 tube. When dry, paint it using silver dusting powder mixed with clear alcohol. Finish the top by adding the floral collar decoration and add 1cm ($^1/_2$in) wide ribbon around the edges of each board.

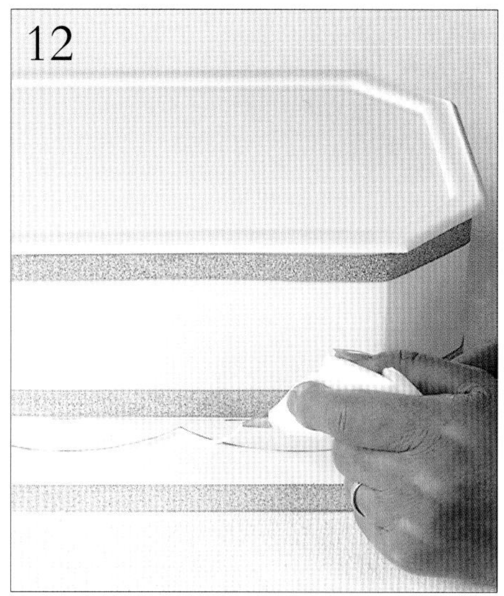

Helpful Hint

Using a suitable cake stand, tilt the top tier so that the wedding message is clearly visible.

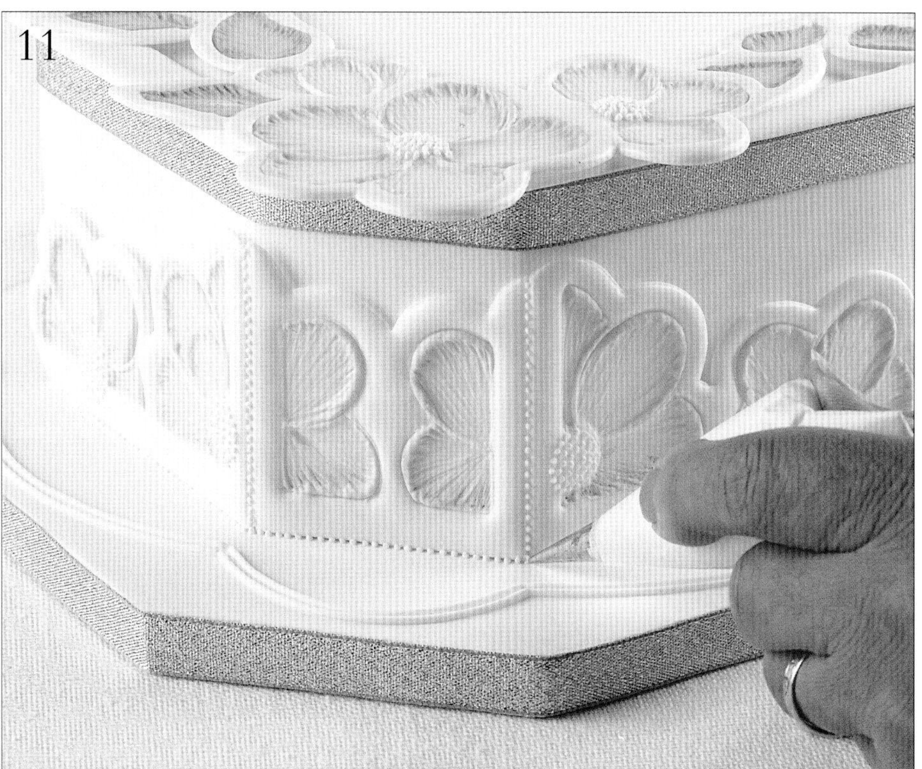

Lily celebration

Create an instant impression with this stunning, but deceptively simple, cake. Its piped collars are as easy to pipe as any other linework, and stronger than imagined when set in place: the strength lies in the original design and the addition of gum tragacanth to the icing before piping.

❋ ❋ ❋

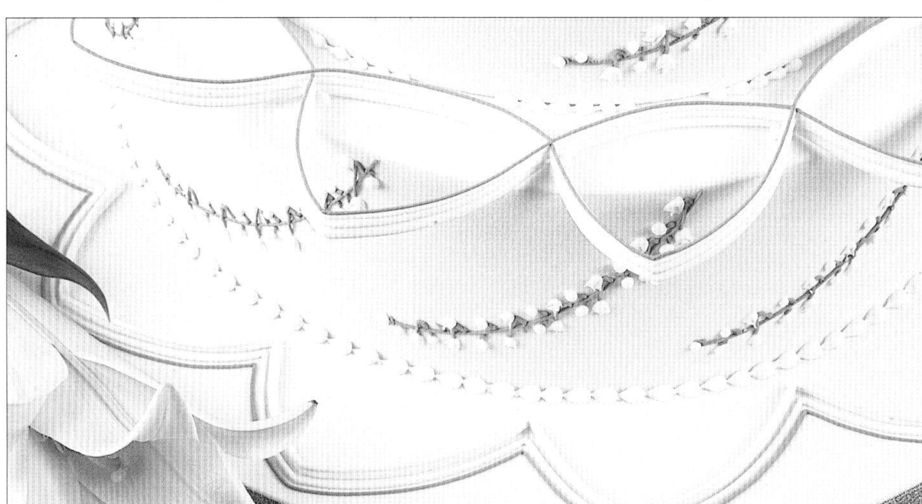

Cake and decoration

25cm (10in), 20cm (8in) and 15cm (6in) round fruit cakes
35cm (14in) and 23cm (9in) round cake boards
20cm (8in) round thin cake board
3kg (6lb) marzipan
3.5kg (7lb) royal icing
Lime-green and leaf-green liquid food colourings
Gum tragacanth
Two sugar, fresh or silk (open) lilies
One bud and three sprays of sugar, fresh or silk lily-of-the-valley
1cm (½in) wide silver ribbon

Essential equipment

Templates and patterns (see pages 144–5)
Run-out film
Nos.1, 2, 3 and 4 piping tubes (tips)
Tilting turntable (optional)
9cm (3½in) perspex tube stand
Perspex cake separator

1 Marzipan the cakes (see page 143). Place the middle tier on the thin cake board, which should fit it exactly, and the top and base tiers on the thicker ones. Check at this stage that the middle cake will fit easily into the space in the centre of the collar pattern.

2 Stand the middle tier, with its thin board underneath, on a spare cake board to make coating it easier. Coat the cakes with three layers of pale lime-green royal icing (see page 12), covering the boards at the same time as the final side coat.

3 Place the patterns on flat boards and cover with run-out film, securing at each corner with masking tape. Paddle some icing to eliminate air bubbles and add a small amount of gum tragacanth for extra strength. If you do not paddle the icing before placing it in the piping bag, the linework will keep breaking during piping, due to air bubbles popping as they come through the end of the

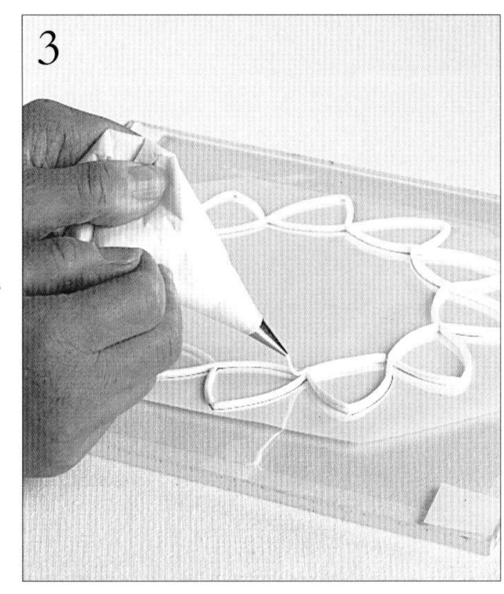

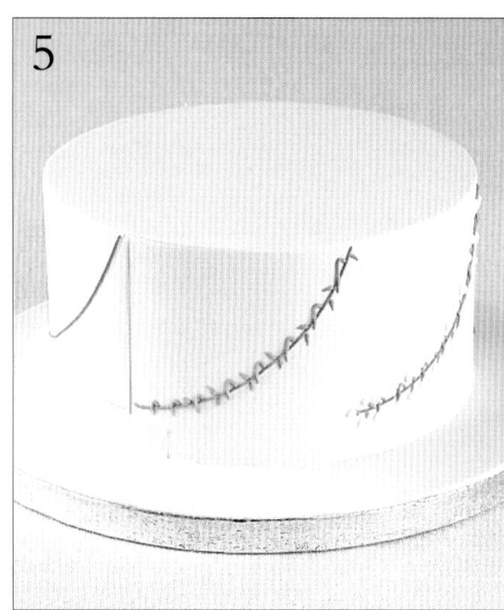

5

tube. Using pale lime-green icing, pipe the outline for the base tier with a no.4 tube. Overpipe with a no.3 tube, then overpipe again with a no.2 tube. Pipe the outlines for the middle and top tiers using a no.3 tube, and then overpipe with a no.2 tube. Finish all the collars by overpiping with a no.1 tube using leaf-green royal icing (see page 12).

All the piping should be dropped down the centre of the line below. Leave each piped line to dry in between each stage, especially if you do not have a lot of piping experience. Pay particular attention to the joins, neatening where necessary with a damp paintbrush as soon as they have been piped.

4 To make the side templates, cut a strip of paper the same depth and circumference as each cake. Fold the top tier template into six equal sections, the middle one into eight, and the base into ten. Copy the template shape onto each section, cut each one out, and fasten them around the cakes.

Helpful Hint

Copy and cut out each template section separately: it is not possible to cut through them all when folded, because of the shape of the template.

5 Pipe a dark green, curved line down each section with a no.1 tube, following the template. It will help if you tilt the cake at this stage on a tilting turntable. Remove the template and pipe short lines at intervals over this line to form stems for the lily-of-the-valley flowers.

6 To make a flower, pipe a no.2 white royal icing bulb on the end of the stem and pull the bottom edge downwards in three points while it is still wet, using a paintbrush. For the buds, just pipe bulbs of various sizes.

7 Cut out the templates (see page 144–5) for the top and base cake boards. Slide these down over the cakes until they rest on the boards with the outer circle against the board's edge. Pipe linework round the inner edge with the nos.3, 2 and 1 tubes in the same way as the collars. Finish the base of the cakes by piping a pearl border with the no.3 tube in the same colour as the cake. Pipe using the same technique as when piping a shell border.

8 Release the collar for the top tier from the run-out film, by sliding a cranked palette knife (metal spatula) underneath and cut away the tape holding the film to the board. Arrange the cake and the collar at the same height next to each other, by placing the collar on the turntable and supporting the cake underneath. Slide

7

✻ ✻ ✻ ✻

Lily celebration

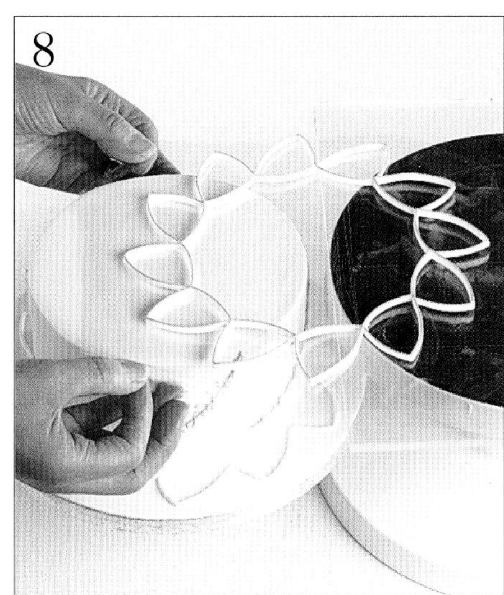

8

the run-out film and the collar over onto the cake. Carefully hold onto the inside edge of the collar while you pull out the film. Immediately take the board and turntable away from the cake to avoid breakages.

9 Check that the collar and the board linework are matching, moving the collar around to fit if necessary. Then pipe no.2 tube bulbs in the inside corners of the collar to attach it to the cake. Proceed in the same way for the other two tiers.

10 Gently release the middle tier cake from its temporary board, by scoring round the base of the cake with a scalpel. Lift it onto the centre of the base tier, keeping the thin board underneath. This is necessary to prevent moisture from the cake staining the one below. Match the position of the middle collar to the base one. Secure with no.3 pearls round the bottom edge.

> **HELPFUL HINT**
> If the collar of the base tier is very close to the side of the middle tier, pipe around the base only where visible and where you can fit in the piping tube.

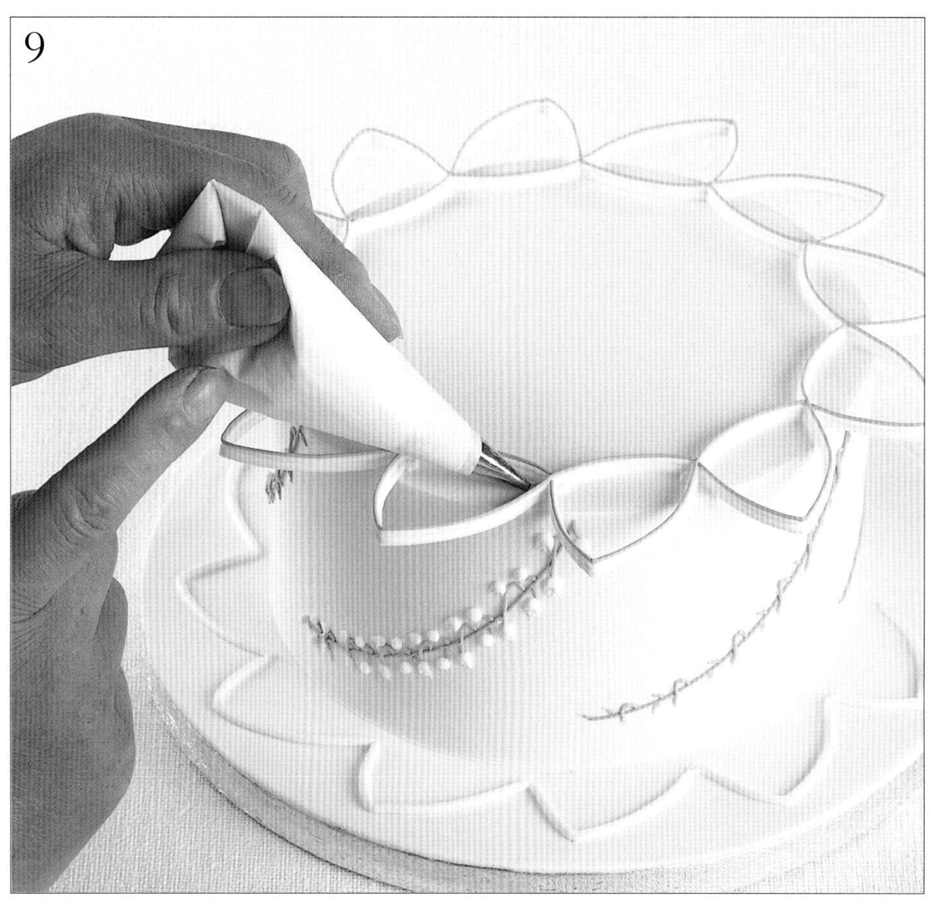

9

11 Trim the two boards with 1cm (½in) wide silver ribbon. A 9cm (3½in) high perspex tube has been used here as a cake separator for the top tier, but this could be substituted with any perspex divider.

12 Finish off the top of the cake with an arrangement of lilies and lily-of-the-valley sprays. You will need two open lilies, one bud and three sprays of lily-of-the-valley. These can be made from sugar, or simply use fresh or silk flowers.

> **HELPFUL HINT**
> Add the top decoration at the venue, because if moved in transit the delicate daisy collars could easily break.

12

Honeysuckle dream

Stencilling is a quick, easy way of decorating a cake which, combined with airbrushing, produces fast, impressive results. Alternatively, colour this beautiful cake with dusting powder or paint on the design with powder or paste food colouring mixed with a little clear alcohol.

Cake and decoration

13 x 18cm (5 x 7in), 18 x 23cm (7 x 9in) and 23 x 28cm (9 x 11in) oval fruit cakes
20 x 25cm (8 x 10in), 25 x 30cm (10 x 12in) and 32 x 38cm (13 x 15in) oval cake boards
3.5kg (7lb) marzipan
3.5kg (7lb) royal icing
Pink, yellow, brown and green liquid food colourings
1cm (1/2in) wide maroon ribbon

Essential equipment

Cake scraper
Polyester honeysuckle stencil [SF9 CSD]
Metal honeysuckle stencil [HS]
Airbrush (optional)
Paintbrush
Templates and patterns (see page 148)
Run-out film
Nos.0, 1 and 2 and piping tubes (tips)
No.51 leaf piping tube
Three tilting cake stands

1 Marzipan the three oval cakes (see page 143). Apply two coats of white royal icing to the top and sides. Prepare a scraper with two holes melted into the side – 2.5cm (1in) from the bottom and 2.5cm (1in) apart. (You may need to rub away the melted plastic from the base of the holes with sandpaper.) Apply a third coat of icing and use the scraper to smooth it around the side to create a pair of parallel lines. Coat the boards while the sides are still wet and later apply the final top coat. Leave the cakes to dry.

2 Using the polyester honeysuckle stencil, apply the complete design to the top of the base tier. Place the stencil on the iced surface of the cake, and hold it in place. With a cranked palette knife, spread a small amount of icing across the top of the stencil and smooth with a scraper. Carefully remove the stencil, without distorting the design. Stencil the second tier in the same way, but you will need to mask off a portion of the

2

3

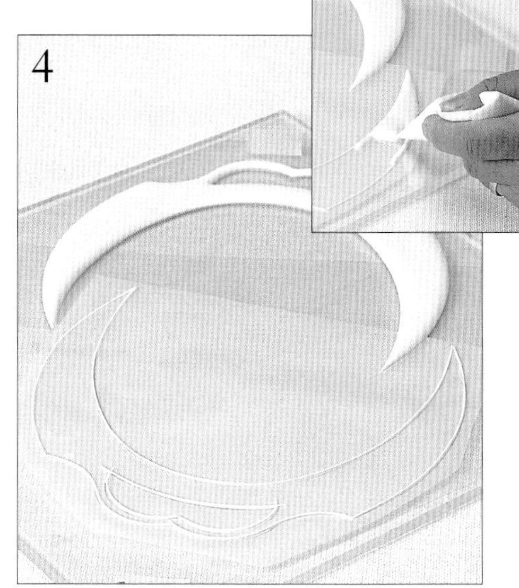
4

design with tape. To decorate the top tier, mask off the whole pattern except for the largest flower. Apply the small stencil design to the edge of the cake boards, at the front and back, using the metal honeysuckle stencil. Leave them to dry out.

3 To colour, put the stencil back on the cake, pressing it down around the raised design. Use an airbrush to apply the colours (see manufacturer's instructions). This will enable you to direct the right colours into each section, but remember to mask off the surrounding area of the cake and board. If you do not have an airbrush, then paint on the colour with a mixture of food colouring and clear alcohol. Colour the board decoration in the same way, carefully replacing the metal stencil and masking off the surrounding area to avoid overspray. Repeat this process on each cake and board and put to one side until the paint is dry.

4 Trace the collar patterns (see page 148), which will frame one half of the top of each cake. Lay them out under run-out film. Pipe in the outline of the collars with a no.1 tube (tip) and white royal icing and fill in this shape pattern with run icing (see page 13). Place the run-out collar under a direct source of heat, such as an angle poise lamp fitted with a reflector bulb. Leave for about 30 minutes, by which time a shiny crust will have formed on the surface of the icing. Leave the collars to dry in a warm place.

5 Place the flower patterns under run-out film. Prepare more run icing, making the consistency thick enough so that it will be able to hold its shape without needing an outline. Place the run icing in a paper piping bag without a tube, and cut a small hole in the end, about the size of a no.2 tube. Pipe bulbs for the centre of each flower and leave it under direct heat to form a shiny crust.

Pipe alternate petals, using the same piping bag, applying extra pressure at the outside tip of each one. Make sure they are anchored well to the

5

6

✻ ✻ ✻ ✻

Honeysuckle dream

bulb in the centre. Allow these to skin over under a lamp before piping in the remaining petals. When dry, overpipe the centres with tiny bulbs using a no.0 tube. Make at least 51 flowers: 12 for the top tier, 15 for the middle, and 18 for the base tier; plus four for the base and middle collars and two small ones for the top collar.

6 To make templates for the board linework, cut out the tracings of the collar patterns from step 4, following the cake line to make the inside edge of the templates. Place the templates around the end of each cake. If they will not lie flat, cut in half at their central point, to improve the fit. Pipe a line around the template at each end of the cake, joining at the centre of each side, using a no.2 tube. Then overpipe the linework using the same tube.

8

9

7 Pipe the detail around the base of the cake using white royal icing and a no.51 leaf tube. Overlap each leaf slightly, working in opposite directions from the central point on each side of the cake. Lift the tube away from the surface after each leaf to avoid them running into each other. Take the piped flowers and carefully remove them from the film. Pipe small bulbs of icing onto the parallel lines on the sides of the cakes. Attach the flowers at intervals of approximately 2cm (3/4in).

7

8 Attach two flowers to the run-out sections of the collars. Remove the collars from the film and attach to the end of each cake with royal icing.

9 Pipe a line along the inside edge and around the tips of the collars with a no.2 tube. Continue the piped line around the edges of the cakes not covered by the collars. Overpipe this linework using the same tube. To finish, trim the edge of each of the cake boards with 1cm (1/2in) wide maroon ribbon, chosen to bring out the colour of the honeysuckle.

Helpful Hint

Position the cakes on three elevated tilting cake stands, with their collars pointing towards the back so that the elaborate designs are shown to best effect.

Wedding favours

The tradition of giving guests wedding favours (bonbonnières), containing sugared almonds or chocolates, on special occasions has been well established in Europe for many years, but the custom is spreading, and cake decorators are discovering a new avenue for their skills.

The quickest way to produce these net favours is to use a favour machine (see below) made for the purpose, which can be hired from any good cake decorating or craft shop. This will speed up the process of making a large number of favours, and will help produce a good, professional finish.

MATERIALS

Stiffened net circles

These can be purchased ready cut, and are available in numerous colours and designs. The number of layers of net used for each favour is your choice, and will depend on the thickness and design of the nets, but it is usually two or three. Several different patterns and colours can be layered together to match the theme of the wedding.

Sugared almonds

Traditionally five sweets are included in each favour, representing health, wealth, happiness, long life and fertility. Use the delicately coloured sugared almonds, or sweets of the same shape containing chocolate. The silver and gold foil-covered almonds are really special.

Dishes

Small plastic dishes can be used to hold the sugared almonds. They also help to give a neat shape to the favour.

Ribbons and decorations

Use ribbon to tie up the tiny parcel, which is usually finished with a bow. Other decorations, such as flowers, can also be added. It is also possible to add tags with the names of the bride and groom and the date of the wedding.

METHOD

1. Pass a length of ribbon under the base plate, and leave at the back.

2. Select the required number of nets and lay them centrally between the hinged perspex plates on the machine. If there is a serrated edge on the nets, alternate the pattern.

3. Slot the tube into the hole in the centre of the plates and push down to form a hollow in the nets. Remove, then insert the small dish and sweets.

4. Take hold of the two ends of the ribbon, pull and tie round the nets, above the dish and sweets.

5. Lift the plates and remove the favour. Finish each favour with a bow or other decoration.

2

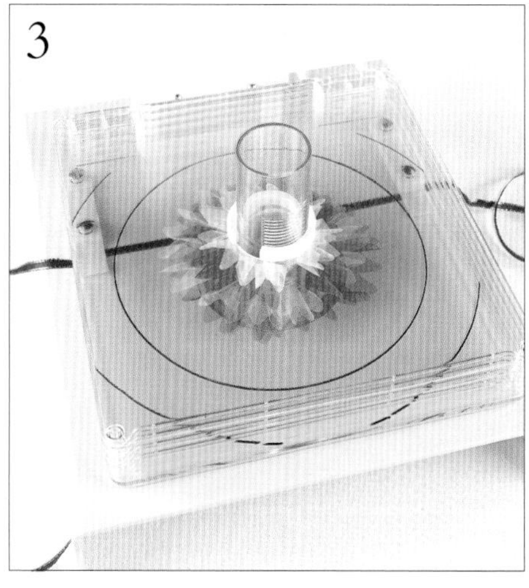
3

4

Stacked wedding cakes

A change has taken place in the traditional style of wedding cakes. Most noticeable is a new absence of pillars between all the tiers, the preference being towards stands, which display the individual cakes better, or stacking the cakes on top of each other. Creating spectacular American-style stacked cakes calls for new skills, working on small, thin boards for the top tiers and inserting dowels into the cake to prevent sinkage.

Stacked cake techniques

A stacked wedding cake is ideal for those who have never tackled a tiered wedding cake before. The beauty of a stacked cake is that there are no pillars involved, just cake dowels and supporting boards in between each tier.

PREPARING STACKED WEDDING CAKES

Always marzipan and cover the cakes (excluding the bottom tier) on a thin cake board the same size as the cake, i.e. if working with a 20cm (8in) round cake, stick it onto a 20cm (8in) round thin cake board. Then place the cake and thin board on another temporary cake board in order to cover it with marzipan.

The marzipan should always cover the cake all the way down to the temporary board it is resting on. This also applies to the final covering, whether it is royal icing or sugarpaste (rolled fondant), so there are no gaps around the base. This should disguise the thin cake board as well. Leave the cakes to harden for up to a week before decorating. This will make handling the cakes easier and they will not get marked by your hands.

HOW TO CREATE A STACKED CAKE

Dowels are inserted into each tier of a stacked cake (excluding the top tier). The thin board underneath each tier to be stacked will prevent the dowels going through to the cake below. When all the cakes are stacked together, all the weight will be supported on the dowels. This is virtually the same principle as using dowels inside cake pillars, except that the dowels here are trimmed level with the surface of the cake and not with the top of the cake pillar, as with a pillared cake.

DOWELS

Always use food quality dowels, available from a good cake decorating suppliers. Do not forget to warn the bride and groom, and whoever will be cutting the cake into portions, that the dowels have been inserted into the cake.

DOWELLING THE CAKE

1. The dowels should be inserted at points towards the centre of the cake, within the area that will be covered by the next tier. If covering an offset stacked cake (for example, the Candles and flowers cake, pages 72–5) it can be useful to create paper templates for the top tiers by drawing round the cake tins onto a piece of paper and cutting out the shape of the cake. Then mark the position of the dowels on the template. Place the template on the cake that you want to insert the dowels into, and mark the position of the dowels with pins.

2. Take the template away, then gently push the dowels straight down into the cake at the marked points, until they will not go in any further, which means that you have reached the thin card at the base of the cake.

3. Holding the dowel with one hand, mark a line with a sharp knife on the dowel at the point where it lines up with the surface of the cake.

4. Gently pull out the dowel, and score it on this line by rolling it back and forth with a sharp knife, then

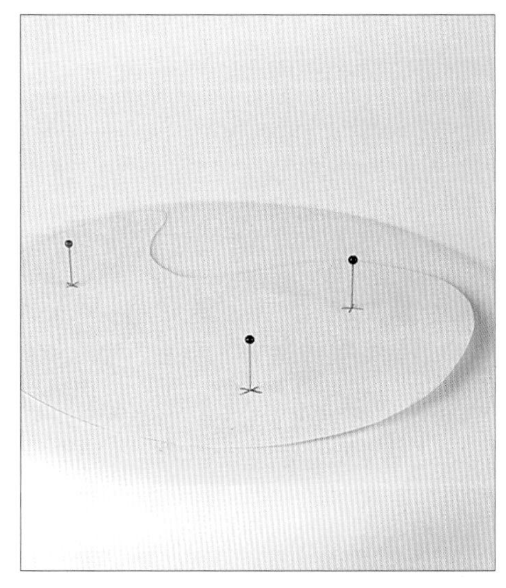

snap the dowel with your hands. Alternatively, cut through the dowel at the marked line with a serrated knife or small saw.

5. Reinsert the trimmed dowel back in the same hole in the cake. Repeat this process for the remaining dowels, making sure that they do not stand proud of the cake surface, otherwise when the tiers are stacked together they may wobble, look lopsided or become unstable.

How many dowels to insert in a cake

As a rough guide to the number of dowels to insert in one cake, it is usually four in square or round cakes, with possibly six in the bottom cake if it is as large as a 30cm (12in) or 35cm (14in) cake with more than two tiers stacked on top. Place three dowels in petal-shaped cakes, and six dowels in a petal-shaped base cake if it is large enough.

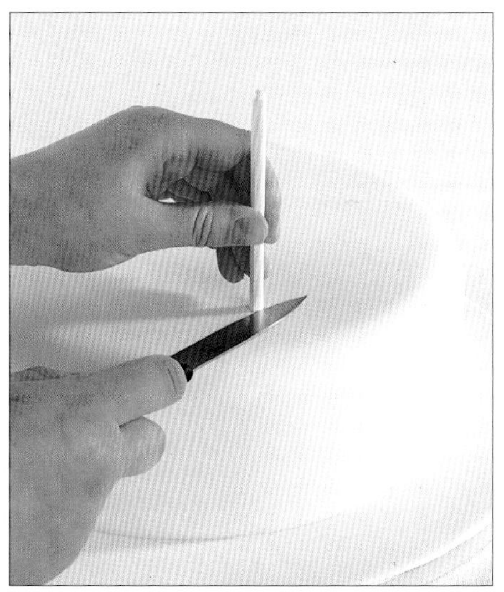

ASSEMBLING A STACKED CAKE

Run a thin-bladed knife around the bottom edges of the cakes to be stacked to loosen them from the boards they were covered on. Leave the thin board intact underneath the cake. Spread some royal icing or softened sugarpaste on the bottom tier in an area a little smaller than the cake to be stacked. Push the cake to be stacked to the edge of the spare board so there is enough room for you to get your hand underneath it, then lift and drop onto the bottom tier.

Do not 'drop' the cake from a great height, but from just above the surface, which will allow enough time to quickly take your hand away from underneath without getting it stuck. With the aid of the soft royal icing underneath you will be able to slide and position the cake. Lowering the cakes too gently can cause problems as it is sometimes difficult to get your fingers out without damaging the icing or getting a hand covered in royal icing.

When happy with the position of the cake, press down on top to make sure the surface of the board under the cake and the surface of the cake it is stacked on are bonded. Repeat for the remaining tiers.

WHEN TO DECORATE

Sometimes it makes for a neater finish if the cakes are stacked first and then decorated. However this is not always practical. For example, if you need space for your hands to pipe and paint at different angles it would

be easier to do this first and then stack the cakes, as having a cake below the one you are working on can be restrictive. Be careful when lifting and stacking the decorated tiers to avoid squashing your work.

Transporting

The only problem with stacked cakes is their weight. Some stacked cakes can be assembled at the wedding reception, but others are better transported in their finished state.

Chocolate drapes and roses

Chocolate wedding cakes are always popular, although they can be offputting to make, requiring ideal temperature conditions. This cake, however, covered with chocolate sugarpaste and decorated with ready-made modelling chocolate, poses no problems and will fulfil any bride and groom's dreams.

CAKE AND DECORATION

13cm (5in), 20cm (8in) and 28cm (11in) round fruit or chocolate cakes
38cm (15in) round cake board
13cm (5in) and 20cm (8in) round thin cake boards
Apricot jam/masking jelly
Clear alcohol
3.5kg (7lb) marzipan
3.5kg (7lb) chocolate-flavoured sugarpaste (rolled fondant) [R]
200g (6½oz) white flower paste
One white, one milk and one plain chocolate 150g (5oz) packets of modelling chocolate [SK]
1.25m (1⅓yd), 15mm (⅝in) wide gold ribbon

ESSENTIAL EQUIPMENT

Varipin [OP]
Cake dowels
Sponge foam
Veining tool [HP]
Set of calyx cutters [PME]
Set of plunger rose leaf cutters [PME]

1 Place the cakes on the boards, then brush with boiled apricot jam or masking jelly and cover with marzipan (see page 143). Leave the cakes for at least 24 hours to harden. Brush with clear alcohol and cover with the chocolate sugarpaste (rolled fondant). This is slightly softer than ordinary sugarpaste; therefore having a firm base underneath will make covering the cake easier. Cover the base board with strips of sugarpaste, and texture by rolling with the Varipin, before trimming round the edge. Leave to dry.

1

HELPFUL HINT

Use icing (confectioners') sugar to roll out the sugarpaste, but be careful to rub in any excess on the top surface as you work.

2 Dowel the base and the middle cakes by cutting out paper templates of the middle and the top cakes. Mark the position of the dowels on the templates, then place

✳ ✳ ✳ ✳

Stacked wedding cakes

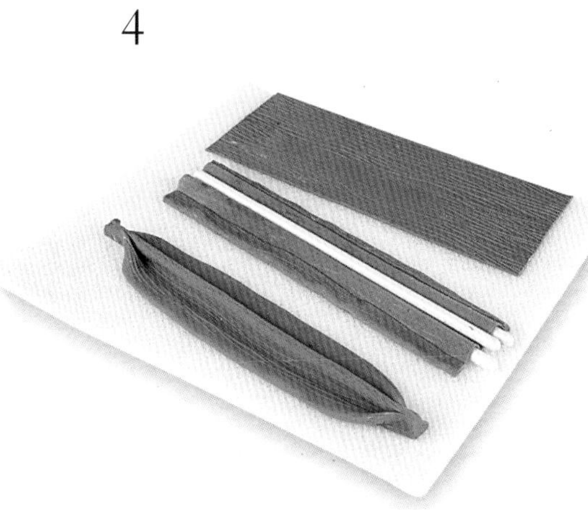

the templates on top of the middle and bottom cakes. Prick through each template to mark the position of the dowels on the cakes. Remove the templates and first insert a narrow tool into the cake at these points, then the dowels. Mark on the dowel where it meets the surface of the cake, then pull it out and cut it off at the mark. Reinsert the dowels, then place the cakes on top of each other, securing underneath with some softened sugarpaste glue (see below).

HELPFUL HINT

To make sugarpaste glue, chop a small amount of sugarpaste into tiny pieces, add some water and paddle with a palette knife (metal spatula) into a soft paste.

3 Mix 360g (12oz) chocolate sugarpaste with 200g (6oz) white flower paste to make the drapes. You will need three large drapes for the front, and about eight smaller drapes for round the bases of the cakes. The larger drapes should measure 20 x 13cm (8 x 5in) and the smaller drapes 20 x 10cm (8 x 4in). Roll out the paste thinly, and texture by rolling with the Varipin. Cut out the large drapes first, turn over and brush each of the long edges with water and turn them inwards.

4 Place two cake dowels on a piece of sponge foam, and cover them with the paste. Place a third dowel on top of the paste, between the two dowels underneath (see left), and press the dowels down onto the foam to create folds in the paste. Remove the dowels, and gather the ends of the paste together to make a drape. Attach one drape from the middle of the top cake, across the front of this cake to the base of the top tier. Secure in position with the softened sugarpaste glue. Repeat this process on the middle and base tiers, keeping the start and finish of each drape in line with the top one, as illustrated.

5 Cut out the smaller drapes and texture as before. Place them around the base of each of the cakes, starting at the bottom of the large drape from the top tier, and finishing at the top of the large drape on the tier below. Repeat this on each tier to form a spiral.

6 For the bow on top of the cake, cut two strips from the same sugarpaste mixture used for the drapes, both 20cm (8in) long and 8cm (3in) wide. Turn in at least 1cm (½in) on each side, then fold the ends into the centre to form loops. Pinch to narrow in the centre. Support the loops with rolls of greaseproof (wax baking) paper until the paste is dry. Attach the pieces to the top of the cake at right angles to each other to form the bow, covering the end of the drape on the top.

✳ ✳ ✳ ✳

Chocolate drapes and roses

7 To make the roses, first roll some white and milk modelling chocolate into long, even rolls, so that it is possible to cut evenly sized pieces off them. For a bud, roll a cone and stand it up on its fat end. Cut three equal pieces off the white roll, and two smaller pieces off the milk chocolate roll. Take one piece of the white and flatten into a disc. Thin out round one half of the edge, and wrap it round the cone, keeping the point at the top tight so that the cone is not exposed. Pair up the two colours

Helpful Hint

Use the excess paste from the base of the bud or flower to make the cone for another one. The mixture of colours will not be seen inside the flowers.

of the remaining pieces on top of each other, then flatten together into discs. Texture with a veining tool, then roll it round the thin edge, and wrap the two petals, interleaving, round the bud, as shown in the picture above. Narrow the base by rolling it between the tip of your fingers, and cut off the excess paste. Roll out some of the plain modelling chocolate, cut out a calyx and add it to the bottom of the bud.

8 To make an open bud, follow the same procedure as above but add another layer with three more petals. For the full blown rose, add a third row of five petals. Finish with a plain chocolate calyx on each rose. Make one full blown rose, one open bud and one closed bud for each of the three tiers of the cake, using the largest of each of the flowers on the bottom tier and the smallest on the top tier, as in the picture.

9 Roll out some plain modelling chocolate and cut out three sizes of rose leaves with the plunger cutters. Cover the joins of the drapes round each cake with a single leaf, and cover up the gap at the base of each cake, between the front drapes, with a line of leaves. Attach the full roses at the front of the cake, at the top of each large drape and arrange the varying sizes of rose leaves and buds to form pretty arrangements.

10 Make another open bud for the top of the cake, and place in the centre of the loops. Arrange a few leaves round the flower, and fill in any gaps round the base also with leaves. Finish off the edge of the board with gold ribbon.

Sophisticats

The inspiration for this cake comes from handmade designer greetings cards, some of which have crimped or corrugated silver paper with a motif on the top embellished with spirals of wire. This fresh and funky wedding cake was created by experimenting with a smocking roller and piped spirals.

Cake and decoration

25cm (10in) square, 20cm (8in) and 15cm (6in) hexagonal fruit cakes
35cm (14in) square cake board
20cm (8in) and 15cm (6in) thin cake boards
10cm (4in) hexagonal cake card
3kg (6lb) marzipan
3kg (6lb) white sugarpaste (rolled fondant)
Two spare cake boards
190g (6½oz) flower paste
600g (1¼lb) royal icing (no glycerine)
Baby blue, grape violet, ice blue and spruce green paste food colourings
Cornflower, jade, ice blue, African violet and silver dusting powders (petal dusts/blossom tints)
Superwhite powder [S]
2.5m (2¾yd), 3mm (1/16in) wide silver ribbon
Eight pieces silver wire
1.5m (5ft) silver braid

Essential equipment

Seven cake dowels
Templates (pages 150–51)
Waxed paper
Nos.0, 1, 1.5 and 2 piping tubes (tips)
Nos.0, 1, 4 and 7 paintbrushes
Two lollipop sticks
Cake box card
Smocking roller [CV]
White floristry tape

1 Stick the hexagonal cakes to the corresponding sized thin boards. Marzipan the cakes (see page 143), then place the hexagonal cakes on temporary boards, and the square cake on the 35cm (14in) square board. Leave for a week. Cover the cakes with white sugarpaste (rolled fondant), using the same amounts as for marzipanning. Leave for a few days, then cover the edges of the square board with white sugarpaste and leave to dry for a week.

2 Insert four plastic dowels into the square cake, and three into the 20cm (8in) cake and trim (see page 50). Run a sharp knife around the bottoms of the hexagonal cakes to loosen them from their temporary boards. Stack the cakes as in the photograph opposite, securing them by spreading a little royal icing in between each layer. Press down to secure and leave to set.

3 Trace the heart, cat and spiral designs (see pages 150–51). Colour 225g (7oz) royal icing blue with baby blue and grape violet paste food colourings, and 125g (4oz) royal icing green, using spruce and ice blue.

4 Place the heart templates under a piece of waxed paper on a board. Pipe the outlines for the hearts with a no.0 tube (tip), moving the tracing along underneath for the next heart, allowing ample space in between. Pipe eight medium and nine long hearts in green, and eight medium hearts in blue. Make spares in case of breakages.

Stacked wedding cakes

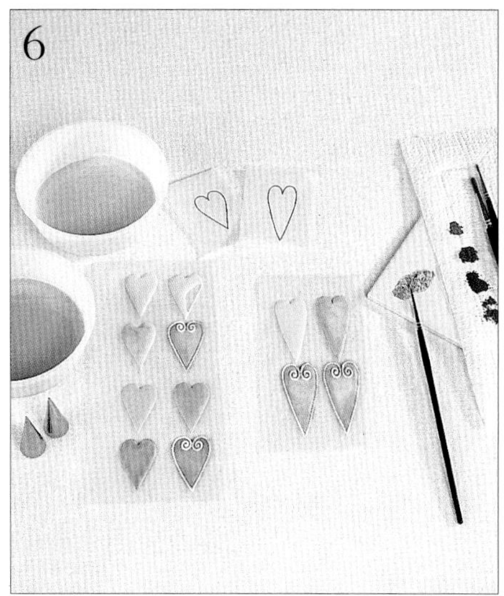

6

5 Add water gradually to each of the remaining colours to make run icing (see page 11). Fit two separate bags with no.1.5 tubes and fill with royal icing. Fill in the hearts with run icing and leave to dry under an angle poise lamp for a few hours.

6 Sprinkle the cornflower, jade, blue and violet dusting powders (petal dusts/blossom tints) onto a clean tile. When the hearts are dry, dust ice blue powder onto the blue hearts with a no.4 brush, then switch to the no.1 brush and dust the edges and points

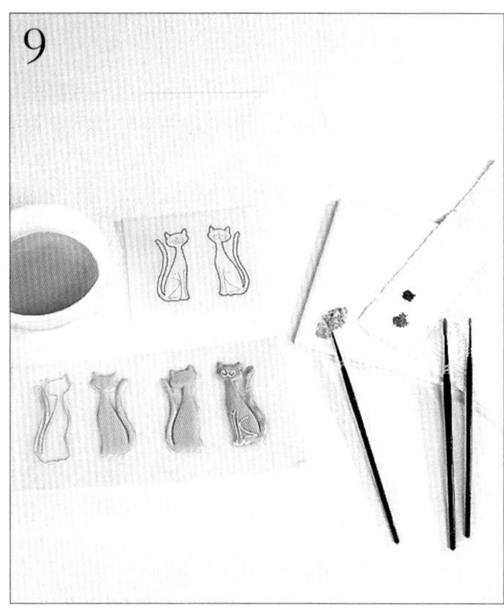

9

of the blue hearts with African violet. Clean the brushes by dabbing in cornflour (cornstarch), then colour the green hearts with cornflower blue using the no.4 brush and finally brush with jade using the no.1 brush.

7 Soften about 30g (1oz) white royal icing with water and pipe around the hearts, forming spirals on the tops with a no.1.5 tube. Pipe the line on the paper touching the sides of the hearts, then pipe onto the hearts at the top in the middle. When the lines are dry, paint silver using the silver dusting powder, dipping solution and a no.0 brush.

8 Pipe the outlines of the cats on waxed paper, using white royal icing. Pipe two large cats with a no.1.5 tube, and eight small cats with a no.1 tube (and a few spares). Leave the outlines to dry and then paint silver. Flood in the cats using the remaining blue run icing (using a no.2 tube for the large cats and a no.1.5 for the small cats) and leave to dry under the lamp.

9 When the small cats are dry, dust with ice blue and African violet, as for the hearts, and give them stripy tails. Pipe the legs and faces freehand, with a no.0 piping tube and white icing. When the lines are dry paint silver with a no.0 brush.

10 When the large cats are dry, slide a cranked palette knife (metal spatula) under each one and turn over. Cut the lollipop sticks to 4.5cm (1¾in) long with scissors. Pipe

11

a little white royal icing onto the back of the sticks at the tops and stick to the cats so they protrude from under the cat by about 3cm (1¼in). Leave to dry for 30 minutes, then pipe the outlines over the existing lines on the reverse of the cat, making sure they match and that there are no gaps where the stick is attached to the cat at the bottom. When dry, paint silver, then flood with blue run icing and leave to dry under a lamp.

11 When dry, dust the reverse side first, then the fronts, and finish by piping the legs and faces with a no.1 tube. Paint the piping silver. Paint a long heart shape on the chest of the cats with grape violet and a little superwhite powder mixed with water, using a no.0 brush.

12 Pipe the spirals onto waxed paper using icing that has been softened with water. Pipe four large spirals with a no.2 tube and 17 with a no.1.5 tube. When dry, paint silver with dusting powder, dipping solution and a no.0 brush.

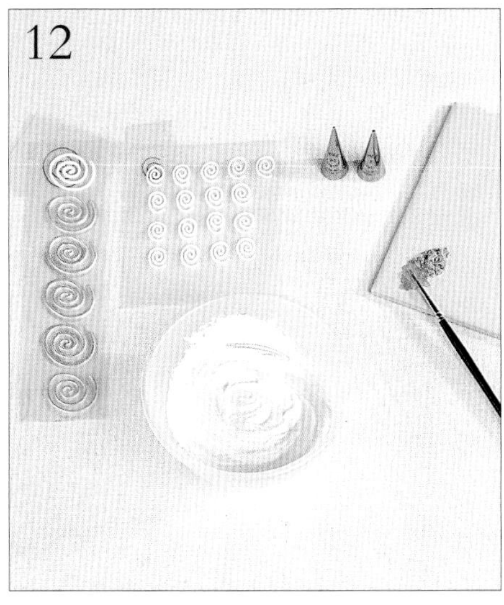

12

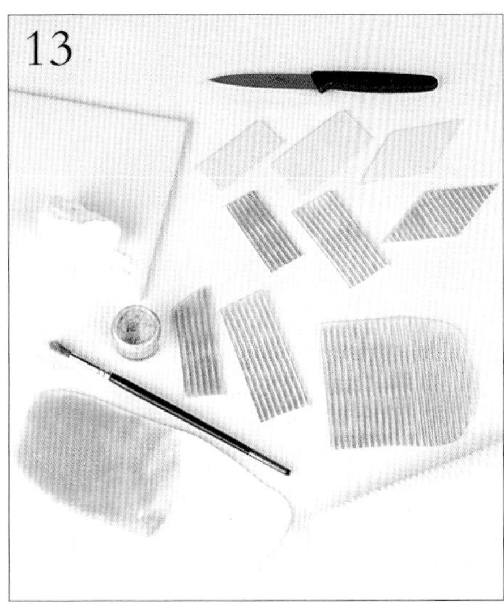

13

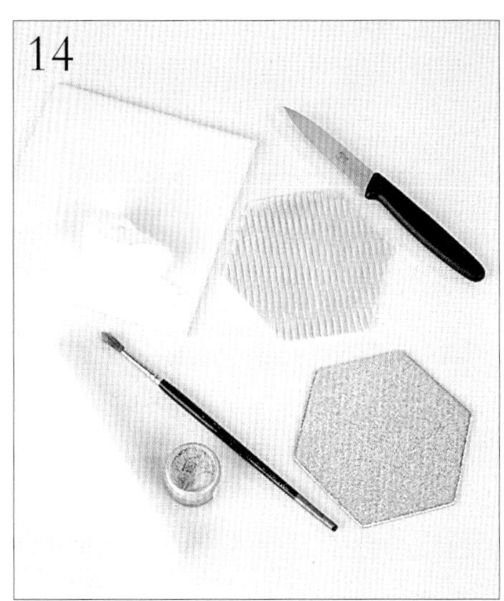

14

13 To make the crimped 'paper', make rectangles and diamond templates with cake box card. Rub a little white fat on the work surface, pull off about two-thirds from 150g (5oz) flower paste, and roll out into a long strip 2.5mm (1/8in) thick. Flip the paste over, and dust with silver dusting powder and a no.7 brush. Roll the paste with the smocking roller from one end to the other without stopping, and cut eight large rectangular shapes. Keep the smocking vertical on the rectangles. Knead the remaining paste and roll out and dust as before (as many times as needed). Cut out six diamonds for the middle tier and nine small rectangles for the top tier. Leave to dry for a few days.

14 Roll out 40g (1¼oz) flower paste on a thin film of white fat, flip over, then dust and crimp with the smocking roller as above, but use the 10cm (4in) hexagonal cake board as a template. Stick to the top of the 15cm (6in) cake. Make two holes in the paste on the top, marking where the large cats will be placed.

15 Fix a length of the silver ribbon around the base of each cake and secure at the back with a blob of royal icing. Carefully run the blade of a cranked palette knife underneath the cats and hearts to release them from the paper. Stick the long green hearts on the small rectangles, two blue hearts on the diamonds and the small cats on the larger rectangles with royal icing, using a bag fitted with a no.1.5 tube.

16 Release the spirals from the paper. Stick one large spiral at each corner of the square cake. Stick two green hearts in the centre of the sides with their points touching, with a spiral above and below. Fix the 'paper' with the motifs to the cake by piping around their shape on the reverse, then pressing gently onto the sides. Place two cats on each side on the bottom tier, a diamond and two hearts on each side of the middle tier, then two long hearts alternating with one heart on the sides of the top tier. Fix the last spirals to the top tier between the hearts and rectangles.

17 Pipe royal icing under each large cat and stick to the top tier by inserting the sticks in the holes. Bend the end of a silver wire round a pencil to form a curve, then roll the wire in your fingers to make a spiral. Make eight spirals of varying sizes.

18 Tape together two lots of four wires so they are at different heights, then stick to the top tier (with royal icing or insert into a ball of flower paste) so there is one spray behind each cat. Bend and fan them out. Attach silver braid to the base.

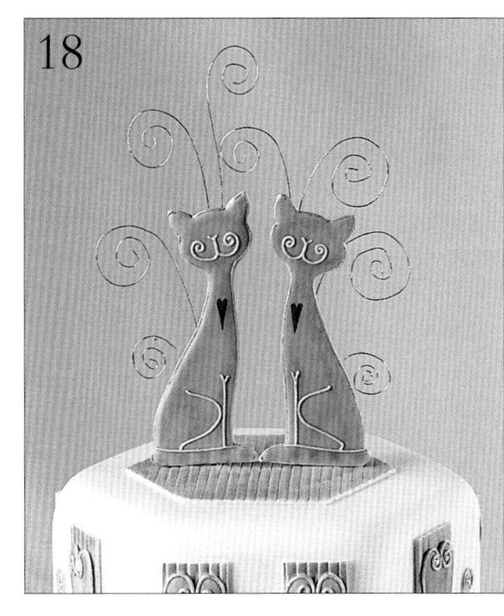

18

Ribbons and bows

Several shades of pink have been used to decorate this pretty cake, which could be altered to complement the varying shades of bridesmaids' dresses or the flowers. The shape of each cake, although unusual, is easy to cut from square cakes, and lends itself well to the draped ribbons.

CAKE AND DECORATION

25cm (10in), 20cm (8in) and
15cm (6in) square fruit cakes
35cm (14in) square cake board
15cm (6in) and 20cm (8in)
thin cake cards
3.5kg (7lb) marzipan
3.5kg (7lb) pale pink sugarpaste
(rolled fondant)
180g (6oz) flower paste
Pink liquid food colouring
2m ($2\frac{1}{4}$yd), 15mm ($\frac{5}{8}$in) wide
silver ribbon

ESSENTIAL EQUIPMENT

Quilting tool [PC]
Open triple scallop crimper [PME]
Silk dupion patterned rolling pin [HP]
Eight cake dowels
Small rose leaf plunger cutter [PME]
Small stitch wheel [PME]

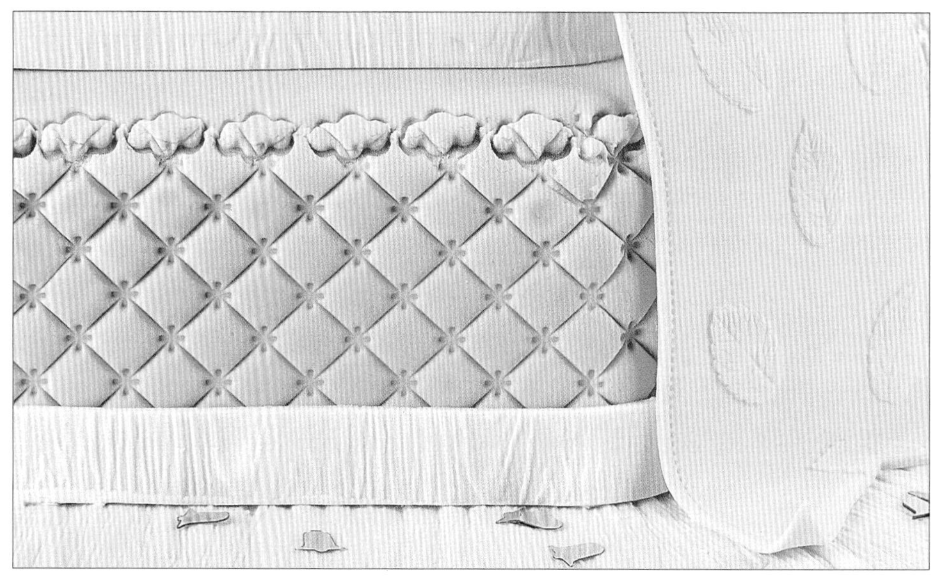

1 If you do not have baking tins (pans) in this shape, cut the corners off square cakes. To do this, measure from each corner along the sides of the cake, and mark at 2.5cm (1in) from each corner for the top tier, 4cm ($1\frac{1}{2}$in) for the middle tier, and 5cm (2in) for the base tier. Cut diagonally across the corners, joining the points, to make the shape of the cake. Dip the knife blade into icing (confectioners') sugar when marking out the cake, it will make it easier to see.

2 Cut cake cards for the top and middle tiers to the same size and shapes to fit underneath.

3 Place the two smallest cakes on the appropriate cards, and place the largest cake on the cake board. Brush each cake with boiled apricot jam or masking jelly and cover with marzipan (see page 143). When dry, brush the marzipan with clear alcohol. Use about 750g ($1\frac{1}{2}$lb) pale pink sugarpaste (rolled fondant) to cover the smallest cake.

4 Add some pink colouring to 1kg (2lb) sugarpaste, creating a slightly darker pink shade than that used to cover the top tier. Roll out this sugarpaste and use to cover the middle tier of the cake.

5 For the base tier, add even more pink colouring to 1.5kg (3lb) sugarpaste, for an even deeper shade of pink. Impress the four sides of the top and the base tiers with the quilting tool, then crimp the top edge of both

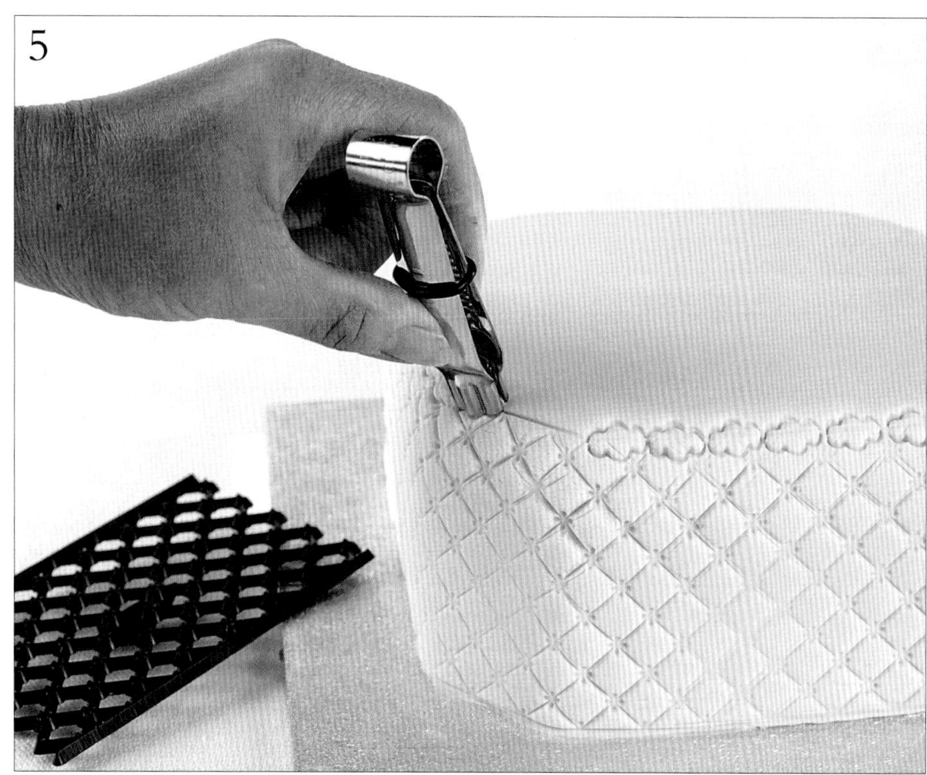

cakes with the crimper. Leave the middle tier plain. Leave all the cakes for at least 24 hours to dry.

HELPFUL HINT
Lightly grease the ends of the crimper with vegetable fat. Hold the edges about 6mm (¼in) apart, and pinch the paste. Ease the pressure slightly before lifting the crimper away. If you release it fully, it may tear the paste.

6 Cover the base cake board by rolling out four long strips of sugarpaste and placing them on each side of the board. Roll out wider squares of paste for the corners. Place these on the corners, overlapping the side strips, then cut through the two thicknesses to make accurate joins. Pinch the cut edges together and smooth. Use a silk patterned rolling pin to texture the paste on the board by rolling it back and forwards, a short length at a time. Radiate the pattern from the centre at the corners.

7 Insert four dowels into each of the base and middle cakes until they are touching the board or card underneath. Mark each piece of dowel where it meets the top of the cake, then remove each one in turn and trim where you have marked it. Reinsert into the cake, then place the cakes on top of each other.

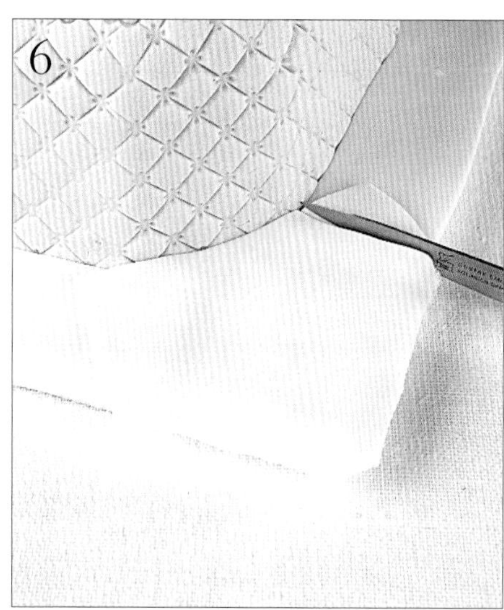

8 Mix the flower paste with 370g (12oz) sugarpaste for the ribbons. Roll out this paste and texture with the silk rolling pin. Cut several 2cm (¾in) wide strips and place round the base of each cake. These will hide the thin cake cards under the top and middle tiers if they are still showing.

HELPFUL HINT
Join the sugarpaste ribbons at the corners of the cakes, where they will later be covered by the hanging ribbons.

9 Roll out a small amount of the same paste thinly. If the paste is thin enough, you should be able to read print through it. Cut out a quantity of rose leaves. Cover with cling film (plastic wrap) until needed.

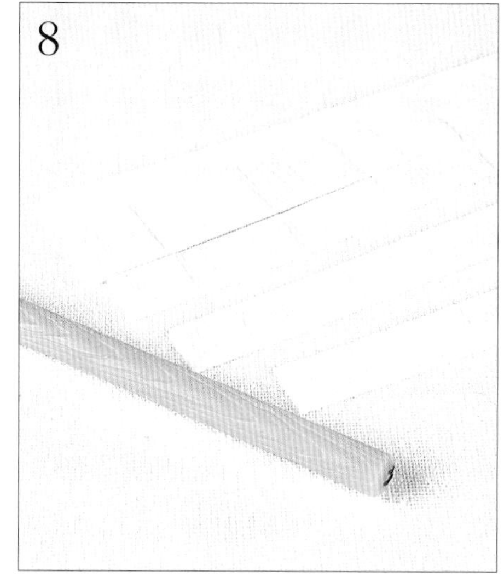

✳ ✳ ✳ ✳

Ribbons and bows

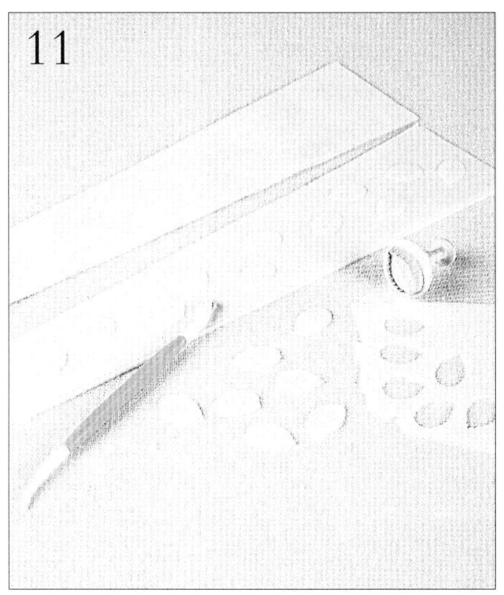
11

10 Measure the cake from the centre of the top tier, down a corner, to the edge of the base board. Make a paper template this length, 5cm (2in) wide at the top, and 10cm (4in) wide at the base, for the longest ribbons.

11 Roll out the paste and cut out a large ribbon using the template. Moisten and add rose leaves at random along the centre of the ribbon. Place a ruler, or similar, along the edges of the ribbon and imprint stitches with the stitch wheel. Attach the ribbon to the centre of the top tier and drape down the corners of the cakes. Trim the bottom edge to fit on the board. Repeat on the other three corners. Work on one ribbon at a time to ensure that the paste remains flexible enough to drape on the cake.

12 Make four smaller ribbons in the same way, each 20cm (8in) long and 2.5cm (1in) wide at the top and 5cm (2in) wide at the bottom. Brush thick sugar glue (see page 54) in three places along the back of the ribbons, place them over the larger ones and push upwards into folds, attaching with the glue patches. Trim the tails.

13 For the loops on the top cake, cut four rectangles, each 8cm (3in) by 13cm (5in). Decorate with rose leaves, fold over and gather slightly at the base. Insert a roll of greaseproof (wax baking) paper through each loop to retain its shape until dry.

14 When dry, use the glue to attach a large loop to the end of each ribbon on the top tier, forming a square. Make some smaller ribbon loops and place in the centre. It may be necessary to trim the bases of the ribbons to fit, and if there are large gaps in the arrangement, fill in with extra, short ribbon tails.

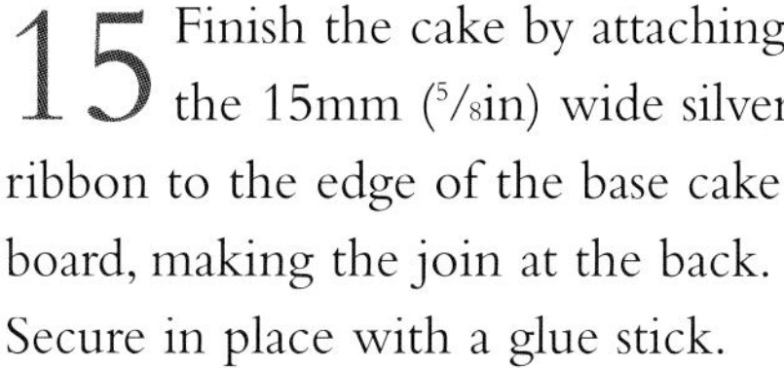
13

15 Finish the cake by attaching the 15mm (5/8in) wide silver ribbon to the edge of the base cake board, making the join at the back. Secure in place with a glue stick.

HELPFUL HINT

Pink sugarpaste can fade in direct sunlight. Keep these cakes in a cake box or a dark cupboard when you are not working on them.

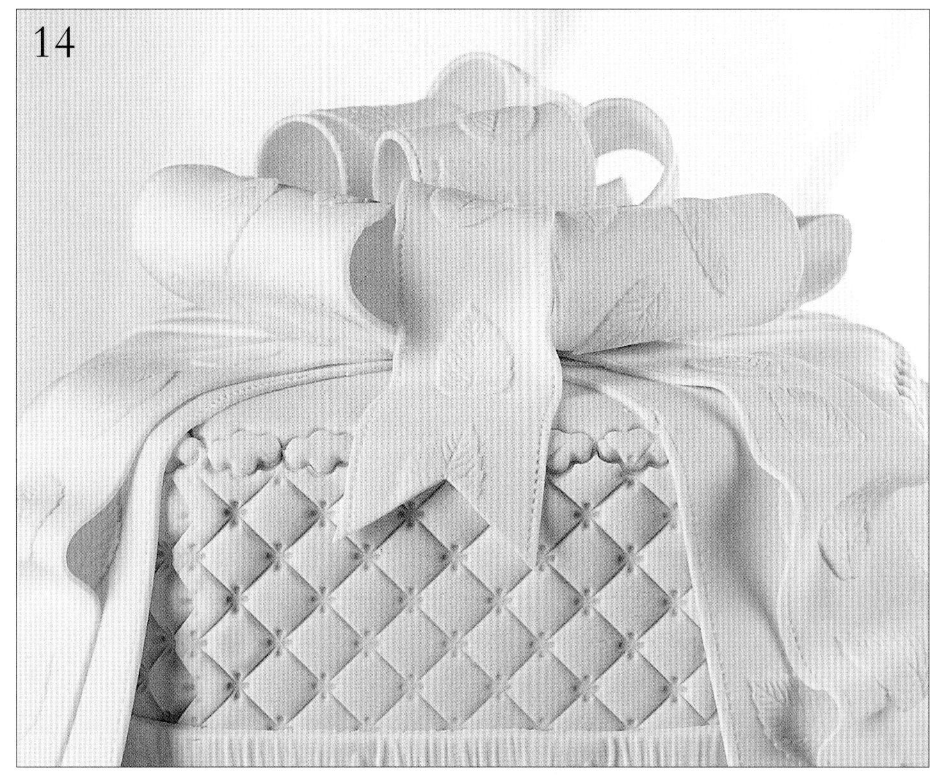
14

Scrolls and ivy

Wedding dresses are no longer just white or ivory and modern trends indicate that the cake is made to match the dress. This cake has been designed with that idea in mind: using two shades of gold on a dark cream base which are currently all very popular colours for brides to wear.

Cake and decoration

30cm (12in), 25cm (10in), 20cm (8in) and 15cm (6in) petal fruit cakes
40cm (16in) petal cake board
25cm (10in), 20cm (8in) and 15cm (6in) thin, petal cake boards
Three spare cake boards
10cm (4in) thin, round cake card
5kg (10lb) marzipan
5kg (10lb) white sugarpaste (rolled fondant)
400g (13oz) modelling paste
25g (3/4oz) flower paste
250g (8oz) royal icing
50g (1 3/4oz) royal icing (no glycerine)
Caramel/ivory paste food colouring
Antique gold dusting powder (petal dust/blossom tint)
Gum tragacanth/tylo powder
50cm (20in), 3mm (1/8in) wide sand dune ribbon
4m (13ft), 7mm (1/3in) wide sand dune ribbon
1.5m (5ft), 15mm (5/8in) wide sand dune ribbon

Essential equipment

Taffeta rolling pin
Pointed ivy cutter [smallest J 714]
Medium ivy veiner [CA]
Nos.1.5 and 2 piping tubes (tips)
Waxed paper
Nos.1 and 7 paintbrushes
12 cake dowels

1 Using apricot jam or masking jelly, stick the three smallest cakes to the thin boards of corresponding size, for example stick the 25cm (10in) cake to the 25cm (10in) board.

Marzipan all the cakes (see page 143). Place the 30cm (12in) cake on the 40cm (16in) board, and the others on spare boards. Make sure that the marzipan covers each cake down to the board. Leave to dry for a week.

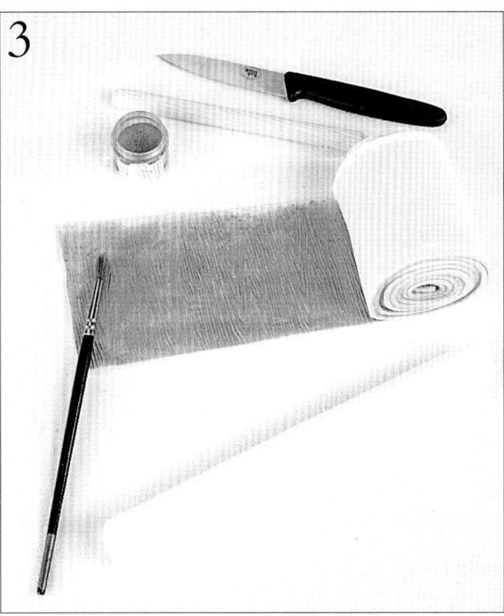

3

2 Add caramel colouring to 5kg (10lb) of sugarpaste (rolled fondant) to make a dark cream colour. Check it is thoroughly mixed by cutting the sugarpaste in half; if it looks streaky, knead the mixture to even out the colour. Cover the cakes with sugarpaste, using 2kg (4lb) for the 30cm (12in) cake, 1.5kg (3lb) for the 25cm (10in), 1kg (2lb) for the 20cm (8in) and 500g (1lb) for the 15cm (6in). Leave to dry for a week.

3 Mix 400g (13oz) modelling paste (see page 142) with caramel food colouring to match the sugarpaste.

Stacked wedding cakes

Roll the paste, on a light dusting of icing (confectioners') sugar, into a strip about 1.5m ($1\frac{2}{3}$yd) long, or long enough to cover the petal cake board. Rub the strip of paste with your hand to remove excess icing sugar, and dust the surface with the antique gold dusting powder (petal dust/blossom tint), using a no.7 paintbrush. Use the taffeta rolling pin to roll over the strip. Trim the lower edge and roll it up like a bandage.

> **HELPFUL HINT**
> It is important not to pull or stretch the paste as you unravel the rolled-up strip, as it will become too thin and lose the impression of the fabric.

4 Moisten the 40cm (16in) petal cake board and unravel the paste onto it, easing the paste gently into the scallops. Use a sharp knife to cut off the excess paste at the back and trim the edge against the edge of the board. (Put the trimmings to one side.) Leave to dry overnight.

5 Roll out the trimmings of paste and dust the surface with the gold dusting powder. Wet the 10cm (4in) cake card, lay the paste on top, and roll over the top with the taffeta rolling pin. Trim the edges.

6 To make the tiny ivy leaves, colour the flower paste the same dark cream as the sugarpaste and modelling paste. Thinly roll out the flower paste and dust over the surface with gold powder, using the no.7 brush. Cut out about 60 pieces of ivy, plus a few spares, and vein them with the ivy veiner. They should not need any balling or shaping, just leave them to dry over a piece of sponge foam.

7 Insert dowels into the lower three tiers; six for the bottom tier, and three each for the other two tiers. Trim them level with the surface of the cake. Do this by marking a line with a knife on the side of the dowel at the top of the cake's surface, remove the dowel and either trim with a sharp knife using a rolling motion to score a line around and snap or cut through using wire cutters. They should not stand proud of the cake's surface (see page 50).

8 Run a clean sharp knife around the bottom edges of the upper three tiers to release them from their spare boards. Then spread royal icing on the 30cm (12in) cake. Lift up the 25cm (10in) cake by sliding it to the edge of the board, put your hand underneath, lift (the thin cake board should remain with the cake) and place it on the 30cm (12in) cake. Position the 25cm (10in) cake so that its scallops lie centrally over the petals of the base cake. Repeat for the two upper tiers, alternating the position of the petals on each cake against the one below (see picture on page 65).

9 Glue 3mm ($\frac{1}{8}$in) wide sand dune ribbon around the edge of the 10cm (4in) cake card, then stick this on top of the 15cm (6in) cake with royal icing. Fix lengths of the 7mm ($\frac{1}{3}$in) wide sand dune ribbon around the base of each cake, making sure all the joins are at the back.

10 Colour 150g (5oz) royal icing the same dark cream as before and add a few drops of water to soften the icing. Fill a bag fitted with a no.1.5 piping tube (tip), then pipe scrolls on all the cakes, starting at the top and working your way down towards the base. Drop pipe lines of icing to form the scrolls on the tops of the cakes, but for the sides this will not be possible. (For the sides it will help if you have a tilting turntable,

✻ ✻ ✻ ✻

Scrolls and ivy

but do not adjust to full tilt or the cake will be unstable.) Pipe against the side of the cake, a few millimetres away from the surface. Move your hand and arm while squeezing the bag, keeping an even pressure and working at an equal distance from the cake's surface. When the scrolls on all the cakes are dry, fix the small ivy leaves to the scrolls and board. Save ten for the top decoration.

11 Trace the scrolls design (see page 150). Colour 50g (1$^{3}/_{4}$oz) royal icing the same dark cream colour and add a tiny amount of gum tragacanth. Mix thoroughly and add it to a piping bag with a no.2 piping tube. On a piece of waxed paper, pipe half a vertical scroll but stop where the horizontal one will join on. Pipe a complete horizontal scrolls then, using a damp paintbrush, ease the end of the first scroll so that it touches and joins it. Leave to dry for about 20 minutes under a lamp. Then pipe a complete vertical scroll, piping over the join. Leave to dry.

12 Carefully slide a cranked palette knife (metal spatula) under the icing to release it from the paper and turn it over. Pipe over the horizontal scroll in one go and leave it to dry. (It is now two layers thick, which should be strong enough to stand up on the cake.) You will need three complete scrolls for the top decoration, two facing one way and one facing the other way.

11

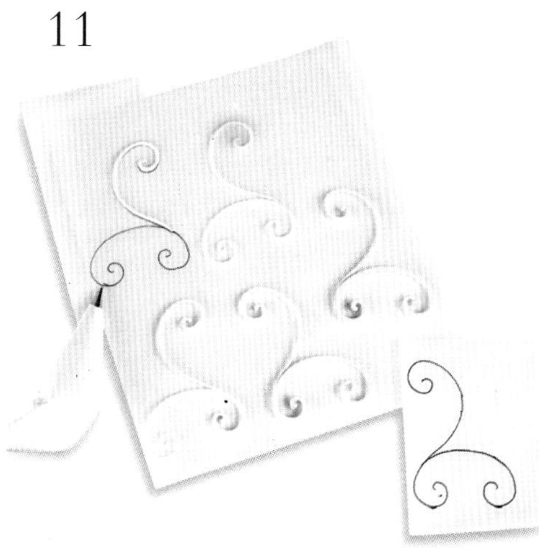

Helpful Hint

You may find it easier to support the first piped scroll with a piece of sponge foam on either side, while you pipe icing on the second scroll prior to fixing it to the cake.

13 Fix the three scrolls to the 10cm (4in) cake card with royal icing, so that they meet in the middle. Stick about seven ivy leaves to the scrolls, plus three on the board in between the scrolls.

14 Finally, glue a length of the 15mm ($^{5}/_{8}$in) wide sand dune ribbon around the edge of the 40cm (16in) cake board.

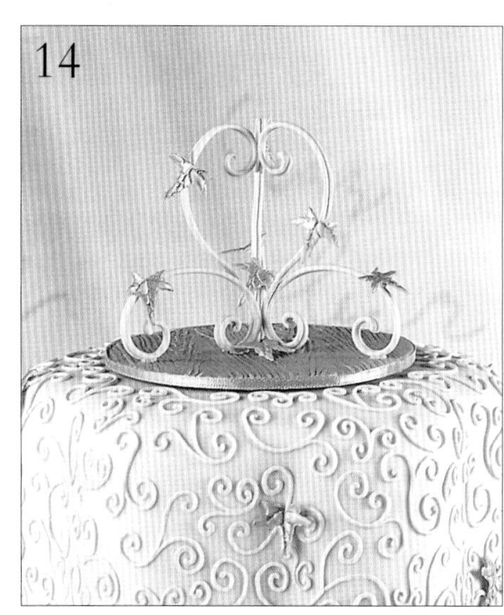

Bridal lace

Any bride would be delighted to have a wedding cake decorated with the same pattern of lace as her dress. This can be achieved by making a mould from a piece of the lace, and using this to make the cake decorations. Add a bouquet of sugar or fresh flowers to complement the bride's bouquet.

Cake and decoration

30 x 25cm (12 x 10in)
and 25 x 20cm (10 x 8in)
oval fruit cakes
20 x 15cm (8 x 6in) teardrop-shaped
fruit cake
40 x 35cm (16 x 14in)
oval, thin cake board
25 x 20cm (10 x 8in)
oval cake card
20cm (8in) square, thin cake card
3.5kg (7lb) ivory coloured sugarpaste
(rolled fondant)
250g (8oz) white flower paste
Mother-of-pearl dusting powder
(petal dust/blossom tint)
Arrangement of sugar or silk flowers
1.5m ($1^2/_3$yd), 15mm ($^5/_8$in) wide
green ribbon

Essential equipment

Small work board
Silicone plastique [CS]
Piece of lace
Veining tool [HP]
Seven cake dowels
Sugarpaste gun and trifoil attachment
Miniature cutting wheel [PME]/scalpel
1cm ($^1/_2$in) wide flat dusting brush
Cake pick

1 Cover the small board with cling film (plastic wrap). Thoroughly mix together equal amounts of the two compounds supplied in the pack of silicone plastique, one white and one blue. Knead together for a few minutes until the mixture begins to feel firm, then roll it out onto the cling film to about 1cm ($^1/_2$in) thick, although this will vary according to the thickness of the lace being used. Press the lace firmly into the paste, using a small sponge, paying attention to small details. Remove the lace and leave the mould to dry. It will be a few hours before you can use it.

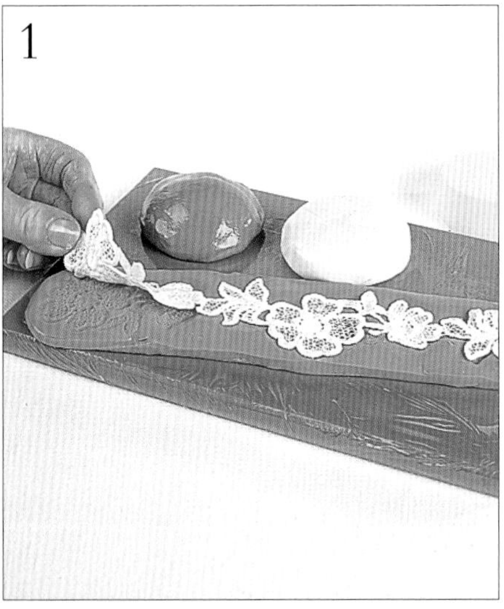
1

Helpful Hint

Have all the necessary materials ready before you start, because once the silicone compounds are mixed, they start to solidify fairly quickly and will only allow a short working time. Mix only the amount you need for the mould you want, as this material is not re-usable.

✳ ✳ ✳ ✳

Stacked wedding cakes

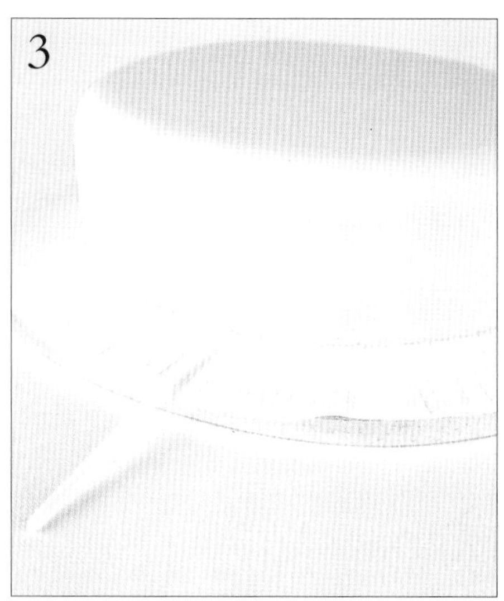
3

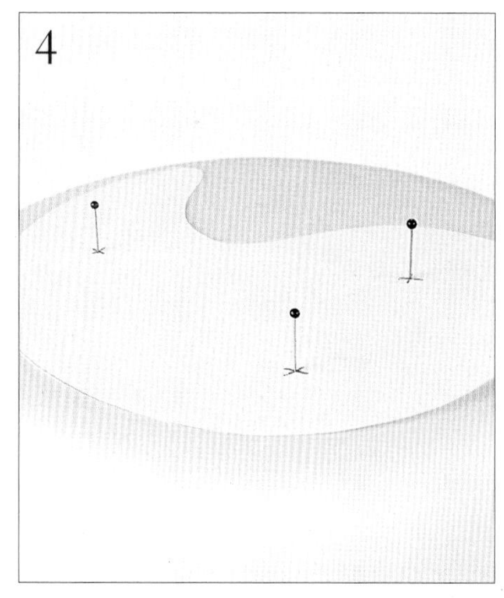
4

5

2 Place the largest cake on the cake board, the medium on the oval, thin cake card, and cut the teardrop shape out of the thin cake card, using the cake tin (pan) as a template. Make sure the cards under the medium and small cakes are exactly the same size as the cake, so that they do not show when the cake is coated.

3 Marzipan the cakes (see page 143). When dry, cover each cake with ivory sugarpaste (rolled fondant). Cover the edge of the base cake board with a strip of ivory sugarpaste and texture with a veining tool. Roll the tool backwards and forwards in short spans, keeping it at 90° to the edge of the board to make sure that the resulting lines radiate from the centre of the cake. Leave the covered cakes to dry for at least 24 hours.

4 Make a template of the top and middle tiers by drawing round the cake tins, then mark the positions of the dowels. There should be four dowels in the base cake, and three in the middle cake, due to the shape of the top tier. Place the templates on the cake below, and prick through to indicate where to insert the dowels.

5 At each point, make a hole in the cake with a narrow tool, then push the dowels straight down until they are resting on the cake card or board beneath. Mark the dowels level with the cake surface, remove, cut at the mark, and insert back in the holes. Position the cakes on top of each other. For safety, a small amount of sugarpaste, softened into a paste, can be spread under the cakes. Check that the cakes are placed centrally on the cake beneath. Remember that the stacked cake will be heavy to carry.

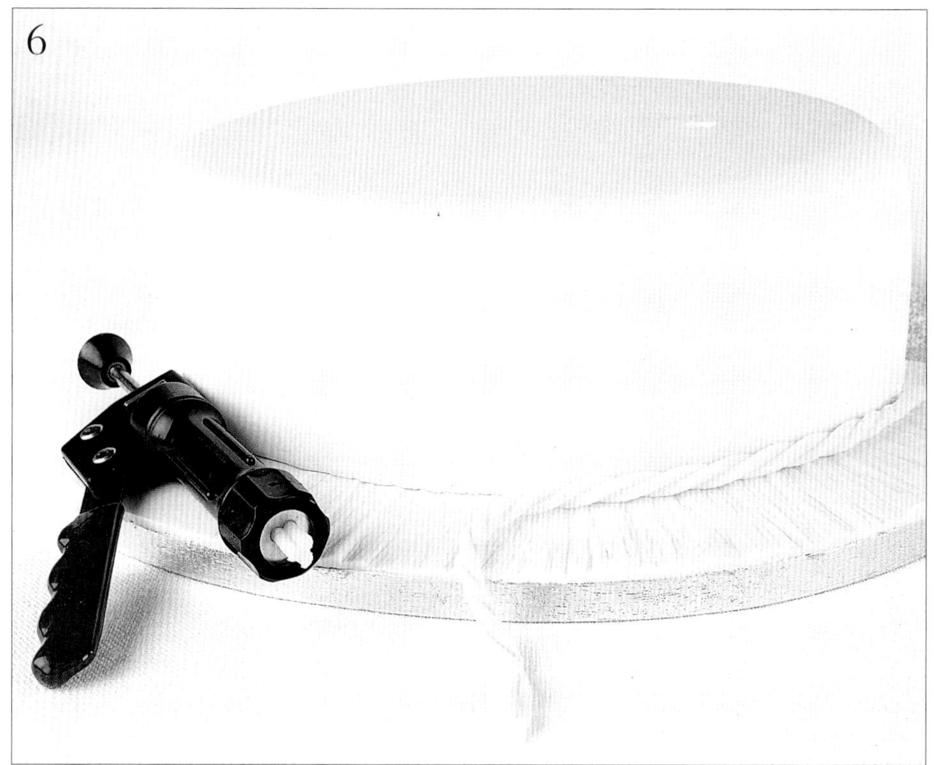
6

✳ ✳ ✳ ✳

HELPFUL HINT

Always use food quality dowels and flower holders, and warn the bride and groom, as well as the person responsible for cutting up the cake, that they have been inserted in the cakes.

6 Load a sugarpaste gun with sugarpaste, and fit it with a large trifoil attachment. Extrude several long lengths of sugarpaste. Soften the sugarpaste slightly with boiled water first, as this will make it easier to push it out of the tool. Twist the lengths of paste and place round the base of each cake, securing with sugarpaste glue. If you need to join two lengths, cut through both pieces at an angle to match the pattern. Alternatively, roll two long, thin sausages of sugarpaste and twist them together.

7 Mix equal amounts of sugarpaste and flower paste together. Roll out thinly on a small board which has been lightly greased with vegetable fat. The fat will enable you to roll out the paste very thinly, and ensures an accurate impression from the mould. Place the paste over the lace mould you have made, with the fat side down, and press it firmly into the mould using a small sponge.

7

8

8 Remove the paste from the mould, turn it pattern side up, and cut round the design with a miniature cutting wheel or a scalpel. Brush with mother-of-pearl dusting powder, and attach to the side of the cake with a little sugarpaste glue. Work with short lengths so it is easier to handle the lace pieces. Cut away part of the design to fill the gap when you reach the end of the cake circumference.

9 Make a hole using a length of dowel in the middle tier cake, just in front of the indent of the teardrop cake. Insert a cake pick, and slot in a bouquet of artificial flowers, using a selection of flowers that will complement the floral arrangements at the wedding. Alternatively, make an arrangement of sugar flowers.

10 Attach a ribbon round the base cake board, matching one of the colours in the bouquet.

10

Candles and flowers

Gone are the days when all wedding cakes were round or square. There is no rule that says all tiers have to be the same shape either. This cake is designed to show that each tier can be different in every way but linked subtly with the use of colour.

Cake and decoration

30cm (12in) oval fruit cake
25cm (10in) teardrop fruit cake
10cm (4in) round fruit cake
30cm (12in) oval cake board
25cm (10in) teardrop-shaped thin cake board (if not available cut your own)
10cm (4in) round thin cake board
3.35kg (6lb 12oz) marzipan
3.4kg (6lb 13oz) white sugarpaste (rolled fondant)
30g (1oz) flower paste
100g (3½oz) royal icing
Navy, spruce and black paste food colourings
Silver dusting powder (petal dust/blossom tint) [SK]
Dipping solution
2.75m (3yd), 3mm (⅛in) wide silver lamé ribbon
1.25m (1⅓yd), 15mm (⅝in) wide antique white ribbon
48 dusky blue silk rosebuds
2m (2¼yd) white shimmer wire
Nine pearl sprays
Small bunch 'iridescent' gypsophila
Two silver candles

Essential equipment

Template (see page 150)
Six cake dowels
Nos.1 and 1.5 piping tubes (tips)
6.5m (7yd) white pearls
Nos.0 and 4 paintbrushes
Blossom cutter [F5, OP]
White floristry tape

1 Using apricot jam or masking jelly, stick the teardrop-shaped cake to the thin teardrop board (cut a board to fit if you cannot find one ready-made), and the 10cm (4in) cake to the thin 10cm (4in) board. Marzipan the cakes (see page 143). Rest the teardrop and top cake on spare cake boards temporarily and the 30cm (12in) oval on the oval board. Leave to dry at least a week.

2 Cover the cakes with white sugarpaste (rolled fondant), using 2kg (4lb) for the base, 1kg (2lb) for the middle and 350g (12oz) for the top tier. Leave to dry for a few days, then cover the oval board around the 30cm (12in) cake with a strip of white sugarpaste. Leave the covered cakes to dry for a week.

3 Insert three cake dowels into each of the two lower tiers, and trim level with the surface of the cake. It is very important they do not stand proud of the surface. Run a sharp knife around the bases of the two upper tiers, then spread a little royal icing on the bottom cake where the teardrop-shaped cake will go. Slide the teardrop-shaped cake to the edge of the temporary board, ease your hand underneath and lift and lower onto the oval cake. Adjust its position if necessary (it should slide around on the royal icing underneath enough for this), then press down gently to secure. Repeat for the top tier.

4 Fill a bag fitted with a no.1.5 tube (tip) with a little royal icing and pipe a line of icing around the

love you

Stacked wedding cakes

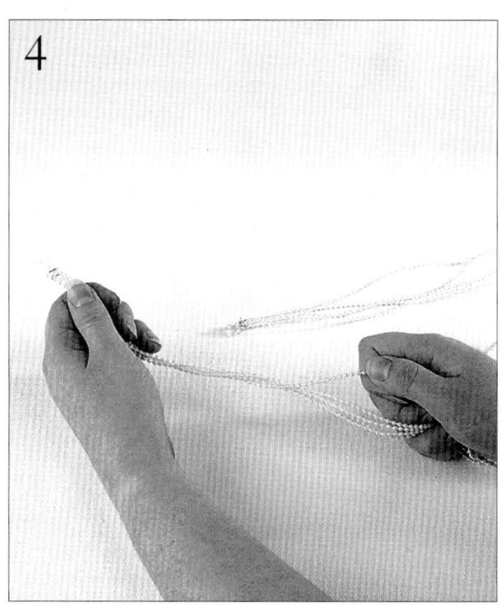
4

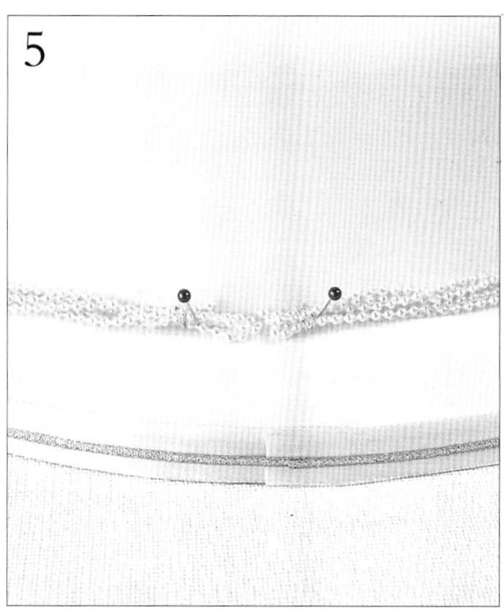
5

base of the top cake. Starting at the back, secure one end of the string of pearls in the icing and press them into the icing all the way around. Snip off the string at the back where it joins. Fix a length of 3mm (1/8in) wide silver lamé just above the pearls and secure at the back with royal icing. Repeat for the teardrop cake with the pearls and ribbon. Measure around the base cake with a tape measure, and fold the remaining string of pearls five times to that length. Bind a piece of wire around the top end temporarily, and around the other, leaving one string of pearls free. Wrap the free string of pearls around all the others, working along its length, then secure at the end with another piece of wire.

5 Squeeze a line of icing around the base of the bottom cake and stick one end of the string of pearls into the icing. Insert a glass-headed pin into the pearls near the wire and into the cake to secure the pearls until the icing has dried. Gently stick the string of pearls into the icing around the base cake, meeting at the back (there should be no overlap), then secure this end with another glass-headed pin. When the icing has dried, the pearls will be set in position, and the pins and wire can be removed.

6 Trace the lettering (see page 150). Transfer to the front and back of the top tier, and then paint with silver dusting powder (petal dust/blossom tint) mixed with a little dipping solution, using a no.0 brush.

7 Fill a bag fitted with a no.1 piping tube and a teaspoon of royal icing (softened with a tiny amount of water) and pipe in the spirals on the middle cake. Start with the centre of each spiral, curl around and trail off. Fill in between the spirals with little dots. Leave to dry, and then paint just the spirals silver with the silver dusting powder, dipping solution and a no.0 brush.

8 For the flowers on the bottom tier, colour 30g (1oz) flower paste dusky blue using navy, spruce and a little black paste food colouring. Roll out the paste quite thinly, and cut out about ten flowers using the blossom cutter. Moisten the backs of the blossoms, using the no.4 brush and stick randomly to the bottom tier. Add a few drops of water to a tablespoon of white royal icing and put some in a piping bag fitted with a no.1.5 tube.

9 Pipe around the blossoms so that the piped icing sits on the cake surface and not on top of the blossom, except where the petals join towards the centre. Pipe spirals in the middle of each blossom and randomly on the cake, and wiggly lines radiating out from the blossoms. When they are dry, paint them with the silver dusting powder, dipping solution and the no.0 brush.

10 Using white floristry tape, tape 24 dusky blue silk rosebuds together in a tight posy shape. Take 1m (1 1/8yd) of the shimmer wire, form continuous loops with it and tape them together with

8

✻ ✻ ✻ ✻

Candles and flowers

the rosebuds. Add five pearl sprays, and then fill in with gypsophila to fill it out underneath. Tape together neatly, trim the end with wire cutters and insert into a cake pick and then into the middle of the top tier. (It may help if you make a pilot hole first in the cake with the end of a paintbrush or something similar.)

11 Trim the candles with a sharp knife so that one is 25cm (10in) long and the other 21cm (8 1/2in) long. Roll 35g (1 1/4oz) white sugarpaste into a ball and stick to the top of the base cake where the teardrop shape goes inwards. Insert the candles side by side into the paste. You may want to remove them and pipe a little royal icing in the hole, then reinsert the candles for added stability. Leave for a couple of hours before adding the flowers. Working in reverse order to before, create a posy with gypsophila, four pearl sprays and 1m (1 1/8yd) shimmer wire formed into continuous loops.

12 Finally, add 24 rosebuds, trimmed to an appropriate length and inserted one at a time around the candles and into the sugarpaste. Stick the 15mm (5/8in) wide antique white ribbon to the edge of the base board, and then glue the 3mm (1/8in) wide silver lamé over the top in the middle. Tie the remaining silver lamé into a bow, trim the ends and fix to the pearls with a blob of royal icing at the front of the base cake.

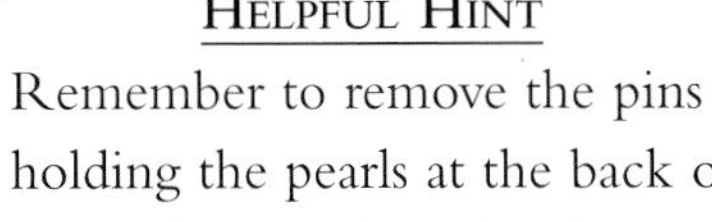

Helpful Hint

Remember to remove the pins holding the pearls at the back of the oval cake when they have dried in position.

Champagne celebration

This fun wedding cake is decorated with ever popular teddy bears, on which simple cut-out shapes of hearts, champagne bottles and glasses are used for maximum effect. The cake is given added sparkle with a length of silver cord draped around each tier and used to trim the board.

Cake and decoration

13cm (5in), 20cm (8in) and 28cm (11in) square fruit cakes
15cm (6in) double thickness and 20cm (8in) single thickness square thin cake cards
35cm (14in) and 38cm (15in) square cake boards
4kg (8lb) marzipan
4kg (8lb) white sugarpaste (rolled fondant)
250g (8oz) Mexican paste
60g (2oz) flower paste
250g (8oz) royal icing
Gold and mother-of-pearl dusting powders (petal dusts/blossom tints)
Egg yellow, brown, pink, blue, green and black liquid food colourings
2m (2¼yd), 15mm (⅝in) wide silver ribbon
6m (6½yd) silver cord
Edible confetti (made with Mexican paste and miniature cutters)
Four 18cm (7in) Grecian pillars

Essential equipment

Templates (see page 147)
Eight cake dowels
Set of heart cutters
No.3 piping tube (tip)
Champagne bottle and glass cutters [PC]
Miniature flower cutters
Small carnation cutter

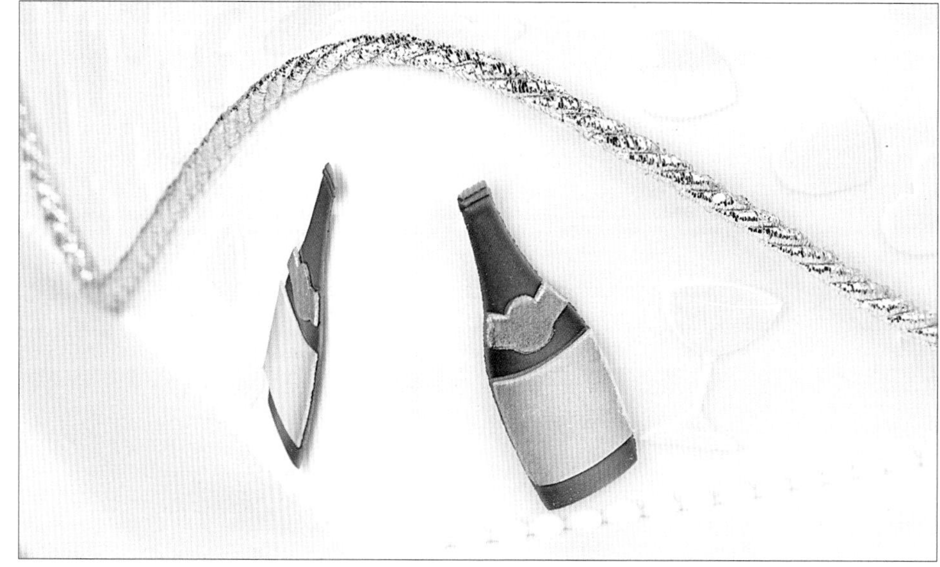

1 Place the 13cm (5in) cake on the 15cm (6in) double thickness card, the 20cm (8in) cake on the 20cm (8in) thin card and the 28cm (11in) cake on the 35cm (14in) board. Cover with marzipan (see page 143). When dry, cover the cakes with white sugarpaste (rolled fondant) and leave to dry.

2 Set the base tier cake and board on top of the 38cm (15in) cake board and fill in the gap between the two boards with royal icing, smoothing it to a slope. Leave to dry.

3 Roll out four long, thin strips of sugarpaste and use to cover each edge of the top tier board, allowing the strips to overlap at the corners. Cut through the overlap, and smooth down to create a neat join. Cover the base tier board in the same way, using long strips of white sugarpaste wide enough to reach down over the slope. Overlap the strips at the corners, then cut through the overlap and finish as before. Smooth and trim the paste level with the top edge of the board.

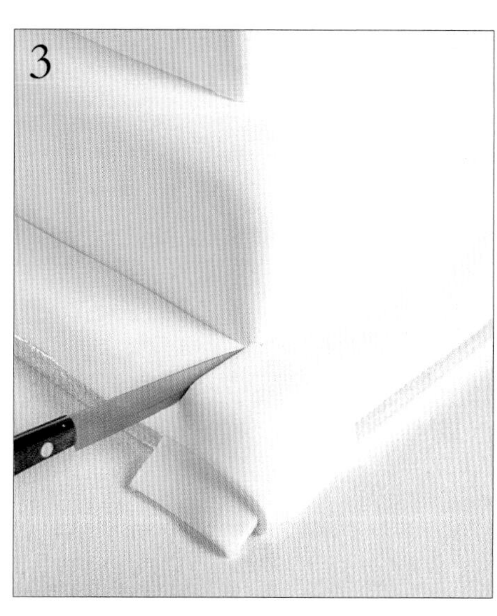
3

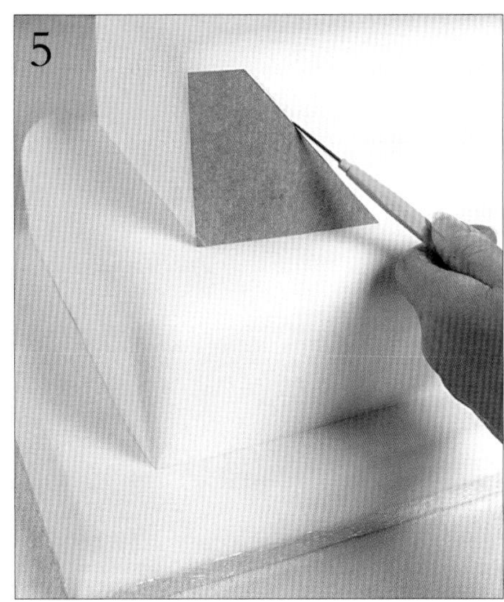

4 Make a template of the middle tier, and mark on this where the dowels should be placed. There should be four dowels in the base cake in order to support the top two tiers. Place the template on the base cake, and prick through the template to indicate where to insert the dowels. Remove the template and at each point, make a hole in the cake with a narrow tool first, then push in the dowels until they are resting on the cake board. Mark the dowels level with the cake surface, remove and cut at this point, then insert back into the holes. Place the middle cake on top of the base cake.

5 Cut out the side templates (see page 147). Place a template against the corner of each cake and score a line along the diagonal edge with a knife to mark the position of the silver cord, creating a 'V' shape on each side of the three cakes.

6 Make 250g (8oz) Mexican paste (see page 142), then roll out, very thinly, on a greased board. Turn the paste over and cut out some small hearts (you will need three different sizes for the three tiers). Dust the hearts with mother-of-pearl dusting powder (petal dust/blossom tint). Moisten the backs and attach to the sides of the cakes. Arrange in a fan shape inside the scored marks.

Helpful Hint

The mother-of-pearl dusting powder will stick to the greasy surface of the Mexican paste, and will form a solid, shiny metallic finish.

7 Mix sugarpaste with water and paddle with a palette knife (metal spatula) to a piping consistency, then place in a piping bag fitted with a no.3 tube (tip). Pipe a line along the marks on the sides and over the corners, and attach the silver cord, securing with glass-headed pins until dry.

8 Make a 15cm (6in) square template, the same size as the board underneath the top tier, and mark the position of the pillars on the middle tier. Set the pillars as close to the corners of the square as

Champagne celebration

11

possible to allow room for the teddy bears. Dowel the middle tier, slot the pillars over the dowels and then cut the dowels level with the top of the pillars, so that the cake above will rest on the dowels, not just the pillars.

9 Pipe a pearl border round the base of the cakes using softened sugarpaste with a no.3 piping tube. Trim the edges of the base board with silver ribbon. Pipe a line of royal icing along the top of the ribbon and attach a line of the silver cord. Secure the cord with pins until dry.

10 Colour some Mexican paste green and roll out on a greased board. Cut out eight small champagne bottles. Cut out labels and glasses from white Mexican paste, adding an extra layer to the bowl of the glass. Smear the labels and glasses lightly with vegetable fat and dust with gold and mother-of-pearl dusting powders as before. Place the labels on the bottles and airbrush down the sides with black, or dust the colour on with black powder. Attach to the corners of the base tier at an angle.

11 Cut out a large heart-shaped plaque in white Mexican paste for the top and trim straight at the bottom to allow it to stand up. Cut a smaller heart for a base plaque. Cut out a large champagne bottle and labels and dry over a small curve. Cut out a large glass and dry flat. Grease and dust the hearts and labels in the same colours as before. Dry the labels on the same curve as the bottle and stick together when dry.

12 To assemble, stick the smaller heart on the top tier. Stand up the large heart, secure with icing at its base, and support until dry. Attach the bottle and the glass to the front of this heart. Finish with twists of flower paste, rolled round a piece of spaghetti, and pink and blue confetti made with miniature cutters.

13 Colour 170g (6oz) Mexican paste a teddy bear colour, using egg yellow and brown food colourings. Each bear is made from 85g (3oz) paste, using 40g (1¼oz) for the body, 20g (¾oz) for the head, 15g (½oz) for two legs, 10g (⅓oz) for two arms and 5g (¼oz) for the ears and muzzle. Roll the bodies into a cone shape, hollowing out on the top for the head, and press in slightly at the base for the legs. Leave to dry. Roll a ball for the head, then add a flattened muzzle. Indent holes for the nose and eyes, and mark the mouth. Stick the head to the body with edible glue, and add the ears. Roll tiny cones of black paste, insert into the eyes and nose and press flat. Shape and attach the legs to each bear.

14 For the female bear, cut out a 13cm (5in) circle and frill the edge for the dress, then place over the body. Cut a strip for the sash and attach a bow. Shape arms and cover with sleeves, then attach to the body and support with sponge foam until dry. For the bouquet, roll a cone and flatten the end. Cover with a green circle cut out with a carnation cutter, and add pink and blue miniature flowers. Place a circle of the same flowers round her head.

15 Make the pieces for the waistcoat with black paste and attach (adjust to fit the body). Add a pink bowtie. Attach arms, supporting until dry, then add a pink heart in his hands. To make a top hat, cut out a cylinder of sugarpaste with a small round cutter. Cover the top with a black disc, using the same cutter, and a strip of black paste round the sides. Place on a larger circle of paste, for the brim. Place the bears inside the pillars, scatter some edible confetti around them. To finish, place the top tier on the four pillars.

15

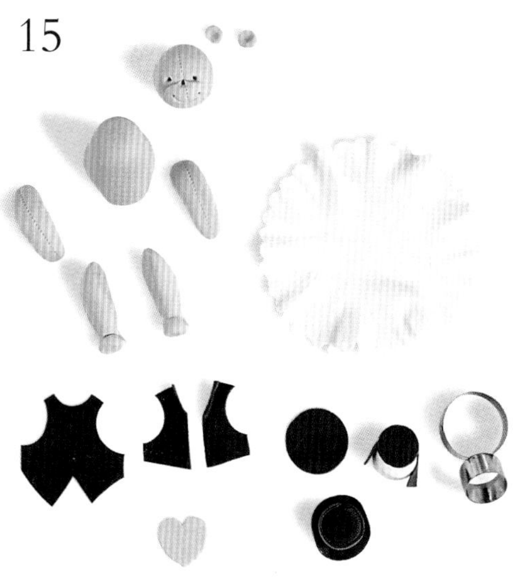

Garlands and tulle

This four-tier wedding cake is not strictly speaking a stacked cake, but with the use of concealed pillars it gives that impression. Draped tulle around each cake and the large bow on top gives the cake a soft romantic look. Simply decorated with piped dots, a garland of rosebuds and ivy adorns each tier.

✻ ✻ 

Cake and decoration

30cm (12in), 25cm (10in), 20cm (8in) and 15cm (6in) hexagonal fruit cakes
40cm (16in), 30cm (12in), 25cm (10in), 20cm (8in) hexagonal cake boards
5kg (10lb) marzipan
5kg (10lb) ivory sugarpaste (rolled fondant)
150g (5oz) royal icing
Caramel/ivory paste food colouring
5.5m (6yd), 15cm (6in) wide eggshell tulle
2.5m (2¾yd), 3mm (⅛in) wide ivory ribbon; 4.5m (5yd), 15mm (⅝in) wide ivory ribbon
Dark green and white floristry tape
20-, 26- and 28-gauge dark green wires; 28-gauge white wire
Silk flowers: ivory gypsophila, dark green ivy leaves, large and small dusky pink rosebuds [DI], large and small claret rosebuds [DI], large and small ivory rosebuds [DI], small pink rosebuds [DI] and ivory pink freesias (see page 82 for quantities)
One flower pick [C]
Nine hidden pillars [W]

✻

Essential equipment

No.1 piping tube (tip)
24 glass-headed pins
A3 paper, pencil and compass
Wire cutters

1 Stick each cake to its board with apricot jam or masking jelly. Marzipan the cakes (see page 143) and leave to dry for up to a week.

2 Cover the cakes with the same amounts of ivory sugarpaste (rolled fondant) as for the marzipan. Leave to dry overnight. Roll out the trimmings into long strips and cover the boards. Leave for a week to dry.

3 Colour 150g (5oz) royal icing with the caramel food colouring to match the sugarpaste. Fill a piping bag with a no.1 piping tube (tip) and pipe small dots all over the surface of each cake. When piping, use a gentle stabbing motion so the tube actually touches the cake. Keep an even pressure on the piping bag as you work, instead of squeezing and releasing. Leave to dry.

4 To calculate for the pinched tulle around the base of each cake, measure across one side of each cake and multiply by six to get the

✻ ✻ ✻ ✻

Stacked wedding cakes

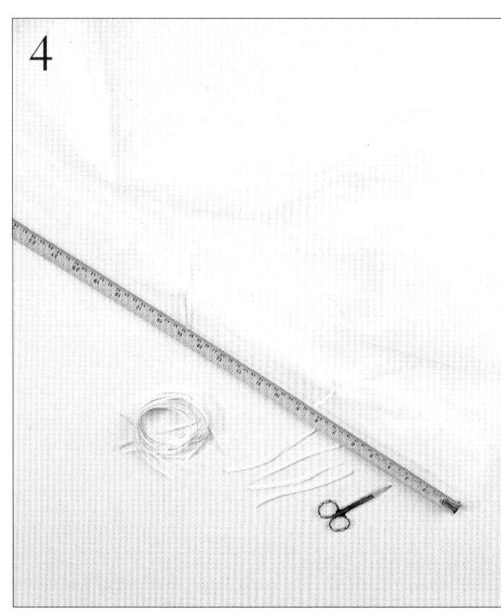
4

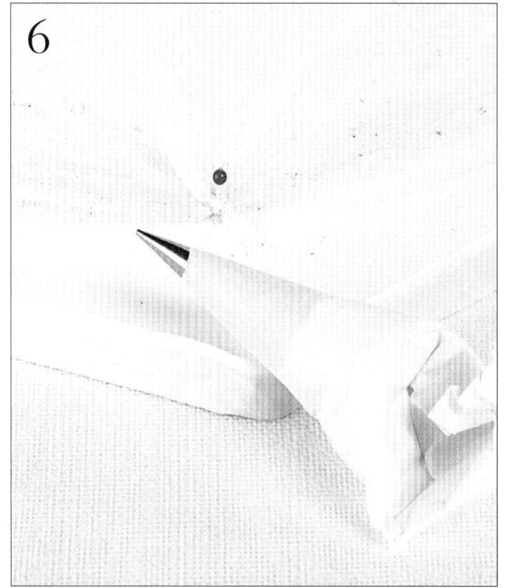
6

circumference, then add 4cm (1½in) for an overlap. Cut four strips from the length of tulle measuring 125cm (49in), 105cm (41in), 90cm (35½in) and 72cm (28in), leaving the rest for the top arrangement. Cut the 3mm (⅙in) ivory ribbon into 24 10cm (4in) lengths.

5 Take the longest length of tulle for the 30cm (12in) cake and lay it out flat on a clean table. Fold the long edges into the centre to make a long cylinder. Turn it over so the ends are underneath and measure 21cm (8½in) in from the left. Use your fingers to gather the tulle across its width at this point and tie a piece of ribbon around it into a double knot. Measure and tie off the tulle at five intervals, spaced 19cm (7½in) apart (if your measurements differ from this use your own measurements instead). Pipe a blob of icing on one of the corners at the back of the cake.

6 Position the first ribbon and tulle on the royal icing at the corner and secure with a glass-headed pin. (Remove the pins when dry.) Work around the cake, securing at each corner in the same way until you get to the last corner. Place a piece of ribbon on the board (easier than threading the ribbon underneath and around with one hand), then overlap the ends of the tulle so that they meet at a corner and pinch the tulle together. Lift up the ends of the ribbon from behind and tie the ends around the tulle in a double knot. Trim the ends of the tulle close to the ribbon, and then trim all the ribbon ends to the same length. Repeat for the other cakes, tying ribbon at the following intervals: 16cm (6½in) intervals for the 25cm (10in) cake, 13cm (5in) intervals for the 20cm (8in) cake and 9.5cm (3¾in) intervals for the 15cm (6in) cake (use your own measurements if different). Add 2cm (¾in) onto the first interval to allow for the overlap.

7 Using a compass or round cake boards, draw four circles on a piece of paper in the following sizes: 30cm (12in), 25cm (10in), 20cm (8in) and 11cm (4½in). These will make the templates for the flower garlands.

8 Commercial silk flowers either have very long stiff-wired stems or plastic floppy stems, neither of which bend very easily. To make them

Cake sizes	30cm (12in)	25cm (10in)	20cm (8in)	11cm (4½in)
Gypsophila	12	12	8	8
Ivy	8	8	8	6
Dusky pink rosebuds				
Large	6	6	4	3
Small	12	6	4	6
Claret rosebuds				
Large	6	6	4	/
Small	/	/	/	3
Ivory rosebuds				
Large	12	6	/	/
Medium	/	6	4	3
Pale pink rosebuds				
small	8	6	6	6
Ivory pink freesia	15	6	12	6

✻ ✻ ✻ ✻

Garlands and tulle

9

10

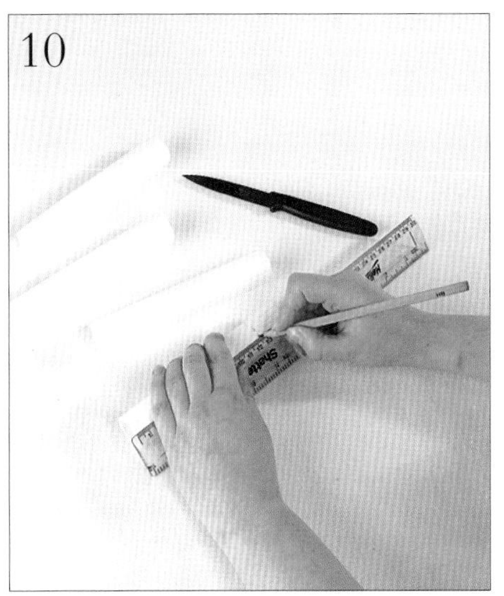

easier to work with, pull out the existing wire and replace it with a more pliable one. Take a piece of green wire and bend it in two, leaving a circle of wire at the bent end. Thread the two cut ends of wire into the centre of the flower and pull through: the circle of wire should stop it from going all the way through.

Wrap green tape along the length of the stem as close to the base of the flower as possible. Rewire the large rosebuds with 26-gauge wire, the medium rosebuds with 28-gauge wire and snipped off single ivy leaves with 28-gauge wire. The smallest rosebuds did not need rewiring and were just taped over. You will need 40 small sprigs of gypsophila on 28-gauge wire with white floristry tape, and 30 separate ivy leaves.

Refer to the chart (opposite) for the correct number of flowers per cake.

9 Wire the garland for the largest cake with 20-gauge wire. Tape a few larger flowers to the wire, and then a couple of the filler flowers, ivy and gypsophila. Every so often lay the wired flowers over the 30cm (12in) template and bend to follow the curve (see above). Group the larger flowers at evenly spaced intervals. When you have completed a circle, trim the wire, leaving about 5–8cm (2–3in), and tape this securely to the starting point. Repeat for the other cakes. For the 15cm (6in) cake, leave about 5cm (2in) of wire at the beginning and the end, then tape them together to stick out at an angle of 90° to the garland, and insert the wire into a cake pick.

10 Measure the depth of the three bottom cakes. Add 5cm (2in) to the depth of the 30cm (12in) and 25cm (10in) cakes, and 4cm (1$\frac{1}{2}$in) to the 20cm (8in) cake, then transfer these measurements to the hidden pillars. Allow three per cake. Mark a line around each pillar and follow this line when cutting, using a sawing motion, to create a level pillar.

11 Lay the garlands on each cake and place the pillars inside the garlands, inserting them into the cake. Insert the smallest garland into the top cake. Tie the remaining tulle into a bow. Thread 28-gauge white wire through the back and fix to the garland. Trim and neaten the tulle.

11

Miniature cakes

Over the past few years there has been a growing interest in the many varied gifts that the bride and groom organize for their wedding guests as a keepsake of their special day. Miniature cakes make lovely individual gifts which can be presented as well as, or in place of, favours and crackers.

Miniature cakes make lovely gifts for wedding guests. These small cakes can also be made and given (or posted with care) to guests unable to attend. They do not have to be mini replicas of the real cake, they can be as simple or creative as you want them to be. By using the same colours, flowers or ribbon they should complement the overall theme quite well.

Baking and shaping

Decide which shape to use. Square cakes will cut down on wastage but round shapes are quicker and easier to cover. It is not advisable to use shapes that are too complicated; all it takes is for a big juicy raisin to be in the wrong place and you could lose a corner when you cut out the shape.

It would be very fiddly to try to decorate a cake smaller than 5cm (2in). The mini round cakes shown here were baked in a 10cm (4in) round cake tin (pan) and presented on a 15cm (6in) thick cake card. The stacked cakes are also presented on a 15cm (6in) card (the bottom tiers are each about 9–10cm [$3\frac{1}{2}$–4in] wide).

For square cakes, bake one large shallow cake, and cut into smaller squares. If you have a lot of mini cakes to produce, cover the top of the large uncut fruit cake with marzipan, flip over so the top is underneath and then cut into squares. Then roll out marzipan, cut into strips and wrap around the sides of each cake. Bake round cakes in individually sized baked bean cans (lined with greaseproof [wax baking] paper as a normal cake tin), buy or hire 10cm (4in) round cake tins and use these, or again bake a large square cake and cut out circles all the same size with a circle cutter.

For the mini stacked cakes, a fruit cake was sliced into layers (as you would a sponge cake before filling) and each layer of fruit cake was used to cut either circles or squares from.

Miniature sponge cakes could be the answer for those who do not like fruit cakes. Cut out the required shapes and cover with a thin layer of marzipan (optional) and sugarpaste (rolled fondant), using buttercream or apricot jam/masking jelly to stick. Remember that sponge cakes do not keep as long as fruit cake so only make a few days before the wedding.

Marzipanning and covering

Treat as you would normal sized cakes. The top and side method of marzipanning may be more time consuming so possibly adopt the all-in-one method and then cover with sugarpaste. Although it is possible to produce beautifully royal-iced miniature cakes, only attempt to do so if you are an accomplished royal icer with lots of patience!

Decoration and packaging

If making a large number of small cakes, keep the design simple unless you have a lot of time to spare. Also, avoid anything too delicate which could break. Silk flowers or tiny sugar blossoms should stand up to quite rough handling. Think about the size of piping tubes as you may need to scale down any piping. Miniature cakes look nice when presented in a decorated box with ribbons and a name tag. Try to find boxes that exactly fit the boards the cakes are resting on so they do not rattle around inside. See-through acetate boxes are excellent and can be bought from most sugarcraft shops.

Amor

Sugarpaste wedding cakes

Sugarpaste is amazingly versatile: not only can it be moulded and used to model with, it can be painted on and coloured, and used to cover a cake in a matter of minutes. Sugarpaste also tastes delicious. With a silky smooth covering of sugarpaste, cakes look more rounded, softer and less formal. These cakes, both classic and modern, all demonstrate the superb effects that can be created with sugarpaste.

Sugarpaste techniques

There was a time when all sugarpaste had to be made by hand. This was a messy and time-consuming business, but the introduction of ready-made and coloured sugarpaste has made life a lot easier.

WORKING WITH SUGARPASTE

Sugarpaste (rolled fondant) is no longer only available in white and ivory, but it now comes in a variety of other colours. No more colour-stained hands! Sugarpaste comes in its own special packaging and keeps very well inside this. However, once opened it must be wrapped closely in cling film (plastic wrap) and then in a polythene bag.

PREPARATION

Before covering a cake with sugarpaste make sure that the work surface is spotless, your hands are clean and you are wearing an apron. Do not wear any sweaters or clothing with loose fibres as when you move they will shed onto the icing and spoil the covering.

COVERING A CAKE WITH SUGARPASTE

1. Knead the sugarpaste until it starts to soften and form a ball. The paste should be a malleable consistency. Use icing (confectioners') sugar to dust the surface when kneading if necessary. You may need a little more icing sugar in very warm weather. Dust the work surface, put the lump of sugarpaste on top, then lightly dust over the paste. Roll out the paste with a rolling pin the right size for the job. If the rolling pin is too small the ends of the pin will leave grooves in the paste which will then be difficult to remove.

2. Turn the paste regularly and dust it underneath, but not so much on top. Do not fold it over onto itself to dust underneath as you will get a crease across the paste which will also be difficult to remove.

Try to get the paste the same thickness all over by keeping your hands level when rolling out and stopping short of the edges.

3. When the paste is large enough to cover the cake, make sure it is not sticking to the table and rub over the surface of the paste with a cake smoother. Slide both hands under the paste one at a time, lift and lower onto the marzipanned cake, which has been moistened with water or clear alcohol (see page 143).

4. Rub over the top of the cake with a cake smoother to expel any air bubbles and to make sure the sugarpaste adheres to the marzipan, then begin to gently ease the paste around the sides of the cake by opening up any folds and patting down gently with the fleshy part of your hand. Start at the top of the cake and work your way round and down to the bottom. Use a cake smoother to smooth around the cake sides. The cake smoothers with a flat bottom edge are excellent as they get right into the lower edge where the cake meets the board.

5. Trim off the excess icing following the line made by the smoother, then smooth for the last time. Lastly, rub over the top rounded edge with the fleshy part of your hand. The warmth from your hand will blend the icing together and any small cracks that may have appeared will disappear.

TIPS FOR WORKING WITH SUGARPASTE

The following tips will help to ensure that working with sugarpaste is both easy and fun.

KNEADING
Always knead and soften the sugarpaste thoroughly so there are no cracks on the surface.

COLOURS
Use paste colours, not liquid, to mix a special colour. Paste colours are more concentrated and will not make the sugarpaste as sticky and wet as a liquid.

STICKING
Use royal icing, not water, to stick two dried surfaces of sugarpaste together. Stick soft surfaces of sugarpaste together with water or sugar glue.

Sugarpaste techniques

COLOURING SUGARPASTE

Place the sugarpaste on a dusted surface. Using the tip of a knife, dot the required paste colour into the sugarpaste, then knead in until completely blended.

Always add colour sparingly as some are much stronger than others. Once the desired colour is achieved, keep the sugarpaste tightly wrapped until ready to use.

PAINTING ON SUGARPASTE

When painting a design on sugarpaste it is easiest to use a template. Transfer the template to the cake as described below. There is an extensive templates section on pages 144–57 of this book.

Transferring your design

1. Trace the design on tracing paper, using an HB pencil. A pencil harder than this means the line will not transfer, any softer and the line will spread and smudge. When tracing the design on a continuous strip of paper, you may need to stick a few pieces of tracing paper together side by side to get a piece long enough. A tape that lets you draw over the surface (sometimes called 'magic' tape) is very useful. Where designs continue around the sides you will need to allow a few extra centimetres of tracing paper for an overlap.

Pay particular attention to the 'base line' under the design as this indicates either the board that the tracing will rest on or the board covering. This will determine the height of the design up the side of the cake.

Covering the board

Sometimes a recipe will ask you to cover the board last of all. This is so the board covering will look neat and fresh, as if already covered when working on the sides of a cake, it can become damaged and marked.

2. Turn the traced image over and retrace on the reverse side.

3. Turn the tracing back the right way. (The sugarpaste-covered cake to be painted on should have been left to dry for about a week.)

If the design is continuous around the sides, hold one end of the tracing at the back of the cake and wrap it around, with the reverse in contact with the surface of the cake. The bottom edge of the tracing, or the 'base line', should be resting on the board (either covered or uncovered, depending on the instructions.) Stick the tracing to itself with tape, making sure the overlap is on top.

If the design is just in one or two places, tape the design to the cake with 'magic' tape (easier to remove than adhesive tape), ensuring the bottom edge of the tracing is on the board.

4. Having correctly positioned the design, rub over the tracing with a veining tool, whilst holding the tracing still with the other hand. This will save time if the design is quite detailed; the alternative is to scribe over the line with a scribing tool. This method requires a lot more care as the tool may pierce the tracing and leave an unsightly hole in the cake.

Photocopying

If you have easy access to a photocopier it is possible to photocopy your design straight onto the tracing paper. This is much quicker as it will cut out the process of tracing the design twice. Then all you will have to do is trace the design on the reverse and transfer it onto the cake as described above.

Another disadvantage of pressing too hard on the tracing is that the transferred image may become too dark and heavy on the cake and will then be difficult to cover up. Try not to move or drag the tracing while transferring; you may get a double image or a smudged line.

Painting the design

Choose something white and without a pattern for mixing food colours on to get a better idea of what colours look like while you mix. A clean, white tile or plate makes an ideal, easy-to-clean palette. Either paste or liquid colours can be used, and dusting powders (petal dusts/blossom tints) mixed with water or alcohol produce lovely watercolour effects.

Food colours mixed with water can look too transparent and watery, but with the addition of a little superwhite powder the colours will become more opaque and cover more easily. However, do not add too much superwhite powder as it will make the paint too thick and difficult to use. It will also look too heavy and will dry patchily. It depends on the effects you want to achieve; why not try colours with and without the superwhite powder and decide on your preferred method.

Paintbrushes

Use the best sable paintbrushes you can afford. A no.1 and no.4 are good sizes for most work. If covering large areas with one colour a large bristle brush works very well.

1. Put a small amount of the food colours you will need on the tile or plate. This cuts down on dipping into each pot of colour and avoids the colours getting mixed up.

2. To start painting, mix a little superwhite powder with water and introduce small amounts of colour to this to mix to the required shade.

3. Start off by painting the palest colours of the design first, then build up layers of darker colour on top. Make sure you have evenly painted one area before starting on another, and always wash the brush when changing to a different colour.

To blend two colours, leave the first to dry slightly so it is tacky, then paint the darker colour on top. Take excess water off a rinsed brush and, using firm brush strokes, paint over the two colours where they meet to create subtle, shading effects.

4. Complete any further outlining or fine detail work when your work is completely dry.

Tips for painting on sugarpaste

Follow these tips to achieve a perfect result. If you make a mistake, rinse the brush, dip it in clean water and paint over the area. Blot immediately with kitchen towel until the colour disappears. Dust with icing sugar to avoid it drying shiny.

Superwhite powder

Do not add superwhite to black, unless you want grey.

Use colours sparingly

Do not overload the paintbrush with paint. Dip the brush in paint and then take off the excess by painting on the tile or plate first a few times.

Water

Using too much water will dissolve the sugar. The brush should be wet enough to leave a trail of colour behind but not flood the whole area.

✻ ✻ ✻ ✻

Sugarpaste techniques

BAS RELIEF AND WORKING WITH TEMPLATES

In quite a few of the following cake designs tracings are used for bas relief work instead of card templates. A tracing is often more accurate as you can see the shape you are cutting

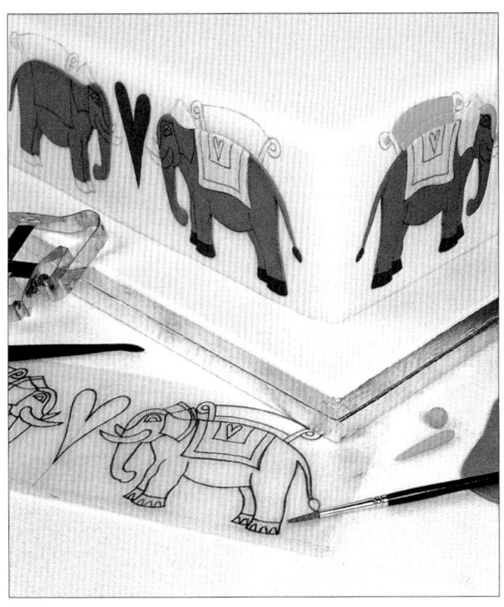

around. Sometimes with a card template the paste underneath can become distorted as you cut around it, and it is not possible to see this until you remove the card. Another advantage of using a tracing is not having to make lots of card templates for different areas. With a tracing simply position it, pencil side down over the paste, rub over the area you want, then remove the paper and cut around the transferred pencil line.

1. Roll out the paste (usually modelling paste, see page 142) to the required thickness, using cornflour (cornstarch) to dust the surfaces. Do not overdust as the paste will just move around when you try to cut around a shape, and it will dry out the paste too much. Just enough is needed to stop it sticking to the table.

2. When you have rolled over the paste for the last time, loosen it from the table with a thin-bladed knife, then 'polish' the surface with your hand to remove the excess cornflour and rub over with a smoother to anchor it to the table. The paste will not move, but will be easy to remove by running a knife underneath.

3. Retrace over the pencil lines every now and again if they begin to get faint. When doing any transferred designs for painting or bas relief it is always best to use an HB pencil. Lay the tracing over the paste (pencil side down) and rub over the tracing with a veining tool in the specific area you require. It does not matter if a little more of the design has transferred than needed as it will be cut away.

4. Cut around the transferred design either with a craft knife or a small thin-bladed knife. To take away the harsh cut edge, gently rub around the edges with fingertips to soften and round them off.

5. Loosen from the table by running a knife underneath, then stick to the cake or plaque. If the design is quite large the piece will be easier to handle if you leave it exposed to the air for a minute or two, as it will keep its shape better. However, only leave it exposed if the design is flat. If it is going on a round cake or over the curved edge of a cake it is best fixed in place straight away.

MARBLING SUGARPASTE

Choose the colour, or colours, you want to use. Dip a knife in one colour at a time, and dot the colour over the sugarpaste. Knead the paste very lightly, just long enough for the colours to start blending. Cut off a portion, and lay the cut edge uppermost: you should be able to see the streaks and lines of colour mixed in which will look like marble when rolled out. Roll out the paste for use.

It is important not to overknead sugarpaste when creating a marble effect. As soon as you have partially mixed the colour into the paste, cover it, and work with one piece at a time. When ready for the next piece, knead in any trimmings from the previous piece, and use it straight away.

Because sugarpaste goes slightly hard when it has been resting for a while, it would not be suitable to be mixed one day and used the next as it would take a bit of kneading to soften it and by then the colours may have been mixed in too thoroughly so there would be no streaks of marble.

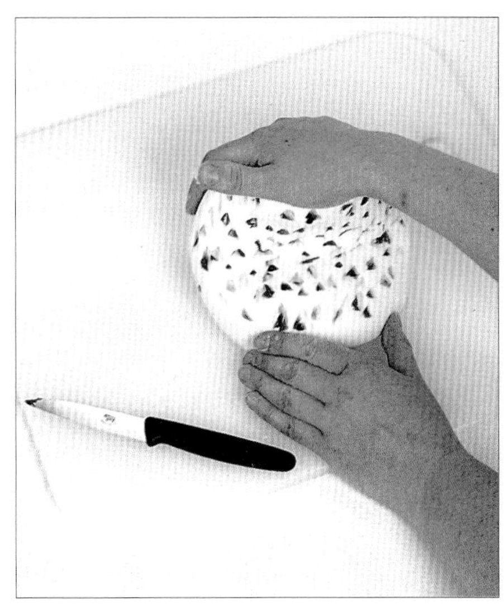

Art nouveau

I recently fell in love with the art and design of the art nouveau period and draw a lot of inspiration from this era when designing. The flower and nasturtium leaf motif used on this cake, with its stylized flowers, flowing stems and dusky, muted colours, has a distinctive art nouveau style.

Cake and decoration

30cm (12in) (10cm [4in] deep) petal-shaped fruit cake, 20cm (8in) and 15cm (6in) round fruit cakes
40cm (16in), 28cm (11in) and 23cm (9in) round cake boards
4kg (8lb) marzipan
4kg (8lb) ivory sugarpaste (rolled fondant)
300g (10oz) royal icing
90g (3oz) flower paste
Holly green, spruce green, mulberry pink, grape violet, chestnut and licorice black paste food colourings
Heraldic black sugartint colour [S]
Champagne, egg yellow, black and foliage green dusting powders (petal dusts/blossom tints)
5m (5½yd), 3mm (⅛in) wide ivory ribbon; 3.25m (3½yd), 1cm (½in) wide featheredge ribbon

Essential equipment

Templates (pages 152–3)
Nos.1, 2 and 4 paintbrushes
Nos.0, 1.5, 2, 3, 4 and 42 piping tubes (tips)
Cake scriber
Butterfly cutter [HH]
24- and 26-gauge wires
Four black stamens
No.2 synthetic paintbrush
Ball tool
Cel pick and cel pad [C]
Nine cake dowels
Nine 15cm (6in) tall plaster pillars

1 Marzipan the cakes (see page 143) and leave to set. Cover with ivory sugarpaste (rolled fondant), using 2.5kg (5lb) for the 30cm (12in), 1kg (2lb) for the 20cm (8in) and 500g (1lb) for the 15cm (6in) cake. Leave to harden for about another week.

2 Trace the templates (see page 152) onto strips of tracing paper and transfer to the sides of the cakes.

3 Using a tilting turntable to rest the cakes on, paint leaves on the cakes. Paint the pale green triangles, with a no.2 brush, mixing spruce green with superwhite and water. Paint the outer leaves with holly green and black, mixed with a tiny amount of superwhite. Use the no.2 brush for the smaller cakes but a no.4 brush for the bottom cake.

4 Colour 100g (3½oz) royal icing pink with a mix of mulberry pink, grape violet and chestnut food colourings. Add water to soften the icing to a 'floppy' consistency. Fill two piping bags; one fitted with a no.2

tube (tip) and the other with a no.1.5 tube. Set up an angle poise lamp on the table to your left so the brush embroidery will dry as you turn the cake to work on the next flower.

5 Begin working on the 30cm (12in) cake with the no.2 tube. Pipe a line of icing down the edge of the centre petal, and a few lines underneath. With a damp no.4 paintbrush held at a 45° angle, draw the icing from the edge of the petal towards the throat of the flower with one smooth stroke. Continue along the edge, drawing the icing inwards until it is all blended. The icing should be thicker at the edges, and thinner towards the centre of the flower. The brush should be damp enough to blend the icing, but not so wet that the icing all runs together. If the icing is blended correctly it will resemble petal veins. Carry on around the rest of the cake working the central petal on each flower. By the time you come round to where you started, the first petal should be dry.

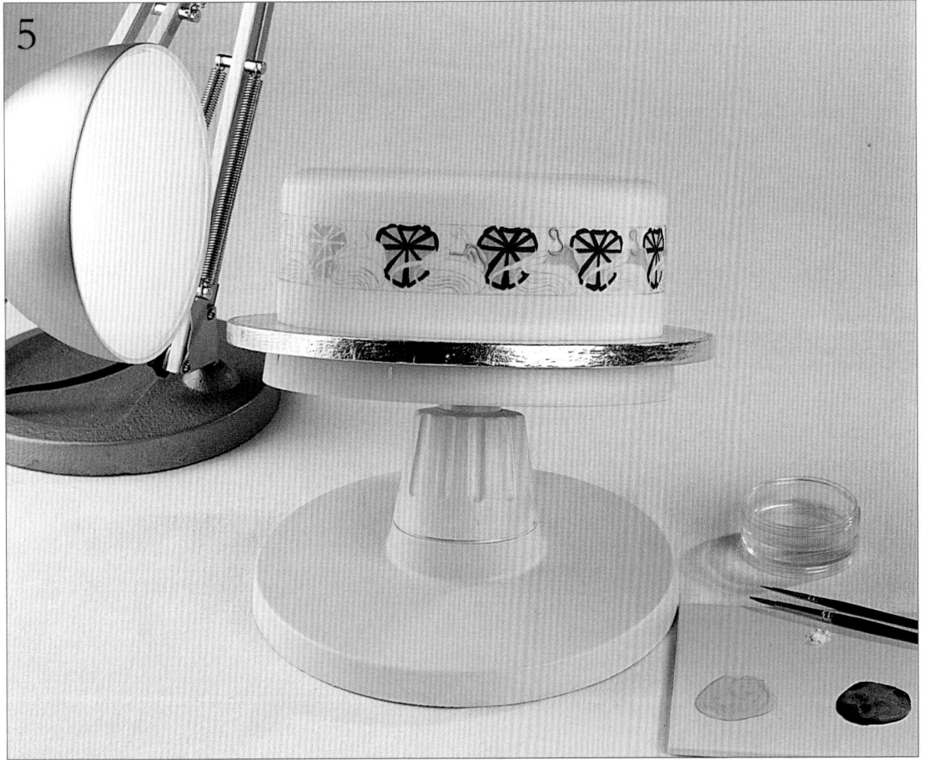
5

6 Work the petal above by piping a line, starting with the furled edge and continuing around to the stem. Blend with the damp brush again. Pipe another line, starting at the base near the stem on the other side and curve round to meet the furled edge. Blend with a damp paintbrush. Work the same petal on each flower.

7 Pipe a line of icing along the top edge for the lower petal to cover the bottom edge of the middle petal, and a few more short lines to give enough icing to blend. Starting with the tip of the petal, blend, following the curve up to the base. Pipe another line on the lower edge of the petal, and blend in the same direction as the previous line. Blend smoothly. Using the no.1.5 tube, work the brush embroidery exactly the same way on the two smaller cakes, blending with a no. 2 paintbrush.

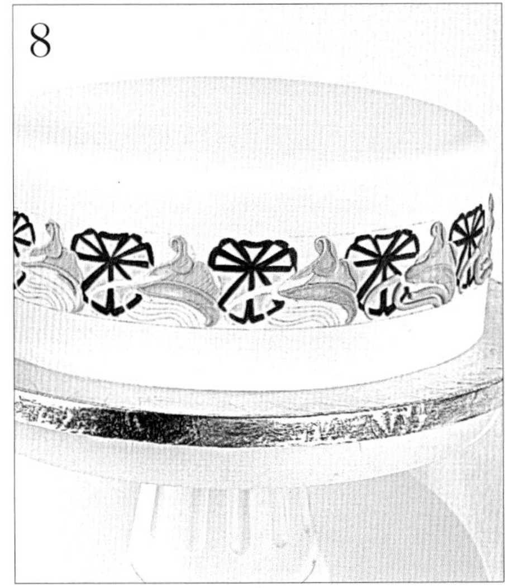
8

8 Colour 100g (3½oz) royal icing pale green to match the leaves. Add a few drops of water. The consistency should be a little stiffer than for the brush embroidery but still form smooth curves. Fill a bag fitted with a no.4 tube and another with a no.3 tube. Using the pencil lines as a guide, pipe two curling parallel stems under the flowers. Use the no.4 on the 30cm (12in) cake and the no.3 tube on the other cakes.

Helpful Hint

You may find it easier to trim the piped lines at the bottom edge by cutting into them gently with a clean knife while the icing is still soft and neaten with a damp brush.

9 Add a little more water to the green royal icing to form the same consistency used for the brush embroidery. Fill a bag fitted with a no.2 tube and one with a no.1.5 tube. Add the stems to the flowers. Begin with the no.2 tube and the 30cm (12in) cake. Hold the bag at a 45° angle, slightly raised off the surface. Starting at the base of the flower, squeeze firmly, letting the icing build up. As it fills up in between the outlines, move your hand away towards the end of the stem, keeping an even pressure. As you approach the end, gradually ease off the pressure and trail off to a nice point. Neaten the take off with a damp paintbrush. Complete the other stems on the cake.

Helpful Hint

When pressure piping, hold the piping bag close to the surface of the cake without touching it, move the bag very slowly, and squeeze firmly and the icing will gradually build up. By wiggling the tip of the tube in the icing it will level it off and get rid of any ridges.

10 Pipe the sepal in the middle of the group of three at the base of the flower. Fill in using the same technique described above. The rest of the calyx is piped in two halves and the join is blended. Start in the middle at the base of the flower and pressure pipe trailing off with the points curling over above the flower. Straight away, pressure pipe from the centre again, in a curve trailing off to a point underneath the flower. Blend the middle of the calyx with a damp paintbrush. Complete the stems and calyxes on the two smaller cakes using the no.1.5 tube.

11 Cover the boards with strips of ivory sugarpaste and join at the back. Leave to dry.

12 Attach 3mm (1/8in) wide ivory ribbon to the sides of the cakes, joining at the back.

13 Trace the scallop template (see page 153) and cut out in greaseproof (wax baking) paper. Place centrally on the 30cm (12in) cake. Gently scribe around the template onto the surface of the cake. Dust away any bits of sugarpaste. Mix a little ivory food colouring into 100g (3 1/2oz) royal icing to match the shade of ivory used to cover the cakes. Pipe, using a no.1.5 tube, on top of the cake, following the scribed line. Pipe another line 6mm (1/4in) inside the first line. Leave to dry.

14 Fit two bags with no.0 tubes and fill with a little of the pale green and dusky pink royal icing. Pipe the embroidery design in between the two lines. The pink flower is made up of three tiny shells, joined at their bases, and the green stems are 'scratched' onto the surface of the cake like piped embroidery, rather than dropped. Pipe shells around the bases of the cakes using the no.42 tube and the remaining ivory royal icing.

15 Fold a piece of thin card to make a former for the butterflies to dry on. Roll out 10g (1/3oz) white flower paste. Cut out two butterflies, pressing into the mould to impress the veins. Run a finger around the cutter to remove excess paste. Leave the butterflies to dry in the card formers. Make a few spares as accidents may happen when it comes to the colouring stage (if they are not used on this cake they may come in handy for future creations).

16 Trace the template for the large wired butterfly (see page 152). Roll out about 15g (1/2oz) flower paste, raised in the middle and thinning out at the sides. Place the template over the top so that the centre of the body fits over the raised bit in the centre of the paste. Rub over the tracing with a veining tool, remove the tracing and cut around the outline of the butterfly. Soften the cut edges by patting with fingertips. With a veining tool mark the separate wings, the body and head. Make hooks on the ends of two pieces of

16

24-gauge wire. Dip one wire in sugar glue and insert in the body of the butterfly from the tail end. Leave to dry on the 'V' former, set at a wider angle than before. Repeat for the second butterfly.

17 Colour the butterflies when they are dry. Mix a little champagne dusting powder with egg yellow dusting powder. Dust with a dry no.4 brush over the butterflies. If you leave them in the 'V' former it will help to support them and cut down on breakages. Dust the body and base of the wings with black dusting powder and a dry no.1 brush. Dust the wing tips to form grey triangles, using the pencil lines as a guide. Paint in veins using heraldic black and the synthetic brush. Cut the stamens in half and trim. Attach the stamens to their heads to create feelers using a little ivory royal icing and a no.0 tube. Support underneath with a little bunched up cling film (plastic wrap). When dry, paint the icing black. Stick the two smaller butterflies to the 30cm (12in) petal and 20cm (8in) round cakes, as shown.

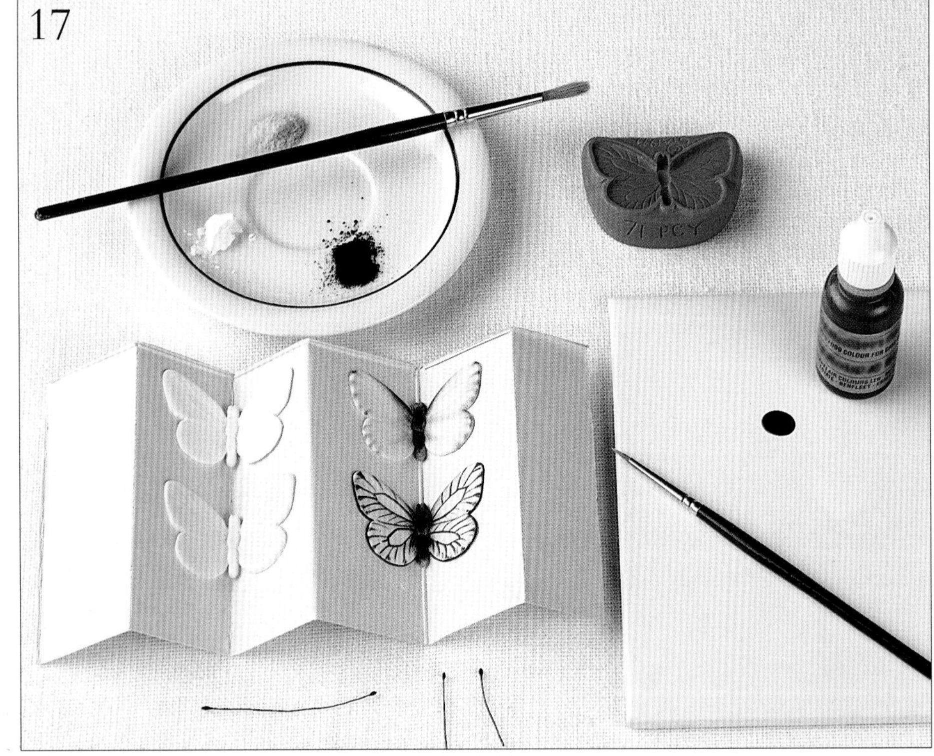

18 Mix spruce green colouring with 40g ($1^1/_3$oz) flower paste to match the green leaves. Make card templates for the nasturtium leaves. Cut out, saving the outer shape. Cut 26-gauge wire into lengths and bend one end with a pair of tweezers to form a circle, then bend the circle to a right angle to the stem. Roll out enough green paste for one leaf, with a raised-up bit in the middle. Position the template over the surface so the raised bit is slightly higher than the centre of the leaf, press the template down and remove. Cut round the outline. Vein the leaf, then thin the edges on a cel pad with a ball tool and turn over so it is face down on the work surface. Hold the wire circle in the flame of a match or a lighter for a few seconds to heat the wire, then press immediately into the back of the leaf. Wait a few seconds for it to cool and crystallize the paste, then thread the stem through the piece of sponge so the leaf is resting on top. Make three small and seven large leaves. When dry, dust with the foliage green dusting powder and paint the outer leaf free hand with holly green and black. Make six pink lily buds and one small pink arum lily, or use silk flowers. Wire together with the butterflies and insert into a cel pick in the middle of the 15cm (6in) cake.

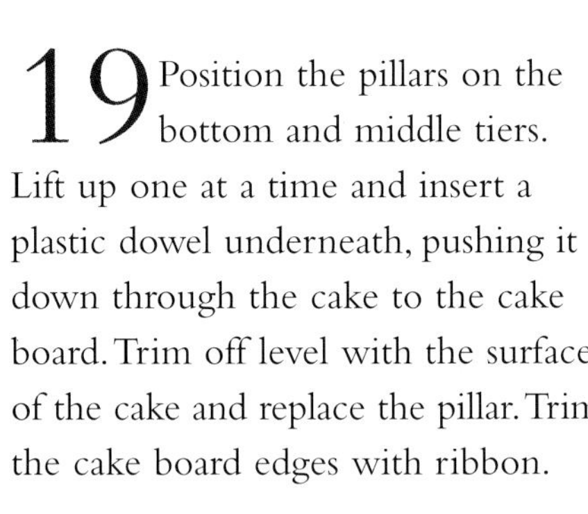

19 Position the pillars on the bottom and middle tiers. Lift up one at a time and insert a plastic dowel underneath, pushing it down through the cake to the cake board. Trim off level with the surface of the cake and replace the pillar. Trim the cake board edges with ribbon.

Cascading waterfall

This wedding cake has a large waterlily on each tier. The cake is the water and the front scallop a waterfall. The cake surface is rippled with rings of water, giving the impression of raindrops falling onto the surface. The result is simple, romantic and almost spiritual.

Cake and decoration

30cm (12in), 25cm (10in), and 20cm (8in) oval fruit cakes; 15 x 9cm (6 x 3½in) rectangular fruit cake
4.5kg (9lb) marzipan
4.5kg (9lb) white sugarpaste (rolled fondant)
38cm (15in), 32cm (13cm), and 28cm (11in) oval cake boards
425g (14oz) royal icing
170g (6oz) flower paste
Baby blue and navy paste food colourings
Heraldic black sugartint colour [S]
Lemon yellow, jade, bluebell, cream, moss green, forest green, foliage green, brown, nutkin brown, black and pink dusting powders (petal dusts/blossom tints)
Ground semolina
5m (5½yd), 3mm (⅛in) wide baby maize ribbon; 3m (3¼yd), 15mm (⅝in) wide featheredge antique white ribbon

Essential equipment

Templates (page 153)
No.1.5 piping tube (tip)
Large stencil brush
Nos.1, 4 and 7 paintbrushes
Dragonfly cutter [HH]
No.2 synthetic brush
Veining tool
Ball tool
Small lily stamens
Three-tiered cake stand

1 As there are no cake tins (pans) available for this shape of cake, cut the scallops out of the rectangular cake and add to the fronts of the oval cakes before marzipanning. Make templates for the scallops with the cake box card (see page 153). Turn the rectangular cake over so the flat base is uppermost. Position all three templates on top of the cake to cut the three scallops. Cut around the largest template with a sharp knife held almost vertical and at right angles to the table. Moving the knife up and down to ensure a clean cut, carefully cut around the template, turning the cake as you go. Neaten the base of the cake by trimming off any rough edges. Repeat this process to create the two remaining scallops.

2 Using apricot jam or masking jelly, stick the scallops to the appropriate cakes. Marzipan the cakes (being careful that the scallops do not move out of position). Position on the appropriate boards so they are slightly off-centre towards the back of the board, leaving enough room in front of the scallops for the waterfall. Leave to harden and set.

1

Cascading waterfall

3 Cover the cakes and boards with white sugarpaste (rolled fondant), using 2kg (4lb) for the 30cm (12in), 1.5kg (3lb) for the 25cm (10in) and 1kg (2lb) for the 20cm (8in) cake. Leave to harden for up to one week

4 Put a couple of teaspoons of white royal icing into a piping bag fitted with a no.1.5 tube (tip) and pipe small shells around the bases of the cakes, leaving the area in front of the scallops clear. Leave to dry.

5 Mix water and a small amount of baby blue paste colouring using the no.4 brush. Mix to a watercolour consistency. Using the large stencil brush, add colour to the 30cm (12in) cake using a stippling technique, dabbing the cake firmly with the brush at a 90° angle. Leave the top edge and side of the scallop unpainted. Paint the other two cakes in the same shade of blue. Add more colour to the largest cake, using a slightly darker shade of blue and shading over the first layer in just a few places. Repeat on the other two. Mix navy paste colouring with water and stipple on top of the scallop at the front of the cake. Stipple the same colour on the board of the largest cake, just in front of the scallop.

Helpful Hint

Do not overload the brush. This is important to remember when painting the surface of a cake, as too much water will start to dissolve the sugar, leaving craters. Load the brush with paint, but dab on a piece of kitchen towel a few times before painting the cake. Practise on the table first or cover an old cake board with sugarpaste and practise on that.

6 For the waterfall effect on each scallop, mix more of the baby blue colour. Dip the no.4 brush in water, then squeeze the bristles with your thumb and forefinger to expel excess water and to leave the bristles flat. Dip in the baby blue and paint light vertical lines on the front of the scallop to give the impression of water flowing down. Add a few lines to resemble water flowing over the top edge of the cakes, then, with a clean brush, paint water over the top edge and down the sides in a few places. When the water dries it will leave a delicate sheen behind.

7 When the cakes are dry, add the ripples. Have some pieces of kitchen towel ready. Dip a clean no.4 brush in water, then take off a little excess water and paint a small circle on top of the cake and then larger and larger circles around that. Wait a few seconds for the water to dissolve the paint on the surface, then lay a piece of kitchen towel on top and blot firmly, leaving white circles on a blue background. Continue painting random sets of circles on the cakes. Repeat on the boards. There will not be room for large complete circles so paint a mixture of small complete circles with large semi-circles.

8 To make the rocks, mix one teaspoon of gum tragacanth or tylo powder into 350g (12oz) royal icing. With a teaspoon, drop varying amounts of this mixture onto a sheet of waxed paper. Lightly dust over the rocks with cornflour (cornstarch) and pat any spiky bits down, then mould and pat lightly to form pleasing rock shapes. Leave the rocks to dry overnight. This mixture will dry quickly so use straight away.

9 Dust the rocks with black dusting powder (petal dust/blossom tint) mixed with cornflour to make grey,

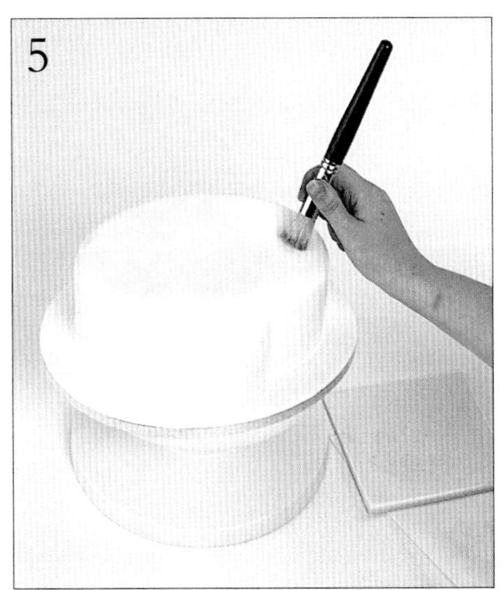
5

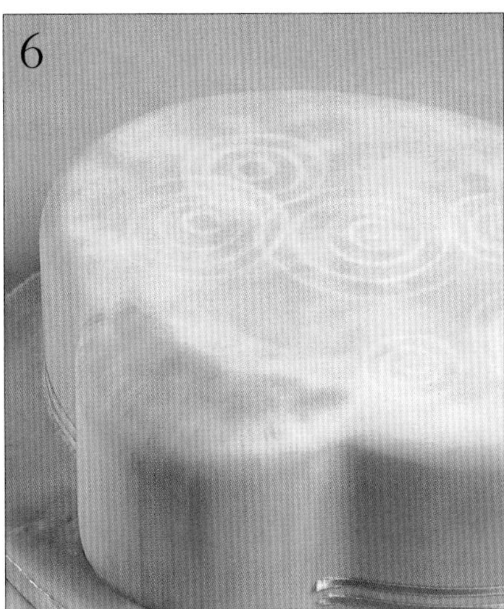
6

using a dry no.7 brush. Dust the rocks again with nutkin brown and a little cornflour, adding some darker shades in a few places. Pour some confectioners' varnish into a container, then dip each rock into it in turn. Shake off the excess and place on cling film (plastic wrap) on a cake board and leave to dry.

10 To make the dragonfly, roll out 10g ($^1/_3$oz) flower paste, using cornflour to dust the surfaces, until quite thin. (This amount will be enough for one dragonfly and a couple of spares.) Cut out a dragonfly shape and turn over so the paste is still in the cutter. Pat the paste down gently so that the impression of the wings, veins and body markings are pressed onto the surface, then take it out and leave it to dry on 'V' shaped former made from thin card (see the photograph below).

11 To colour the dragonfly, mix together cream and yellow dusting powders with cornflour and dust the wings and head, using a no.1 brush. Using jade dusting powder mixed with cornflour, dust the head leaving two yellow circles for the eyes at each side. Dust the upper body with moss green and yellow, and the lower body with bluebell, mixing all the colours with a little cornflour to tone them down a bit. Paint the veins on the dragonfly's wings using the no.2 synthetic brush and diluted heraldic black colour. Use a slightly darker paint for the body markings.

12 Trace templates for the water lily petals (page 153) and make templates with thin card. Mark each template clearly with the appropriate number. Cut out the following sizes, using 75g ($2^1/_2$oz) white flower paste: for the bottom tier four no.1, eight no.2, six nos.4 and 6; for the middle tier four no.2, eight no.3, six nos.4 and 6 and for the top tier: four no.4, eight no.5 and six nos.6 and 7. Vein on corn on the cob husk, then ball and cup each petal and leave to dry on a piece of sponge foam.

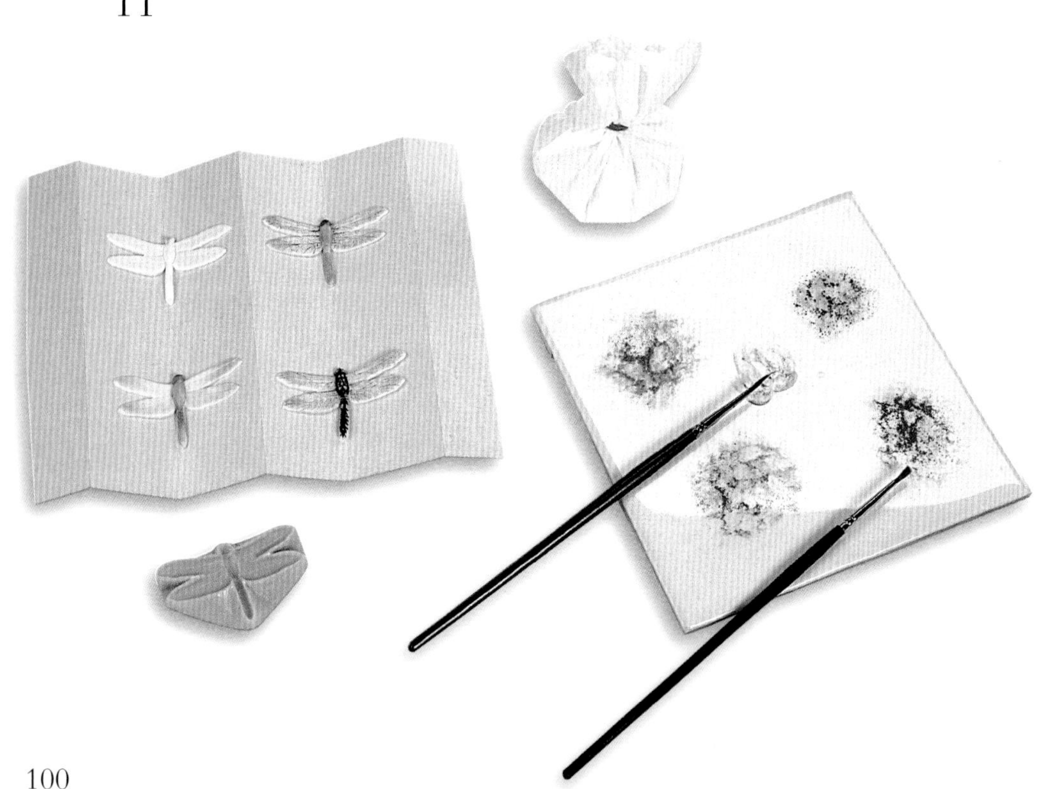

13 To assemble the flowers, cut out a square of waxed paper for each flower. Pipe a circle of white royal icing on one square, then lay the four largest petals on the icing to form a cross. Pipe another circle of icing on top of those and add another layer of petals and so on. Support in between each layer with small pieces of sponge foam until dry.

14 Dip the ends of the lily stamens into sugar glue, then into finely ground semolina coloured with lemon yellow dusting powder. Pipe a little yellow icing in the centre of each water lily and sprinkle with ground semolina, then push in the stamens. Dust the petals with pink

dusting powder at the centre of the flower and under the tips.

15 Cut out templates (page 153) for the lily pads. Cut three of each size from 45g (1½oz) pale spruce green flower paste. Vein, using a real lily pad or a veining tool. Ball the edges (so the ends curl upwards) and leave to dry on sponge foam. Dust triangle shapes on each pad with yellow and a no.7 brush. Dust further triangle shapes in moss green. Mix some foliage green and black together and use a no.1 brush to dust around the edges. Add a few lines radiating towards the centre, and also dust the centre. Mix some brown and black together and dust in a few places. Dip the pads in a mix of five teaspoons of confectioners' varnish and seven teaspoons of dipping solution, then leave to dry on cling film.

16 Attach two bands of 3mm (⅛in) wide maize ribbon just above the piping at the base of each cake, making the joins at the back and leaving the scallop clear at the front. Stick the white featheredge ribbon to the edges of the cake boards, leaving a gap at the front where the waterfall will flow over.

17 Set the cakes up on a three-tier stepped stand with the scallops at the front. For the waterfall effect on the 25cm (10in) and 20cm (8in) cakes, trace the templates (page 153) and make templates with thin card. Roll out 50g (1¾oz) flower paste until about 3mm (⅛in) thick. Place the template for the 20cm (10in) cake on top and cut around it. Position the paste on the board of the 20cm (10in) cake so it flows over the edge and onto the top of the cake

below. Pat with your fingertips, to make sure it hangs down vertically and there is no gap underneath where it flows over the board. It may take a bit of time to make sure it is hanging correctly. Repeat for the top tier. Allow to dry for at least 24 hours, then remove both pieces and lay them on a piece of sponge foam so that the underneaths can dry.

18 Position the waterfall pieces on the cake boards and paint a waterfall effect, using the same baby blue colouring as on the cakes. When dry, store these pieces with the rocks, ready to be taken to the venue.

To assemble, stick the waterfalls, lily pads and lilies to the cakes with royal icing. Fix the dragonfly to the lily on the top with royal icing and support it from underneath with sponge foam until dry. Pipe random bulbs with royal icing and a no.1.5 tube at the bottom of each waterfall and at the bases of the cakes. Blend with a damp no.4 brush to resemble splashes of water. Stick the rocks in place either side of the waterfall.

Art deco

The design for the bottom tier of this cake was inspired by the executive suite bathroom in one of New York's art deco buildings, using clean, modern motifs such as the fan and chevron. The rest of the cake is covered with decorative panelling and a marble staircase for the newly-weds to sweep down.

Cake and decoration

Three 20cm (8in) square fruit cakes and two 15cm (6in) square fruit cakes
30cm (12in), 20cm (8in) and 15cm (6in) square cake boards
Two 15cm (6in) and one 13cm (5in) double thickness cake boards
3.4kg (6lb 13oz) marzipan
4.65kg (9lb 5oz) white sugarpaste (rolled fondant)
770g (1½lb) modelling paste
1 tablespoon royal icing
2g (1/16oz) red sugarpaste
Autumn leaf, licorice black, navy, red and paprika paste food colourings
Dusky pink, black and silver dusting powders (petal dusts/blossom tints)
3m (3¼yd), 15mm (⅝in) wide; 25cm (10in), 3mm (⅛in) wide and 75cm (¾yd), 7mm (⅓in) wide white ribbon
6m (6½yd), 1.5mm (1/16in) wide black ribbon

Essential equipment

Templates (see page 152)
Nos.0, 1 and 4 paintbrushes
No.1 piping tube (tip)
Sugarpaste gun with 3mm (⅛in) wide ribbon disc
Scallop shell moulds [SS]
2cm (¾in) and 6mm (¼in) circle cutters
Bamboo skewer (wooden stick)
Veining tool
Eight long cake dowels

1 Level the cakes. Stick one of the 20cm (8in) cakes in the middle of the 30cm (12in) board, then stack the other two on top of that with a little apricot jam or masking jelly in between. Stack the two 15cm (6in) cakes together in the same way, on the 20cm (8in) board. Fill in any gaps around the sides with marzipan. The stacked 20cm (8in) fruit cakes should measure about 24.5cm (9¾in) high and the 15cm (6in) fruit cakes about 13.5cm (5¼in) high.

2 Marzipan the cakes, using 2.4kg (4lb 13oz) marzipan for the 20cm (8in) cake and 1.5kg (3lb) for the 15cm (6in) cake. Paint the top of each cake with jam or masking jelly and place a piece of 6mm (¼in) thick marzipan on top. Smooth and trim. Roll out another portion the same thickness to cover one side. Stick against the side of the cake, smooth and trim. It is important that the sides are flat and the corners are square. Marzipan the 15cm (6in) cake in the same way. Leave to dry for a week.

3 Roll out 2.5kg (5lb) white sugarpaste (rolled fondant) to 6mm (¼in) thick. Moisten the top of the 20cm (8in) cake with water. Cover and trim as before. Decide which will be the front of the cake, then cover the back, followed by the two sides and finally the front. This way there will only be one join on each side of the cake and no joins at the front.

4 For the 15cm (6in) cake, knead 1.1kg (2lb 3½oz) sugarpaste until

4

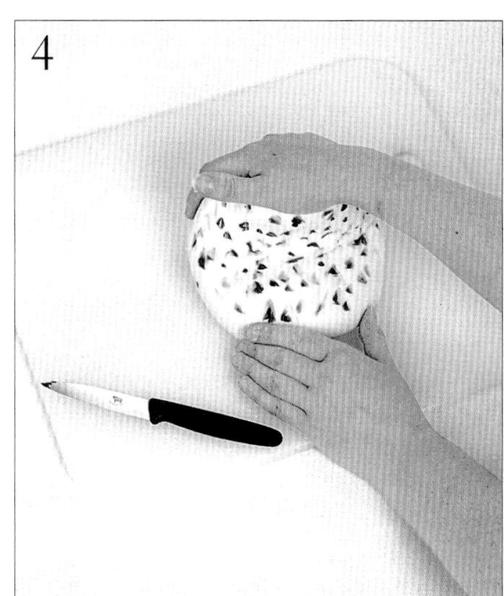

HELPFUL HINT

Do not use a sawing motion when trimming the paste. To get a better finish, hold the paste to be trimmed in one hand so it is stable, then slice straight down. It is also important to use a clean sharp knife, as any build-up of paste on the knife blade will cause it to drag and tear the paste instead of making a clean cut.

smooth, then colour using a little autumn leaf and black to create a marbled effect in the sugarpaste, (see page 91). Roll out to 6mm ($^{1}/_{4}$in) thick and cover the 15cm (6in) cake. Cover the top first, then the back, the two sides and finally the front.

5 Cover the boards with the same marbled sugarpaste. Take the remaining 300g (10oz) sugarpaste and marble as before. Use to cover the boards by rolling out long strips of paste and laying them on the boards, before making the joins at the back

6

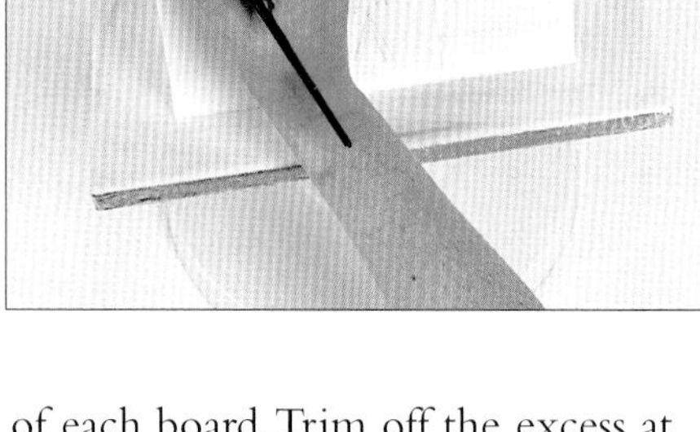

of each board. Trim off the excess at the board edge. Leave to dry for a few days before decorating the cakes.

6 Trace the template (page 152). If your cake is a little taller or shorter, just adjust the depth of the cornicing at the top and bottom. What is important is that the tiles are full squares vertically and horizontally. Transfer the design to the sides of the base cake. Put a little autumn leaf food colouring on a white tile or plate and mix with water and superwhite powder. Paint the design on the cake, starting from the top and working downwards. Outline one tile with a no.0 brush, then fill in with a no.4, but stop at three tile depths from the bottom. Decorate each side in the same way, trying to keep to the same shade of autumn leaf colour.

7 Mix a small amount of royal icing with a little black food colouring and thin (if needed) with dipping solution. Paint the black tiles by first outlining, and then filling in each tile.

Black food colouring takes a long time to dry, so by mixing it with dipping solution or clear alcohol instead of water, it evaporates more quickly and therefore the drying time is reduced. The addition of a small amount of royal icing to the food colouring improves its coverage and prevents streaking.

8 Paint in the triangles using a no.1 brush and silver dusting powder (petal dust/blossom tint) mixed with dipping solution. Fill a piping bag with a teaspoon of white royal icing. Have the cake on a tilting turntable (full tilt will not be possible with a cake this deep, so tilt as far as is stable), and use a no.1 tube to pipe the chevrons above each triangle, starting at the point and then piping a line to each side. Pipe the horizontals. Leave to dry, then paint silver.

9 Roll out 25g ($^{3}/_{4}$oz) white modelling paste to 1.5mm ($^{1}/_{16}$in) thick. Using the same tracing used for the cake sides, transfer the design for the strips with the curved tiles (a pair for each side of the cake). Cut out, then paint the corresponding area of the cake with water, and stick the strips of paste to the cake. The

9

horizontal lines should match the square tiles on the cake. If they look uneven pat them back into a straight line using the edge of a knife. When in position mark horizontal lines in the paste to define each tile using the blade of a knife. Paint the lower half of each tile silver with a no.1 brush.

10 Colour 100g (3½oz) modelling paste dark gold using the autumn leaf food colouring and 60g (2oz) modelling paste black. Cover and set aside. Roll out 25g (¾oz) gold paste and transfer the design for the sunburst onto the surface. You will need four, one for each side. Cut out and stick in position on the sides of the cake.

11 Fill the sugarpaste gun with 10g (⅓oz) black paste and fit the 3mm (⅛in) wide ribbon disc. Extrude about 40cm (16in) of paste. Cut the strip into eight sections. Stick the first strip of black in the centre of the sunburst and then two along the straight edge at the bottom. Stick another two in the middle to divide it into four. Do not trim the ends coming into the middle at this stage. Stick another four in between the gaps, making sure they are all equally spaced. Take the 2cm (¾in) circle cutter and cut into the black lines at the line marking the smaller semicircle and take away the excess black. Roll out 10g (⅓oz) black and cut two circles with the 2cm (¾in) cutter. Cut in half to make four semicircles, then stick to the sunburst. Trim the bottom edge of the black semicircle with a sharp knife.

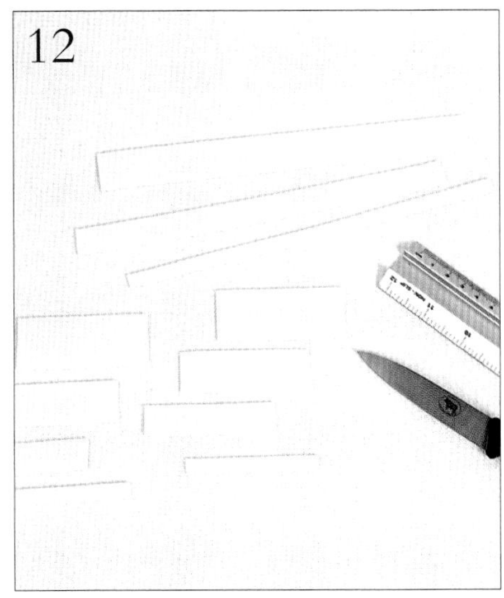
12

12 Use 200g (6½oz) white modelling paste for the upper and lower cornicing. Roll out half of this to a 3mm (⅛in) thickness. Cut four strips 3cm (1¼in) wide and 20cm (8in) long, then cut each strip in half widthways. Paint the base of the cake where the lower cornicing will go, and cut into the edge of one of the strips on the table at a 45° angle to make mitred corners. Stick the strip to the cake base on the left side and trim vertically on the cake at the doorway on the right. Go around the cake like this, cutting firstly the angle on the strip and trimming to the right length on the cake. Repeat the procedure by rolling out the paste and cutting four strips 20cm (8in) long and 2.5cm (1in) wide, and again 3mm (⅛in) thick. Stick these over the first layer of strips and trim as before. Add a further two layers of strips for the cornicing, using four strips 15mm (⅝in) wide and 3mm (⅛in) thick, and four strips 7mm (⅓in) wide and 3mm (⅛in) thick.

13 For the cornicing on the upper edge of the cake use the same technique, except that there are only three layers of paste and

13

there is no break in the middle. Cut strips the same length as specified for the last three layers. Trim one edge of the strip while on the cake, at an angle on the corner. Hold the knife at a 45° angle and push into the paste to make a neat cut, do not drag the knife downwards. Repeat for the other layers.

14 To make the fan shells for the centre of the sides of the 15cm (6in) cake, roll a piece of sugarpaste into a ball and then press it into the smallest of the shell moulds. It should be about 6mm (1/4in) thick. Take it out of the mould and cut around the top edge of the shell to make a curve, and then use a veining tool to indent a line on each side to mark a line to cut on. As a guide for width, the first fan at the top should have seven ridges on it. Then make a clean cut with a knife. Pat and smooth the cut edges with fingertips. Stick to the cake, then cut off at the bottom on the line marked for the top of the next shell, using the 2cm (3/4in) cutter on the cake. Smooth this cut edge, then define the ridges by marking in with the veining tool.

Make another seven fans, two for each side. The next fans should be five ridges wide (two per side) and the smallest fan at the bottom should be three ridges wide (cut off the bottom edge in a straight line).

15 For the window panels, roll out half of the remaining gold paste to 3mm (1/8in) thick. Transfer the design (page 152) to the surface of the paste. Cut four window panels on the outer line, then moisten the cake and stick each panel in place with the lower cut edge resting on the board. Repeat the procedure with the remaining paste, then cut another four. Cut out eight window panels, following the inner line, using 70g (2 1/4oz) white modelling paste (cut four at a time) and stick on the gold panels on the cake. Soften all the cut edges by rubbing over with a finger. Mark horizontal lines across the window panels from point to point. Roll out 10g (1/3oz) white modelling paste and cut out four 4mm (1/4in) wide strips, each about 3mm (1/8in) thick. Stick these to the top side of the cake, then mitre the corners.

16 Use a small amount of black food colouring to make 110g (3 1/2oz) grey modelling paste. Put aside 45g (1 1/2oz), leaving 65g (2 1/4oz) for the decorative tiered sconces. Roll four balls 2cm (3/4in) wide, four 15mm (5/8in), four 1cm (1/2in), and four 7mm (1/3in) wide. Work one at a time, placing the rest under cling film (plastic wrap). Pat the top of each ball down onto the table so it has a flat bottom and a domed top, then cut in half. Try to keep each ball circular. Stick to the sides of the 15cm (6in) cake in the middle at the bottom of the window panels using a little sugar glue. The dome should be underneath and the cut edge against the side of the cake with the flat bottom uppermost. Layer them centrally in each window panel and stick in place with sugar glue. Roll two 6mm (1/4in) balls into a sausage, then cut in half widthways to make four pinnacles. Stick one to the top of each sconce with the rounded edge uppermost. Paint silver, using a no.1 brush.

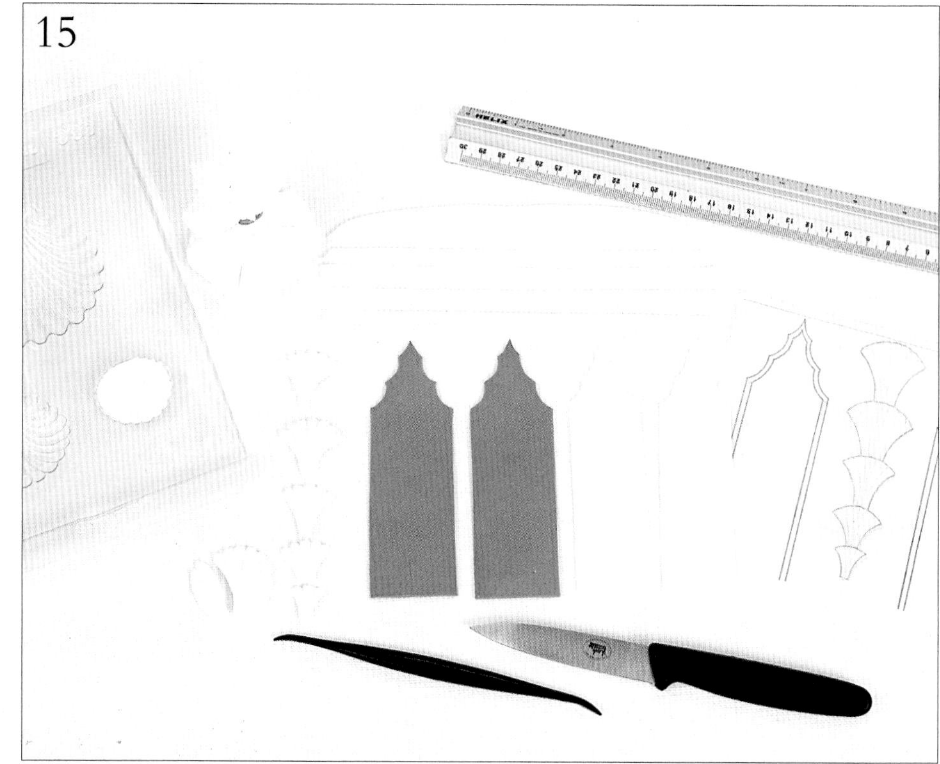
15

✻ ✻ ✻ ✻

Art deco

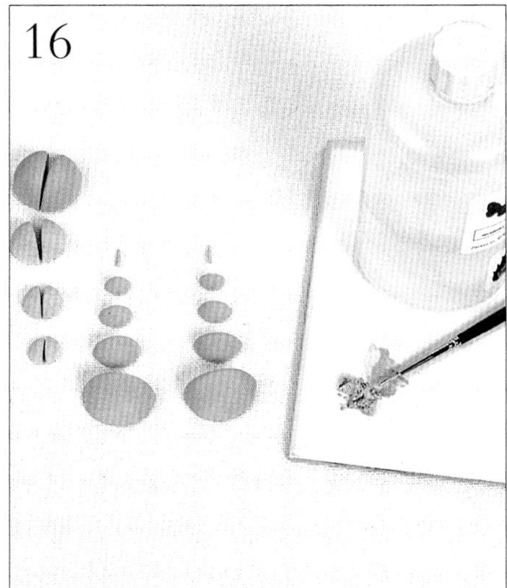

16

17 Cut lengths of 15mm ($^5/_8$in) wide antique white ribbon for the top edges of both cakes. Mitre the corners and stick in place using a little royal icing.

18 For the staircase, make three square card templates in varying sizes: 13cm (5in) square, 11cm (4$^1/_2$in) square, and 9cm (3$^1/_2$in) square. Knead two teaspoons of gum tragacanth or tylo powder into 750g (1$^1/_2$lb) white sugarpaste and mix thoroughly. Marble the icing using autumn leaf and a little black (see page 91), then roll out to 1cm ($^1/_2$in) thick. Lay the paste on a spare cake board and use the templates to cut out one of each of the sizes. Lightly knead the trimmings together and roll out a piece large enough to cover the 15cm (6in) cake board. Leave to dry for a few days, then stick the layers together with royal icing. Place the largest at the bottom, on top of the 15cm (6in) board.

Helpful Hint

By laying the paste on the board before cutting you will not have to handle the cut shapes so they will keep their crisp edges. Dust the boards thoroughly with icing (confectioners') sugar first.

19 Make and assemble the two figures of the bride and groom, as described on page 108. Gently pick up the groom, and hold him above the staircase to decide where to position him. Make a mark where the skewer meets the icing, and make a hole with a bamboo skewer. Do not attempt to force the figure into the paste without first making a hole as the figure could be damaged with the pressure from your hands. Pipe royal icing under his feet and lower the figure with its skewer into the hole. Pipe icing on the base of the bride, and stick her next to the groom. Leave to set for a few hours.

Assemble the figures' arms, and attach. Make the bride's scarf, and position it around her neck, draping it at the back. Where the scarf touches the dress, lift and dot with sugar glue, then pat back down to secure. Attach the heads, then make their hair and the bride's headdress. Carefully paint in the facial features.

20 Stick the two double thick 15cm (6in) boards together with royal icing and leave them to dry. Stick a length of 7mm ($^1/_3$in) wide antique white ribbon around the edge. Stick 3mm ($^1/_8$in) wide antique ribbon around the edge of the 13cm (5in) double thick board. Stick the 15mm ($^5/_8$in) wide antique white ribbon around all the cake boards and then stick two lengths of 1.5mm ($^1/_{16}$in) wide black ribbon on top, making all the joins at the back.

Insert four cake dowels in each cake and trim level with the cake surface (see page 51). Stick the 15cm (6in) double thickness boards to the top of the 20cm (8in) with royal icing, and the 13cm (5in) to the top of the 15cm (6in). The tiers will rest on top of the boards without the use of pillars but will still be stable due to the dowels in the cakes.

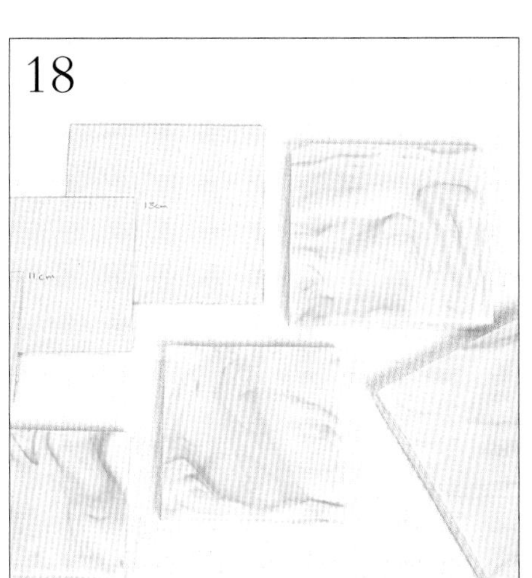

18

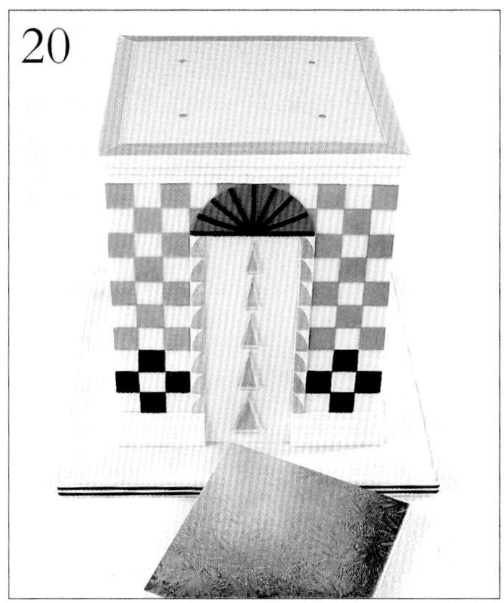

20

Figure modelling ~ Art deco

Follow these guidelines when making the figures for the top of the Art deco and Folk art cakes, checking against the photographs for extra guidance.

BRIDE (about 12cm [4¾in] high)
Roll 50g (1¾oz) white modelling paste into a ball, then a tapered sausage. Trim the fat end. Square off thin end, and stand up. Roll to make a waist. Insert a skewer in the centre. Dry.

Colour 30g (1oz) paste flesh using paprika. Roll out a thin rectangle 1.5 x 3cm (⅝ x 1¼in). Cover the chest and back. Smooth the cut edges.

Roll a 4mm (¼in) ball into a neck. Use a cocktail stick to make a hole in the centre. Paint the skewer with sugar glue, lower the neck over the skewer onto shoulders. Secure and trim.

Using 10g (⅓oz) white paste, roll eight cones and trim the fat end flat. Stick to figure to make fabric folds.

Roll eight smaller cones and stick in between. Roll out 25g (¾oz) white paste, moisten and wrap around the figure. Ease into dress folds and around body. Cut the neckline of the dress. Define fabric with a veining tool. Cut a piece of white into a thin strip about 2mm (⅛in) wide for a belt. Leave to dry.

GROOM (about 12.5cm [5in] high)
For the legs, roll 45g (1½oz) grey modelling paste into a ball, then a long cigar shape. Bend so both the thin ends are together. Trim ankles.

Flatten the upper body and make the shoulders square. Indent at the waist. Insert a bamboo skewer through the central body and out between the ankles, protruding no more than 3cm (1¼in). (Make sure the skewer is not visible.) Dry lying down overnight, turn over and dry overnight again.

Flatten two balls for shoes. Stick side by side on a piece of oasis covered in cling film. Paint with sugar glue, then lower the figure onto shoes and into the oasis. Cut a piece of grey paste into a 6mm (¼in) wide strip for turn-ups. Moisten and fold the edge over. Cut into two and stick in place.

Roll 7mm (⅓in) flesh-coloured paste into a neck. Stick on figure. Cut a strip of white paste 6mm (¼in) wide. Moisten the neck, then wrap round the collar, easing out the corners to make a wing collar. Cut a white waistcoat. Mark a line down the centre, cut out a curved dart for the neckline, and a 'V' at the bottom. Trim the lower edges at an angle and stick to figure. Mark buttons. Roll a 1cm (½in) ball into a cone and flatten to make a cravat. Use a veining tool to mark folds and attach.

Cut out a black rectangle for the jacket. Cut a slit up the back. Trim to form jacket tail. Wrap around, check fit and trim. Trim at the front from the knees in a curve up to the centre front. Roll a black collar, trim and attach. Cut small 'V's for lapels. Roll a tiny red carnation buttonhole for lapel.

FINISHING TOUCHES
Make the groom's arms by rolling two 15mm (⅝in) balls of white modelling paste into sausages with a lump at the ends. Flatten the lumps and cut out a 'V' to form thumbs, and make three cuts to form fingers. Roll out 15g (½oz) of black paste to make sleeves. Cut into rectangles and use to encase the arms. Make the bride's arms in the same way with flesh-coloured paste. Assemble and finish the figures on the cake (see page 107).

Figure modelling ~ Folk art

Cover the individual pieces of paste with cling film (plastic wrap) while not working on them to prevent them drying out and cracking.

BRIDE (about 8cm [3in] high)
Roll 35g (1¼oz) white modelling paste into a cone for skirts. Roll 10g (⅓oz) paste into a smaller cone and roll halfway down one side to make a bust. Cut off lower portion, moisten and stick to skirts. Insert a cocktail stick down centre. Roll a small flesh-coloured sausage for the neck. Dry.

Roll eight long, thin cones using terracotta paste and stick to skirt.

Roll smaller sausages tapering at each end and stick in between around waist. Roll out 15g (½oz) terracotta into a strip 5 x 14cm (2 x 5½in). Wrap strip around figure, joining at back.

Roll out and cut two 2.5cm (1in) squares. Add definition with a veining tool, and add a few lines radiating out from waist. Cut a small semi-circle from one edge on each square. Moisten the front of her body and stick one square in place around the neck. Trim, then repeat for back. Roll a small sausage for a collar and position.

Mark a row of horizontal fastenings on front of the body.

GROOM (about 8.5cm [3¼in] high)
Knead ¼ teaspoon tylo powder into 15g (½oz) black sugarpaste. Roll into a ball, then a long sausage. Bend in half and trim to 4cm (1½in) for legs.

Knead remainder into two balls about 6mm (¼in) across for shoes. Roll into cones, flatten on top, moisten and position. Place on a piece of oasis, wrapped in cling film, and moisten, then stick the legs on top. Insert a cocktail stick down the centre of the legs and into the oasis, making sure it is not visible.

Roll out trimmings to about 3mm (⅛in) thick and cut out a 2cm (¾in) circle. Roll out remainder to 3mm (⅛in) deep and cut out a 15mm (⅝in) circle. Stick small circle on the larger one to make his hat. Dry.

Roll 10g (⅓oz) into a cone and flatten on top. Trim the lower half, moisten the tops of the legs, and lower the body centrally onto the cocktail stick. Roll a white neck and stick on the cocktail stick. Dry.

Cut out a black 2cm (¾in) square. Cut out a deep 'V' for the neck line, a smaller 'V' at the bottom and trim each lower edge at an angle. Moisten body, and position waistcoat. Trim.

Roll out a piece to 5 x 4cm (2 x 1½in). Cut a semicircle at the centre of one edge, and a vertical cut on the opposite edge. Wrap around moistened figure and trim.

Roll a collar and position. Cut out small 'V's for the lapels. Cut a long white triangle for the groom's stock. For arms, roll a black sausage, cut in two, then cut at an angle at the top of each arm. Bend and stick in place.

Roll tiny flesh paste cones, fold for thumbs and cut to make fingers.

FINISHING TOUCHES

When the two figures are on the cake (see page 115) attach a piece of raffia to the bride's dress where her hand will go. Roll the bride's terracotta arms and two ivory hands. Roll 1cm (½in) (bride) and 13mm (⅝in) (groom) ivory balls for the heads and stick in place. Cut the top off the groom's head and position his hat. Roll and indent two ears, and use dark brown paste for his hair and beard. Make a cream bonnet for the bride.

Folk art

This cake captures the folk art style, using familiar motifs from the style of New England interiors: hearts, homesteads, countryside, angels and gingham in rich, earthy colours. Deceptively straightforward to execute, the backgrounds are washes of colour with bas relief images over the top.

CAKE AND DECORATION

30cm (12in), 25cm (10in), 20cm (8in) and 15cm (6in) round fruit cakes
40cm (16in), 32cm (13in), 28cm (11in), 23cm (9in) round cake boards
5kg (10lb) marzipan
5kg (10lb) ivory sugarpaste (rolled fondant)
30g (1oz) black sugarpaste
575g (1¼lb) modelling paste
Navy, grape violet, autumn leaf, paprika, spruce green, gooseberry, dark brown, black, tangerine, chestnut, melon, Christmas red and caramel/ivory paste food colourings
Rose, skintone, peach and cream dusting powders (petal dusts/blossom tints)
5 teaspoons royal icing
One third of a hank of raffia
1m (1⅛yd), 1cm (½in) wide and 2.5m (2¾yd), 7mm (⅓in) wide gingham ribbon; 4m (4⅓yd), 15mm (⅝in) wide tan ribbon

ESSENTIAL EQUIPMENT

Templates (page 154)
Nos.0, 1, 2 and 4 paintbrushes
Nos.3, 5 and 11 flat bristle brushes
Nos.0 and 1.5 piping tubes (tips)
Veining tool
Set of two dove moulds [HH]
12mm (½in), 15mm (⅝in), 2cm (¾in) and 8.5cm (3¼in) circle cutters
Nine concealed pillars [W]

1 Place the cakes on the boards and cover with marzipan (see page 143). Leave to dry. Cover with ivory sugarpaste (rolled fondant), using 2kg (4lb) for the 30cm (12in), 1.5kg (3lb) for the 25cm (10in), 1kg (2lb) for the 20cm (8in) and 500g (1lb) for the 15cm (6in) cake. Leave overnight, then cover the boards with strips of sugarpaste. Leave for up to a week.

2 Divide the circumference of each cake into three, making a little mark with a knife at the base. Trace the templates for the sides (see page 154). There are three pattern repeats per cake so only trace one image and transfer it to the cake sides by simply moving the tracing along. Line up the centre of the design with one of the marks. At this stage, the only lines required are the horizon lines on the 30cm (12in) and 20cm (8in) cakes (just rub over the lines you require on the tracing), but transfer the whole design to the 25cm (10in) cake, as the colour wash will wash away any pencil lines in the way.

3 Mix autumn leaf and paprika paste food colourings with water to an apricot-coloured watercolour consistency with the no.4 brush. Add a tiny amount of superwhite powder and apply to the surface of each cake, just above the horizon line, using the no.5 flat bristle brush. Paint an area about as deep as the width of the brush on the 30cm (12in), 20cm (8in), and 15cm (6in) cakes and paint an area about half that deep for the 25cm (10in) cake.

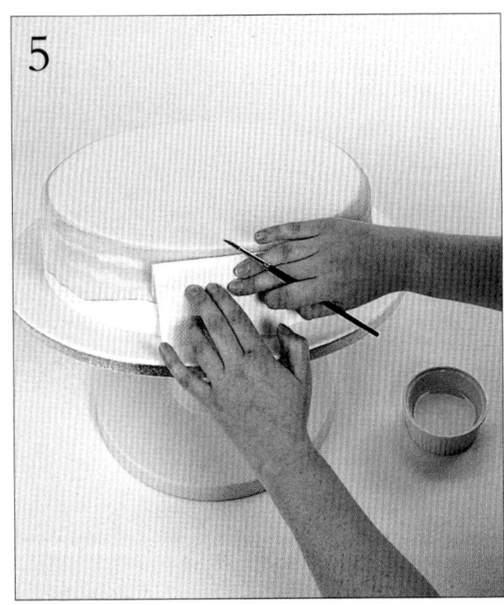
5

7

HELPFUL HINT

Applying water over a painted colour takes off that colour when blotted with a piece of kitchen towel. Useful if you have made a mistake but not suitable for very large areas. It works for the clouds because painting a paler colour over the blue would not work, and painting blue around the clouds would result in a patchy background.

4 Mix a wash for the sky with navy, grape violet and water. Add a little superwhite. Start painting at the top edge of the 30cm (12in) cake with the no.11 flat brush, using a side to side painting motion, until halfway down the side of the cake. Try not to add too much paint at once. If too wet, simply brush over that area with the brush until it blends in. Make the wash paler by adding more water, and continue painting as before, blending the two shades of blue together and blending into the top of the apricot wash. Repeat for the other cakes.

5 To create the clouds, use a clean no.4 brush to paint a horizontal line of water across the tops of each hill on the sides of the 30cm (12in) cake. Circle the brush as you paint to resemble straight puffy clouds, then blot with kitchen towel to reveal the ivory sugarpaste beneath. Create a thinner cloud just above the previous one. Repeat this process above the other two hills and then add a few random clouds. When dry, paint in the clouds with apricot. The brush should not be too wet, just damp with colour. Blend in the cloud areas with swirling movements. Add a few darker shades of apricot.

6 When dry, transfer the designs for the homestead and trees to the 30cm (12in) cake, and the angels to the 20cm (8in) cake. Then mix spruce and gooseberry food colourings into 100g (3½oz) modelling paste and knead well. Roll out 75g (2½oz) into a long strip until it is about 3mm (⅛in) thick. Lay the tracing for the 30cm (12in) cake over the top and transfer the design for the hills. Trim against the lower edge of the tracing and remove, then cut along the pencil line. Repeat for another two strips. Moisten the area on the cake and stick the strips of green to the sides. Round off the edges and blend all joins. Use the remaining 25g (¾oz) of green for the hills on the 20cm (8in) cake and repeat the procedure.

7 Roll out 15g (½oz) white modelling paste to 3mm (⅛in) thick. Lay the homestead tracing over the top and transfer the image three times onto the paste, then cut it out carefully. Stick the homesteads to the side of the 30cm (12in) cake and round off the edges. Make sure there are no air bubbles trapped.

Paint the roofs and windows black using a no.1 brush. Paint the tree trunks and branches dark brown. Paint the flag poles grey. Roll out a little white paste and rub over the tracing for the flag. Cut out and stick on the flag pole. Paint red stripes and a navy square in the corner.

Put a teaspoon of royal icing into two separate containers, and add water to soften slightly. Add gooseberry and a little dark brown food colourings to one, and spruce with a little black food colouring to the other. Mix thoroughly. Stipple the spruce colour above the trees to resemble leaves, using a no.2 brush and a stabbing motion. Repeat with the gooseberry colour, to highlight a few areas.

8 Add water and superwhite to a little gooseberry and dark brown colourings, to create a shade just

darker than the paste, with a watery consistency; take off the excess on kitchen towel. Stipple, using a no.3 bristle brush, onto the green strip of paste around the base for grass, being careful not to get any on the board (do not paint all the way down to the board as the lower bit will be covered with ribbon). Mix a darker green with spruce and black and stipple over the pale green at the base. Blend the two shades of green where they join with a damp brush. It should look as if the darker green is in the foreground, fading to paler green in the distance. Repeat on the 20cm (8in) cake.

9 Mix a little gooseberry and dark brown food colourings with water and superwhite powder to a watercolour consistency, and paint with the no.5 bristle brush onto the side of the 25cm (10in) cake for the fields in the background. Stop about halfway down each valley. Mix a little spruce and black, less watery than before, and stipple at the base of each valley, blending the two shades of green as you go. Leave to dry.

10

10 Colour 25g (¾oz) modelling paste with spruce and black to make a dark green, 20g (¾oz) with spruce and gooseberry to make pale green, and 50g (1¾oz) with tangerine, paprika and chestnut to make terracotta. Roll out each colour to 3mm (⅛in) thick and lay over the tracing for the 25cm (10in) cake to transfer the design for the fields, three of the same shape per colour. Stick onto the side of the cake. Make sure all the joins are clean and neat.

Paint in ploughing lines with dark terracotta over the terracotta area, spruce and black over the pale green, and a watery black over the dark green. To do this, paint in a few lines with a no.4 brush, then stipple over the lines with a no.3 bristle brush.

11 Take two teaspoons of royal icing and mix in a little autumn leaf colour to get a warm ivory colour. Fit a piping bag with a no.0 tube (tip) and fill with the icing. Pipe in the fence freehand, working from left to right. Pipe one vertical, then two horizontals and so on. Pat down any peaks on the ends with a damp no.1 brush as you go. Pipe the small section of picket fence on the 30cm (12in) cake over the tree.

12 Colour 15g (½oz) modelling paste gold with autumn leaf, using 5g (¼oz) for the angels and saving the rest for the hearts on the 15cm (6in) cake. Colour 10g (⅓oz) orange/red with Christmas red, tangerine and brown; 5g (¼oz) dusky yellow with melon and dark brown colourings and 30g (1oz) flesh with paprika and dark brown. Use 5g (¼oz) of flesh for the angels and save the rest for the figures.

13 Use 15g (½oz) white paste for the wings, banners and two houses. Trace the house design on a piece of tracing paper. Roll out a small piece of leftover terracotta about 3mm (⅛in) thick, and transfer the tracing to the paste. Remove the tracing and cut out the houses, including the roofs. Keep covered with cling film (plastic wrap) until needed. Cut out six more houses in the same way with the following colours: two white, two gold, and two orange/red. Stick randomly on top of the green paste on the sides of the 20cm (8in) cake, sticking a few on the green paste.

14 Trace the angel template. Roll out 5g (¼oz) dusky yellow paste and cut out six trumpets. Stick in position on the sides of the cake. Roll out 10g (⅓oz) white and cut out six banners and six wings. Stick in position, softening the cut edges

14

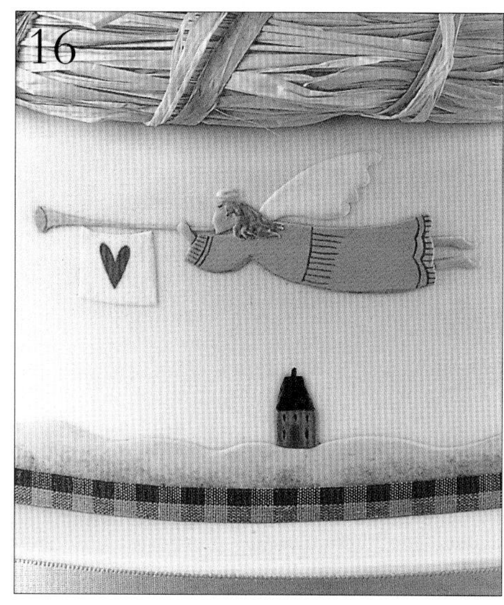

with your fingertips. Roll six tiny teardrop shapes using the flesh colour paste and stick over the trumpet for hands. Roll 12 longer teardrop shapes for the feet, two at a time, then stick in position. Roll out 10g (1/3oz) gold and cut out two angel bodies. Stick in position over the hands and feet, hiding the joins. Soften the edges.

15 Roll out the remaining orange/red and 10g (1/3oz) of leftover paprika paste. Transfer the angel template onto the rolled out paste, cutting out two angel bodies in each colour. Stick in place on the sides of the 20cm (8in) cake. Roll out 5g (1/4oz) flesh paste and cut out six heads and stick in place, the hair overlapping onto the body a little. Paint the edges of their wings and shade the banners with an apricot colour, using a no.4 brush. Add detail on the angels' gowns using dark brown mixed with a little black, with a no.0 brush. Paint the ends of the trumpets with the same brown colour and the windows and roofs of the houses with black. Paint hearts on the banners with red and brown.

> **HELPFUL HINT**
>
> Do not use a sawing or chopping motion for straight lines, simply lower the knife edge over the line to be cut.

16 Colour a teaspoon of royal icing a gold colour, using autumn leaf, and use to fill a bag fitted with a no.0 tube. Pipe lines of icing onto the angels' heads to resemble hair, trailing the ends off onto the gowns with a damp no.1 brush. Pipe in the haloes above their heads. Leave to dry. Paint over the crowns of the angels' heads with dark brown, leaving some areas gold. Shade part of their haloes darker apricot colour using a no.1 brush. When they are dry, dust their cheeks with skintone and rose dusting powders (petal dusts/blossom tints) mixed with a little cornflour (cornstarch) using a dry no.1 brush.

17 Cut three lengths of raffia, 1cm (1/2in) long and fold over into a 'V' shape. Stick to the side of the top cake at the divisions made earlier. Using 25g (3/4oz) white modelling paste, make three pairs of doves, using the moulds. Stick the doves in place so they are facing each other and their beaks look as if they are holding the strands of raffia. Pipe small hearts using a little of the ivory colour mixed earlier for the picket fence, and a no.0 tube. Dust the doves with a mixture of cream and peach dusting powders and a no.1 brush.

18 Trace the heart design (see page 154) onto tracing paper. Roll out the remaining 10g (1/3oz) gold modelling paste to 3mm (1/8in) thick, lay the heart tracing over and transfer three times. Cut out the hearts and stick to the sides of the cakes in between each pair of doves.

19 Roll out 5g (1/4oz) terracotta paste and cut out tiny pairs of holes using the no.1.5 piping tube. To make the buttons, cut around each pair of holes, making sure the holes are in the middle, with the 12mm (1/2in) circle cutter. Stick to the sides of the cake, one each side of a heart. Cut six lengths of raffia about 2cm (3/4in) long and stick to the sides of the cake so it looks as if they are coming out of the doves' beaks.

20 Colour 200g (6 1/2oz) modelling paste ivory and knead in half a teaspoon of gum tragacanth or tylo powder. Roll to 15mm (5/8in) deep, and cut out a circle using the 8.5cm (3 1/4in) circle cutter. Leave to dry.

Folk art

23

21 Make the sugarpaste figures of the bride and groom, as described on page 109. Using a little royal icing, stick the ivory plinth to the top of the 15cm (6in) cake, then fix a length of the gingham ribbon around it and leave to dry for a few hours. Stick the bride to the plinth with royal icing, and then mark where the groom will go. Make a pilot hole with a cocktail stick (toothpick), pipe royal icing under the groom's feet, then lower him into the hole next to the bride. Leave to dry for a few hours.

Complete the finishing touches to the figures, adding their arms, hair and the groom's hat and bride's bonnet, using the photograph as a guide. Finally, dust their cheeks with a mixture of rose and skintone dusting powders with cornflour, using a no.1 brush.

22 Attach lengths of the gingham ribbon around each cake, making sure the joins are at the back. Use the 1cm (½in) wide ribbon around the bottom cake. Stick the 15mm (⅝in) wide tan ribbon to the edges of the cake boards.

23 Measure the depth of each cake then add the following measurements: 4cm (1½in) to the depth of bottom two cakes and 3.5cm (1⅜in) to the depth of the 20cm (8in) cake. Transfer this measurement to the concealed pillars, allowing three per cake, and cut them to size. Rest the concealed pillars on the corresponding cakes, positioning them at an equal distance away from the edge and from each other. Push right down into the cake to the board below. Check that the pillars are all level. Tie a raffia bow for the bottom tier.

24 From the main bundle of raffia, pull away three bundles, each 3cm (1¼in) thick. Wrap an elastic band around one end of each bundle to keep the ends together. Gather another bundle about 2cm (¾in) thick and again wrap an elastic band around it. Starting with the bottom cake, lay the raffia strands on top to form a circle, then, with another single strand, bind loosely and tie the bundle together where they overlap. Trim, allowing enough to tuck in neatly after binding. Bind along the length with a piece of raffia secured at one end, working from left to right with a single piece. Tie the ends neatly, then snip the elastic band with scissors and remove it. Tuck in the ends where they overlap and trim. Repeat for the other lengths of raffia using the 2cm (¾in) thick bundle for the 15cm (6in) cake.

25 Lay the garlands on the cakes. The garlands should be large enough to sit on top of the cake and disguise the join of the sky onto the cake edge. Finally, stack the cakes.

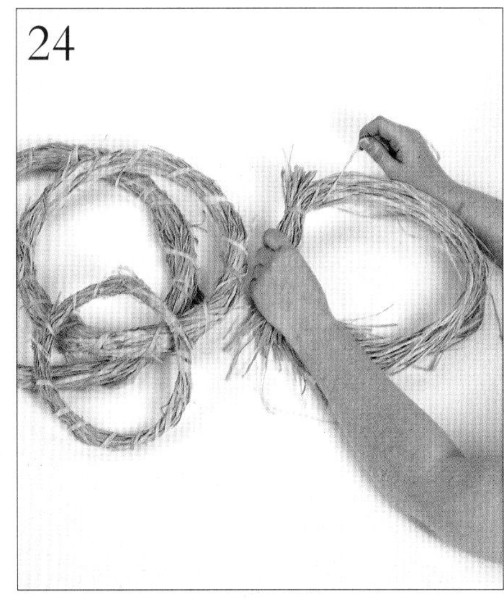

24

Calligraphy cake

The inspiration for this cake came from the popularity of calligraphy as a decorative motif. Combined with music, it shows how you can successfully link two design elements together to represent the two people getting married. Incorporate a favourite piece of music or poem to personalize the cake.

Cake and decoration

25cm (10in), 20cm (8in) and 15cm (6in) fruit cakes
35cm (14in), 28cm (11in) and 23cm (9in) round cake boards
3kg (6lb) marzipan
3.2kg (6lb 6½oz) ivory sugarpaste (rolled fondant)
20cm (8in), 15cm (6in) and 13cm (5in) thin cake boards
Autumn leaf, caramel/ivory and licorice black paste food colourings
75g (2½oz) ivory flower paste
Cream, tangerine and primrose dusting powders (petal dusts/blossom tints)
50g (1¾oz) royal icing
200g (6½oz) ivory modelling paste
3m (3¼yd), 15mm (⅝in) wide and 1.75m (2yd), 3mm (⅛in) wide sand dune ribbon
Six brass candlesticks
Five pieces gold wire, curled

Essential equipment

Templates (pages 150–51)
No.10 bristle brush
Nos.0, 1 and 4 paintbrushes
No.1.5 piping tube (tip)
Small [549, 550, 551 TKT] and large rose petal cutters [276–280 TKT]
20-, 24-, 26- and 28-gauge wire
Medium lily cutter and veiner [HH]
Lily and white flower stamens
Caladium leaf veiner [GI]
Jasmine leaf cutter set [SC]
Ivy cutters [J] and medium ivy veiner

1 Marzipan the cakes (see page 143) and leave to dry. Cover each cake with ivory sugarpaste (rolled fondant) using 1.5kg (3lb) for the 25cm (10in) cake, 1kg (2lb) for the 20cm (8in) and 500g (1lb) for the 15cm (6in) cake. Leave the cakes to dry for up to a week. Use some of the remaining ivory sugarpaste to cover the three thin cake boards.

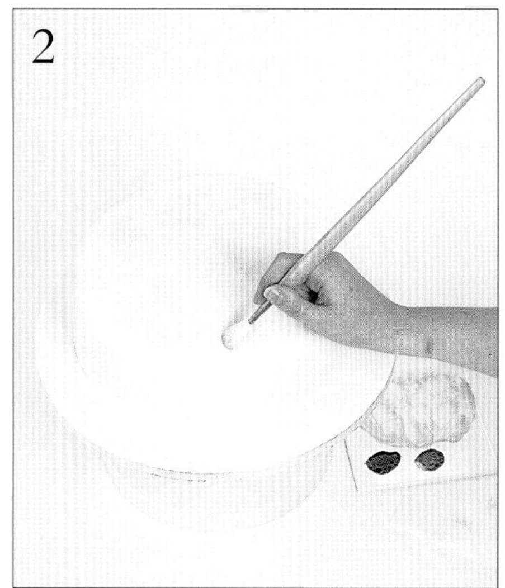

2 Mix superwhite powder and water to a watercolour consistency. Add autumn leaf and caramel food colourings to obtain a parchment colour. Dip a no.10 bristle brush in the mixture (take off any excess with kitchen towel) and paint the surface of one cake, using a stabbing motion and leaving some areas uncovered. Mix a darker parchment colour and shade in some of the blank spaces. Repeat on the other cakes, and the three thin cake boards.

3 Trace the calligraphy templates (see pages 150–51) onto a continuous strip of tracing paper for

Anna
dolce
credo. ad Theotimum devenit
vectabere cymis, nec te fortis
formam, di tibi divitias dederunt artemque
etiam Ascraes norunt mea carmina fontes

Sugarpaste wedding cakes

4

each cake. Flip the tracing over and pencil over the lines on the back. Secure the tracings around the 25cm (10in) and 20cm (8in) cakes. Rub over the calligraphy to transfer it onto the sides of the cakes.

4 Trace and transfer the calligraphy flourish to the front of the 15cm (6in) cake, in the middle: Trace separate words of your choice and transfer them randomly at angles around the sides of the cake. Mix black food colouring with water and paint over the calligraphy on each tier using a no.0 brush for the outline and a no.1 brush for any filling in. Paint tiny music notes around the top cake. You may find it easier when painting on the sides to use a tilting turntable.

5 Cover the cake boards with strips of sugarpaste. Trim where the paste overlaps and smooth over the surface to hide the join. Make sure that all the joins are at the back.

6 To make the manuscript and poetry fragments, roll out some ivory flower paste. Cut out six strips measuring 6 x 3cm ($2\frac{1}{2}$ x $1\frac{1}{4}$in), six 4cm x 15mm ($1\frac{1}{2}$ x $\frac{5}{8}$in), eight 2 x 3cm ($\frac{3}{4}$ x $1\frac{1}{4}$in) for the bottom tier and eight 3 x 3.5cm ($1\frac{1}{4}$ x $1\frac{3}{8}$in), five 4cm x 15mm ($1\frac{1}{2}$ x $\frac{5}{8}$in) and five 2 x 3cm ($\frac{3}{4}$ x $1\frac{1}{4}$in) for the middle tier. Make a few spares. Roll out a small amount of paste at a time to prevent it from drying out. Ball the edges on a cel pad and leave to dry on a 20cm (8in) thin cake board, bent to the same curve as the cake.

7 Mix together cream, tangerine and primrose dusting powders (petal dusts/blossom tints) with cornflour (cornstarch) to match the colour of the cakes. Using a dry no.4 brush, lightly dust over the strips.

8 For the bottom tier, paint music on the larger strips using a no.1 brush dipped in black food colouring. (Copy some real music.) On the smaller shapes, paint lines of poetry in a similar style. For the middle tier, paint poetry on the larger pieces and manuscript on the smaller ones.

6

9 Colour the royal icing a parchment colour. Using a piping bag fitted with a no.1.5 piping tube (tip), pipe a small snail's trail of icing around the base of each cake.

10 Stick the large fragments of poetry and manuscript to the cakes with small blobs of icing, then overlap them with the smaller ones.

11 Using a glue stick, fasten the 15mm ($\frac{5}{8}$in) wide sand dune ribbon around the cake boards, and the 3mm ($\frac{1}{8}$in) wide ribbon to the edges of the thin cake boards.

12 Insert four dowels into the bottom and middle tiers and cut off level with the surface of the cakes. Stick the thin cake boards on the top with a little royal icing and push down gently. Make sure the boards are level and secure. Place three candlesticks between the tiers.

13 To make the book, roll out 200g ($6\frac{1}{2}$oz) ivory modelling paste to 15mm ($\frac{5}{8}$in) thick. Cut out a

8

❋ ❋ ❋ ❋

Calligraphy cake

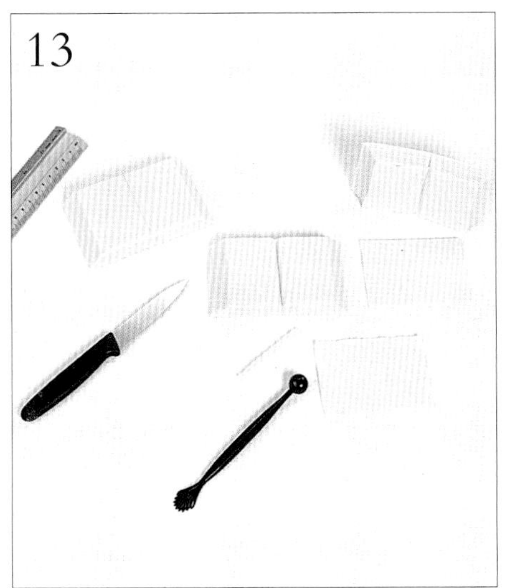
13

rectangle measuring 11.5 x 6.5cm ($4\frac{5}{8}$ x $2\frac{5}{8}$in). Mark a line down the middle and cut out a small 'V' shape. Cut away at an angle of 15mm ($\frac{5}{8}$in) from each of the short edges. Mark horizontal lines for the pages. Pick up the book and bend inwards slightly. Leave to dry in this position, resting on one long side. Cut out a rectangle of ivory flower paste measuring 9 x 6.5cm ($3\frac{1}{2}$ x $2\frac{5}{8}$in). Thin the edges with a ball tool, then stick on top of the book with water. Mark a line down the centre. Leave to dry then paint in the lettering with black food colouring, using a no. 0 brush.

14 Use the large rose petal cutters and 24-gauge wire to make the large roses, then stub them onto 20-gauge wire. Use the smaller cutters and 24-gauge wire to make the smaller roses and buds from ivory flower paste. Dust the roses with a mix of cream, tangerine and primrose dusting powders. Make the lilies with a medium lily cutter and 26-gauge wire. Use yellow lily stamens dipped in sugar glue and some crushed semolina mixed with yellow dusting powder. Dust flower centres with lime green. Make 30 lily buds on 26-gauge wire and wire into six sprays.

15 Make two large and two medium caladium leaves using the template (page 150) and ivory flower paste on 26-gauge wire. Vein and paint with a mix of spruce, gooseberry, holly and black. Make 65 jasmine leaves with pale gooseberry flower paste, using the three smallest cutters and 28-gauge wire. Dust with a mixture of green and yellow dusting powders. Wire into 13 sprays.

Make 90 ivy leaves in various sizes on 28-gauge wire, using Christmas green paste and the ivy cutters. Vein and dust with moss green and black. Dip the ivy and jasmine leaves in a half-and-half mixture of confectioners' varnish and dipping solution.

15

16 Roll 150g (5oz) ivory sugar-paste into a ball and stick onto the 13cm (5in) thin cake board. Attach the open book to the paste with a little royal icing. Stick the board to the top tier with a little royal icing. Finally, build up the flower and leaves arrangement around the book; starting with the leaves.

16

Summer garden

This cake is ideal for a beginner to try. The brocade-effect sunflowers, daisies and strawberries are made with flower cutters and flower paste, then simply stuck onto the surface of the cake. Tiny dots of royal icing are filled in between, with narrow ribbons and tulle cascading down to finish.

Cake and decoration

25cm (10in) and 15cm (6in) hexagonal fruit cakes
35cm (14in) hexagonal cake board
20cm (8in) hexagonal thin cake board
2kg (4lb) marzipan
2kg (4lb) white sugarpaste (rolled fondant)
210g (7oz) flower paste
Autumn leaf and dark brown paste food colourings
2 tablespoons royal icing
3.5m (3¾yd), 3mm (⅛in) wide; 1.5m (1⅔yd), 7mm (⅓in) wide; 1m (1⅛yd), 15mm (⅝in) wide antique white ribbon; 2m (2¼yd), 3mm (⅛in) wide fawn ribbon
1.5m (1⅔yd) white tulle

Essential equipment

Nos.2, 3, 4 and 5 daisy cutters [FMM]
No.4 paintbrush
Thin card
28mm (1⅛in), 15mm (⅝in) and 1cm (½in) circle cutters
2cm (¾in) wide heart cutter
Veining tool
D1 daisy cutter [FMM]
Blossom cutter set [PME]
Medium heart cutter [PME]
Cel stick [C]
Nos.0 and 1.5 piping tubes (tips)
32-gauge white wire
White floristry tape
Two-tiered tilting cake stand

1 Marzipan the cakes and leave to dry (see page 143). Then cover the cakes with sugarpaste (rolled fondant), using 1.5kg (3lb) for the larger cake and 500g (1lb) for the smaller cake. Cover the edges of the cake boards with a continuous strip of sugarpaste, preferably the following day. Leave to harden for up to a week.

2 Colour 75g (2½oz) flower paste pale gold using autumn leaf colouring, and 20g (¾oz) toffee colour using a mixture of autumn leaf and dark brown food colourings.

3 Roll out a portion of the pale gold paste very thinly and cut out three sunflowers using the no.2 daisy cutter. Have the cake ready in position on a tilting turntable at maximum tilt. Flip one of the sunflowers over onto a small piece of thin card, and moisten the back of the petals, using a no. 4 paintbrush. Do not paint the centre of the flower. Hold the card at an angle in the centre of one side of the 25cm (10in)

cake, with the card resting on the cake board where the cake joins the board. Push the card up and onto the side. Pat the petals down firmly with fingertips to make sure they are stuck.

4 Cut out the centre of the flower on the cake with the 28mm (1 1/8in) circle cutter, then repeat for the remaining five sides. Cut out six more sunflowers (three at a time) and stick on top of the cake positioned at the corners, cutting out the centres on the cake as you go. Roll out a piece of the toffee-coloured flower paste and cut out 12 circles with the 28mm

HELPFUL HINT

This card technique works well with large flowers as picking them up would cause the petals to flop and stick to each other. Do not cover flowers that are waiting to be put in position, because if they are exposed to the air for a few minutes they will keep their shape and be easier to handle.

(1 1/8in) circle cutter. Moisten the centres of the flowers on the cake and stick the circles inside. Make sure there is a neat join and that there are no air bubbles underneath.

5 Cut 12 daisies from white flower paste with the no.4 daisy cutter. Cut pale gold centres with the 15mm (5/8in) circle cutter. Position on the cake, using the card, so that there is a daisy on each bottom corner and one on each top corner. Add another six daisies on top of the cake so that they fit in between the sunflowers.

6 Roll out a piece of gold paste and cut out 12 sunflowers with the no.5 daisy cutter. It may not be necessary to use card for support as they are small enough to handle. Stick one either side of the main sunflower, cut out the centres and leave blank.

7 Roll out a piece of white flower paste and cut out 18 hearts for strawberries with the 2cm (3/4in) heart cutter. Moisten the backs, one at a time, and stick to the middle of the corners of the cake in pairs, with their points touching. Mark seeds with the fine end of the veining tool. Stick the remaining six on the cake in between the sunflowers. Roll out another piece of white flower paste and cut out 12 calyxes (the strawberry leaves) with the D1 daisy cutter. Moisten the top of each strawberry and stick the calyx in place. Make a hole in the centre of each calyx at an angle with a cake stick.

8 Roll out another piece of white flower paste and cut out 36 large blossoms and 18 medium blossoms, using the blossom cutter set. Moisten their backs before using them and arrange in groups on the sides of the cake, bottom left and top right of the main central flower. Each group should have three large blossoms and two medium blossoms overlapping.

9 Cut out 48 hearts using the medium heart cutter and 12 small blossoms. Moisten each heart before using it, and arrange in groups of four with the points touching on the cake

sides, top left and bottom right of the central sunflower. Cut out the centre using the smallest blossom cutter and replace with a small blossom flower.

10 The flowers used on the smaller cake are slightly different sizes, but the techniques are the same. Cut 12 white daisies with the no.3 daisy cutter. Position six at the base on the corners of the small cake, and six centrally below the top edge. Cut out the centres with the 15mm (5/8in) circle cutter and replace with a toffee-coloured circle.

11 Cut out six pale gold sunflowers with the no. 3 daisy cutter and stick to the small cake at each corner. Cut out the centres with the 15mm (5/8in) circle cutter and replace with a toffee-coloured circle. Cut out six more sunflowers using the no. 5 cutter, and position under the main central daisy on each side. Cut out the centres with an 1cm (1/2in) circle cutter and replace with circles the same size made with toffee-coloured paste.

12 Cut out 12 white hearts with the 2cm (3/4in) heart cutter and stick to the top corners of the small cake. Cut out 12 calyxes with the D1 daisy cutter, and finish as in step 7. Cut out six medium white hearts and stick in between the sunflowers on the top of the cake.

13 Cut out 24 medium and 24 small white blossoms. Stick in groups of two medium and one small at the top right and bottom left on

each side, and single small blossoms at the top left and bottom right.

14 To make the strawberries, divide 35g (1 1/4oz) white flower paste into 12. Roll a portion into a ball, then a cone. Mark tiny lines on the surface with the veining tool to resemble seeds and insert a cel stick into the fat end to make a hole. Moisten and attach a calyx, made with the D1 daisy cutter. Insert the cel stick again to open up the hole, then pipe a stalk using royal icing and a no.1.5 piping tube (tip). Leave to dry for a few hours. Place one strawberry at each corner of the large cake. Arrange the last six on top of the small cake with their points facing inwards. Secure with royal icing.

15 Fill a small piping bag with white royal icing and fit with a no.0 tube. Pipe a mixture of tiny white dots, blossoms and five pointed flowers in between the brocade. Pipe dots on both cake boards. Fill the centres of the small sunflowers on the bottom tier with small dots.

16 Stick 15mm (5/8in) wide white ribbon to the base tier board edge and 3mm (1/8in) wide white ribbon to the top tier board edge.

17 Decorate the top tier board with three 40cm (16in) wide sections of tulle. Cut each section in half length ways. Gather the end of each piece, twist a length of 32-gauge wire around and finish with floristry tape. Tape over six pieces of the 32-gauge wire individually and wrap around a rolling pin to curl. Cut the white and fawn ribbons into varying lengths long enough to hang from the stand onto the cake. Divide into two, mixing the colours equally, then wire and finish with tape. Assemble, beginning with the tulle, then the wire and finally the ribbon. Tape together.

Trim and fix to opposite corners of the top board by inserting into a piece of sugarpaste stuck to the board. To cover the join, tie two bows with 7mm (1/3in) wide ribbon and secure with royal icing. Tie a bow with the remaining 3mm (1/8in) wide ribbon and attach to the front of the top tier.

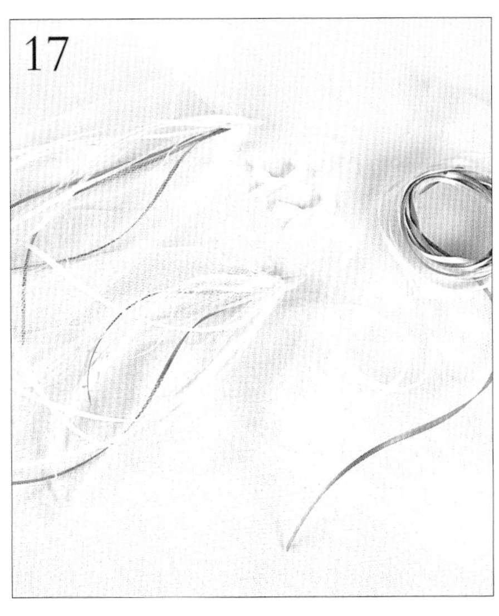

Indian elephants

The country of India conjures up a riot of colours, textures and a feeling of opulence, with its images of exotic animals and air of mystery. The Indian elephant, with full ceremonial dress and gold toenails, seemed an excellent theme to build on for so grand an occasion as a wedding.

Cake and decoration

30cm (12in), 9cm (3½in) deep square fruit cake,
25cm (10in), 20cm (8in), 15cm (6in) and 10cm (4in) square fruit cakes
6.35kg (12lb 12oz) marzipan
3.85kg (7lb 11oz) ivory sugarpaste (rolled fondant)
2kg (4lb) white sugarpaste
Two 40cm (16in) thick cake boards
23cm (9in) thick cake board
25cm (10in), 20cm (8in) and 10cm (4in) thin cake boards
725g (1½lb) modelling paste
Navy, grape violet, licorice black, pink, ice blue, egg yellow, melon, Christmas red and spruce green paste food colourings
Antique gold dusting powder (petal dust/blossom tint) [SK]
Ice pink pearl lustre [SK]
25g (¾oz) pastillage
500g (1lb) royal icing

Essential equipment

Templates (see page 155)
Veining tool
Sugarpaste gun (with discs)
Umbrella mould
Bamboo stick (wooden skewer)
Silk/taffeta rolling pin
Nos.0, 1 and 4 paintbrushes
Nos.1 and 1.5 piping tubes (tips)
2cm (¾in) circle cutter
16 cake dowels
Four wooden pillars

1 Stick the 25cm (10in), 20cm (8in) and 10cm (4in) cakes on the corresponding thin cake boards, then place on larger spare boards. Stick the two 40cm (16in) cake boards together with royal icing to form the base for the bottom cake. Place the 15cm (6in) on the 23cm (9in) board. Marzipan all the cakes (see page 143). Leave to set for up to a week.

2 Cover the 30cm (12in) cake and board and the 20cm (8in) and 10cm (4in) cakes with ivory sugarpaste (rolled fondant). Colour 2kg (4lb) sugarpaste porcelain blue with navy and grape violet food colourings. Use 1.5kg (3lb) blue sugarpaste to cover the 25cm (10in) cake and 500g (1lb) for the 15cm (6in) cake and board. Leave to set for up to a week.

3 Trace the elephants templates (see page 155), then transfer the design onto the sides of the 30cm (12in) and 25cm (10in) cakes. To decorate the 30cm (12in) cake, colour 100g (3½oz) modelling paste grey with licorice black food colouring. Roll out a quarter of the paste to about 3mm (⅛in) thick. Transfer the elephant design onto the paste. Cut around the elephant and at the line marking the elephants' ankles (they will be replaced with purple feet later). If you have an elephant cutter, use this to cut out the elephant instead, then flip it over to cut its mirror image.

4 Moisten the position of the elephants on the cake sides, then stick in place using the pencil outline

as a guide. Smooth away any hard edges with your fingertips so all the outlines are nicely rounded. Mark the elephants' legs, belly and neck lines on the paste with the veining tool. Repeat for the remaining sides, working with enough paste to cut out two at a time.

5 Colour 25g (¾oz) modelling paste deep purple with the grape violet food colouring. Roll it out until it is about 3mm (⅛in) thick, lay the tracing on top and rub over just where the outlines of the feet and ankles are. Repeat eight times (four each way). Cut carefully around the shapes. Moisten the sides of the cake where the feet will go, then stick each set of feet in place matching up with the bottom of the elephants' legs. Smooth the edges, then mark in the feet with the veining tool.

6 If you have used a cutter make the tails separately. Roll small balls of grey into sausages tapering gently towards the ends, and stick on the side of the cake using the pencil line as a guide. Blend with a little water onto the body. Roll tiny balls of purple with points on the ends and stick at the ends of the grey tails.

7 Colour 60g (2oz) modelling paste red. Roll half of it out to about 3mm (⅛in) thick and transfer the heart design onto the surface. Carefully cut out the hearts and stick to the sides of the cake in between the elephants. Smooth the edges so they are nicely rounded.

8 To make the ornamental cloth, roll out 50g (1¾oz) white modelling paste quite thinly, and rub over the cloth part of the tracing, to make eight. Cut out the shapes, and stick on top of the elephants, using the pencil lines as a guide, and smooth the edges. Repeat for the ears using the rest of the white paste, starting with the ear in the background and then the one in foreground. Ease the paste forward a little to raise it up.

6

9 For the carrying seat, colour 100g (3½oz) modelling paste yellow/orange with egg yellow and melon food colourings. Roll out about 25g (¾oz) thinly (save 75g [2½oz] for the top of the cake) and transfer the image for the seat (without the curly ends) onto the paste eight times (four each way). Stick on the sides of the cake above the elephants making sure the joins are neat and all the edges are smooth. Roll eight tiny balls of paste for the centres of the curls and stick in place with water, then squash flat with a finger. Roll out 10g (⅓oz) of paste and cut eight 6mm (¼in) wide strips and stick over the seat, trimming at the ends. Fit the 3mm (⅛in) plain rope disc into the sugarpaste gun and extrude approximately 50cm (20in) of yellow/orange paste. Cut off sections long enough to curl around the ends of the carrying seat. Start with the inside of the curl and finish by cutting the excess paste away on the elephant's back.

10 Roll out the rest of the paste for the headdress. Cut out the headdress shapes, using the tracing, and stick over the elephants' foreheads. Colour 15g (½oz) modelling paste sea green with ice blue and spruce green food colours. Roll out a small

✳ ✳ ✳ ✳

Indian elephants

amount and transfer the image for the background tusk onto the paste. Cut out eight tusks and stick to the sides of the cake, smoothing over the edges. Roll the remaining paste into balls and then into long cones to form the tusks in the foreground. Stick over the elephant in a curve and flatten the fat end slightly. Roll out a small amount of white modelling paste thinly and cut out eight eyes. Stick in position on the elephant.

11 Paint the ornamental cloth with a pink outline, ice blue on the inside. Paint the hearts red, and hearts on the carrying seat. Paint stripes on the ears with navy and grape violet mixed together. Paint the outer eye with the same colour and the rest of the eye, pupil and lashes with black. Use a no.0 brush, mixing all food colours with a little superwhite and water (except black as it will go grey). Paint the toenails and ankle band with gold dusting powder (petal dust/blossom tint) mixed with dipping solution. Paint gold stripes on the tusks, gold lines to separate the colours on the ornamental cloth and gold spots on the headdress. Finally, paint a few dark grey feathery lines on the knees and the trunks.

12 Roll out a quarter of the modelling paste taken from 100g (3½oz) of white until about 3mm (⅛in) thick. Cut out three elephants at a time and stick to the sides of the 25cm (10in) cake, marking the legs and belly with the veining tool. Use a quarter of the paste for every three elephants. Build up the elephants in the same way as before, working with the remaining white paste for all the features in the following order: tail, ornamental cloth, background ear, foreground ear, background tusk, foreground tusk. Omit the headdress, which will be painted onto the forehead later.

Paint the ornamental cloth with the same colours as the 30cm (12in) cake but with a gold heart on a red background. Paint dark grey feathery lines on the knees and trunks. Paint the eyes in the same way as above and finish by painting all the gold details (toenails, headdress and outlines on the cloth).

13 Insert four plastic dowels into the 30cm (12in), 25cm (10in), 20cm (8in) and 15cm (6in) cakes, and trim level with the surface of the cake (see page 50). Gently release the 25cm (10in), 20cm (8in) and 10cm (4in) cakes from their spare boards. Place some of royal icing on the 30cm (12in), the 20cm (10in) and 15cm (6in) cakes. You can now begin to stack them up, assembling the cakes as in the photograph on page 125. Push down on top to make sure they are well stuck together and leave to set.

14 Colour 100g (3½oz) modelling paste turquoise blue using ice blue food colouring with a little spruce green. Fit the sugarpaste gun with the big clover leaf disc, load with paste, and extrude 26cm (10½in). Extrude enough paste for a continuous rope without joins, without having to reload the clay gun. Twist the paste from the centre outwards all along the length. Paint a gentle curve onto the side of the cake with water from corner to corner,

15

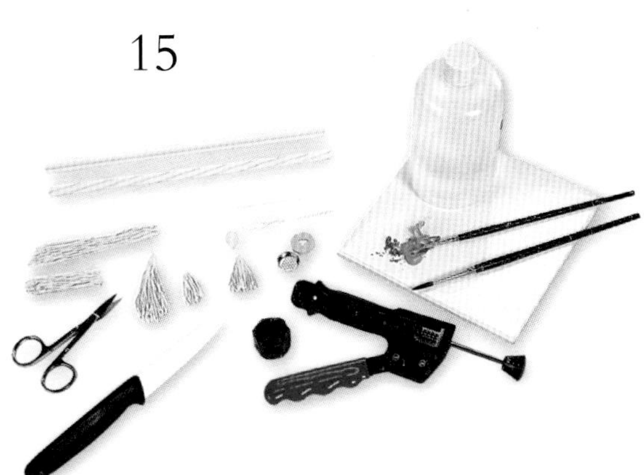

then stick the rope in place, working from left to right. Push the rope against the side of the cake with the flat of your hand to make sure it is stuck well but try not to distort the shape of the rope. Trim at both ends making vertical cuts. Repeat for the other three sides. Indent the paste at the corners by squashing gently with a finger to make room for the tassels.

15 For the tassels, fit the sugarpaste gun with a fine mesh disc and reload with paste. Extrude 8cm (3in) paste and cut off. Paint a line of water down the middle, then fold over end to end. Pat the folded end to make sure the strands are stuck to themselves, then pick it up and roll a few times between your fingers. Mark a line at the top of the strands, then measure down 3cm (1¼in) and mark a line across. Trim at this line with a small pair of scissors, holding the bulb of icing at the top of the tassel. Make sure the strands are separate at the bottom of the tassel. Lay it down and trim off the bulb of icing.

Stick the tassel onto the corner of the cake with water. Make another three tassels the same way and stick in place. Roll four balls about 1cm (½in) in width and then roll into cones. Moisten the corners of the cake and stick each cone in place with the pointed end downwards. Flatten the edges of the cone to the cake leaving a dome in the middle.

16 Change the disc for the 1.5mm ($^1/_{16}$in) plain rope and extrude about 24cm (9½in) blue paste. Cut into four. Paint a line of water on half of one piece and fold it over end to end. Twist to make a small rope. Repeat for the other three ropes and attach to the tassels with a little water over the join. Trim neatly at each end. Give the large rope a striped effect by painting with gold powder mixed with dipping solution, and paint the small rope on the tassel. Fill a piping bag with ivory royal icing. Use a no.1.5 tube (tip) to pipe small hearts above the rope swag and onto the top of the cake, but stopping clear of where the stand or pillars will go. Leave to dry, then paint gold.

17 For the 15cm (6in) cake, fill a piping bag with royal icing coloured the same blue as the cake. Use a no.1.5 tube to pipe small hearts all over the surface. First pipe a long thin teardrop shape, and then pipe another one next to it at an angle so that they taper off to a nice point together. When dry, paint some hearts gold and leave some blue.

18 For the 10cm (4in) cake, trace the design (see page 155) and transfer the image onto the sides of the cake. Make a tracing for one side, then reposition the same tracing on the other sides. Using the same technique for the heart design on the 30cm (12in) cake, take 15g (½oz) of the red modelling paste and cut out four hearts. Stick to the sides of the cake with a little water. Colour a dessertspoon of royal icing ivory, and fill a piping bag fitted with a no.1.5 piping tube. Pipe the scrolls onto the side of the cake. Colour a teaspoon of royal icing turquoise blue to match the rope on the 20cm (8in) cake and pipe small dots next to the scrolls. When the scrolls have dried, paint gold using the no.0 brush.

> **Helpful Hint**
>
> For ease, use a tilting turntable or a tilting board because the cake can be tilted away from you and the piping can be dropped onto the surface to create lovely smooth curves. Alternatively find something similar to prop up the cake.

19 Knead 500g (1lb) marzipan until soft and roll into a ball. Form the ball into a square-based dome by patting down on top with your palms and smoothing diagonally from corner to corner. Mark an 8cm

19

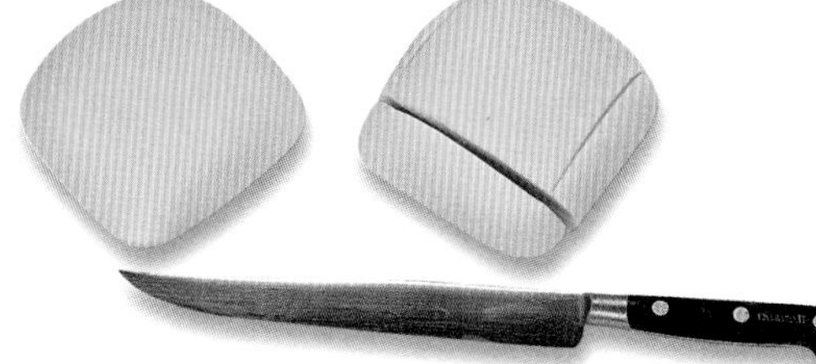

(3in) square on top, then cut the sides so that they curve inwards from this line. Leave to set overnight.

20 Moisten the top of the marzipan. Roll out a portion of orange/yellow modelling paste and cover the top, then trim. Roll out a long strip, trim the edges square, roll up and unravel to cover the sides, making a join at the back. Trim the excess away. Rub the top edge with your finger to blend the join. Moisten the base of the seat. Roll out another long strip and trim to about 1cm (½in) wide. Roll up and unravel around the seat, joining at a corner. Fill the sugarpaste gun with yellow/orange paste and fit with the 6mm (¼in) thick rope disc. Extrude about 35cm (14in) and stick it to the top edge of the seat, making a join at a corner. Mark a line with the blade of a knife at all the corners at a 45° angle. Stick the seat to the top of the 10cm (4in) cake with royal icing.

21 Change the disc in the sugarpaste gun for the 3mm (⅛in) rope and extrude about 30cm (12in) of paste. Cut into four. Moisten halfway along the top of each piece and roll up, starting with the wet end. Make sure they are all the same size, then stick to the corners of the seat using sugar glue. Trim the ends of the coils when attached to the seat at their bases. Support the coils with a piece of sponge foam. Roll out 10g (⅓oz) white modelling paste and cut out four shapes for the sides of the seat. Cut each shape into four and stick to the seat. Repeat for the other

21

sides. Paint a red heart in the centre of each shape and outline with gold.

22 Colour 175g (6oz) modelling paste bright pink using the pink food colouring. Roll 10g (⅓oz) pink paste into a ball, flatten slightly, and stick on top of the seat with a little water. Roll out 15g (½oz) paste quite thinly, and then dust the surface with the pearl lustre using a no.4 brush. Roll over the top with the silk-effect rolling pin, then cut out a 10cm (4in) square. Turn over and fold the edges in about 3mm (⅛in), securing with water. Moisten the ball of icing and over the top of the seat. Gently pick up the fabric, textured side up and place on top of the seat so that the corners drape in between the coils on the seat. Arrange into pleasing folds and leave to dry.

23 To make the umbrella, insert the bamboo skewer into the centre of the seat, down to the cake below. Mark the depth on the skewer where it enters the cake. Take out the skewer and mark from this line how

22

tall you would like the umbrella to be. Trim the remainder. Roll out 10g (⅓oz) turquoise blue modelling paste, paint the skewer with masking jelly and wrap the paste around it. Trim, then seal the join. Cut off the excess paste at the line marking the depth of the seat, and at the top. Leave to dry in an upright position. When dry, insert in the seat. Colour 25g (¾oz) pastillage turquoise blue and roll out to about 3mm (⅛in) deep. Dust the inside of an umbrella mould with cornflour (cornstarch) and ease the pastillage into the mould. Trim the ends and leave to dry for six hours.

24 Gently tip out onto a piece of sponge foam so the dome is facing upwards and dry for a further six hours. Fill the gun with turquoise blue modelling paste and fit with the 1.5mm (1/16in) rope disc. Extrude double the circumference of the umbrella, moisten one half, then lay the other half on top. Twist to make a rope. Lay the umbrella upside down on the sponge foam and paint sugar glue on the edges. Stick the rope

around the edge of the umbrella. Leave to dry. Turn the umbrella the right way up. Cut out a circle of turquoise modelling paste using the 2cm (¾in) cutter, and stick it in the centre on top. Roll a small cone using the same paste, trim the fat end so it has a flat base and stick on top of the circle. Pipe hearts on the sides of the umbrella with a no.1 piping tube and turquoise blue royal icing. When dry, paint with gold dusting powder and dipping solution. Paint one half of the rope to look stripy, and the circle and spike on top.

25 To model the hearts, knead 25g (¾oz) red modelling paste until smooth. Divide into two and roll into balls and then long cones. Lie on the table and cut a 'V' in the fat end. Smooth away the hard edges. Stick on the seat using sugar glue, one resting against the umbrella pole and the other lying next to it. Support with a piece of sponge until dry. Stick the umbrella on the pole with blue royal icing and leave to dry.

26 Fix a length of 3mm (⅛in) wide sand dune ribbon around each cake. Tie eight bows using the remaining ribbon and stick to the corners of the 30cm (12in) and 15cm (6in) cakes with royal icing. Stick 1cm (½in) wide sand dune ribbon around the 23cm (9in) board and 2.5cm (1in) wide sand dune ribbon to the double thick base board with a glue stick, making joins at the back.

27 Place the pillars on the cake. (These pillars were made for this cake, and were screwed onto plywood, painted and then gilded. The underside was covered with gold board covering paper, and the edges trimmed with ribbon.) Roll 100g (3½oz) pink paste into a ball, then stick between the pillars. Roll out the remaining 50g (1¾oz) pink paste with the silk-effect rolling pin. Stick the pillars or stand to the cake with royal icing. Either add the fabric, with its corners draping out between the pillars, and transport the cake with the pillars in place (bearing in mind that it will be taller and heavier with the pillars); or preferably transport the pillars/stand separately and put the fabric in place when assembling.

Oriental splendour

Several different oriental themes are incorporated in this wedding cake, with alternating colours on each tier. The result is an unusual cake which is also elegant and dramatic. For a more subtle finish, cover all four tiers with the willow pattern, or just decorate each tier with swags and Chinese characters.

Cake and decoration

30cm (12in), 25cm (10in), 20cm (8in), 15cm (6in) round fruit cakes
40cm (16in) and 28cm (11in) round cake boards; 15cm (6in) square cake board; (25cm) 10in, 15cm (6in) round thin cake boards
5kg (10lb) marzipan
10cm (4in) square polystyrene dummy, 13cm (5in) deep
500g (1lb) royal icing
3kg (6lb) poppy red sugarpaste (rolled fondant)
2.45kg (4lb 14oz) white sugarpaste
350g (12oz) modelling paste
25g (¾oz) flower paste
Baby blue, grape violet, caramel/ivory, black, Christmas red and autumn leaf paste food colourings
725g (1lb 7oz) black sugarpaste
1.15kg (2½lb) ivory sugarpaste
Gold, yellow, green and brown dusting powders (petal dusts/blossom tints)
60g (2oz) red flower paste [SK]
35g (1¼oz) spruce green flower paste
Red petal cream [J]

Essential equipment

Templates (pages 156–7)
Nos.0, 1 and 4 paintbrushes
23mm (⅞in), 15mm (⅝in), 12mm (9/16in) and 1cm (½in) circle cutters
Nos.1.5, 2 and 3 piping tubes (tips)
Rose petal cutters [TKT]
Flower former [J] and flower stamens
1m (1⅛yd) wooden/eight cake dowels

1 Stick the 25cm (10in) and 15cm (6in) thin cake boards to the bottom of the corresponding cakes, then place on spare boards for marzipanning and decorating. Place the 30cm (12in) cake on the 40cm (16in) board and the 20cm (8in) on the 28cm (11in) board. Marzipan the cakes, making sure the ones with the thin boards underneath have no gaps at the bases. Leave to set and harden for up to one week. Stick the 10cm (4in) dummy in the centre of the 15cm (6in) square cake board.

2 Cover the largest cake with 2kg (4lb) red sugarpaste (rolled fondant) and the 20cm (8in) cake with 1kg (2lb) red sugarpaste. Then cover the 25cm (10in) cake with 1.5kg (3lb) white sugarpaste and the 15cm (6in) cake with 500g (1lb) white sugarpaste. Leave the boards uncovered at this stage.

3 Measure the circumference of the base tier cake and divide it into six. Mark these divisions on the side of the cake with a veining tool. Colour 100g (3½oz) modelling paste ivory. Roll out the paste with a small rolling pin until 3mm (⅛in) thick. Cut into strips 2cm (¾in) wide and a little longer than each division of the cake. Cover with cling film (plastic wrap). Paint a gentle curve on the side of the cake with water using a no.4 paintbrush. Pick up one section of paste and, working from left to right, gently stick it to the wet surface. Trim the ends. Apply the remaining swags in the same way.

Oriental splendour

Neaten the joins at the divisions by overlapping each swag over one that has been trimmed and pushing the knife into the paste at the join. Remove the overlaps and smooth. Leave to dry overnight.

4 Place red, black and a mixture of baby blue and grape violet food colourings with a little water and superwhite powder on a tile. Paint characters on the swags with a no.0 paintbrush. It may be easier to trace some Chinese text and transfer the characters onto the swags as a guide. Be sure to cover the pencil lines.

HELPFUL HINT

Try to be accurate when painting sugarpaste with water as any excess water on the surface which is not covered by the swag will remain visible and will dry shiny.

5 Trace the willow pattern (see pages 156–7) on a continuous strip of tracing paper, using an HB pencil. Transfer the pattern onto the side of the 25cm (10in) round cake. Mix baby blue, grape violet and a little superwhite powder together with a no.4 paintbrush and colour the background with a thin wash of colour. When dry, build up further layers of colour with slightly thicker paint, gradually getting darker and darker. Finally, paint the fine details in the darkest shade of blue with a no.0 paintbrush. It may help if you have a willow pattern plate in front of you while you paint, to see in more detail which areas should be shaded.

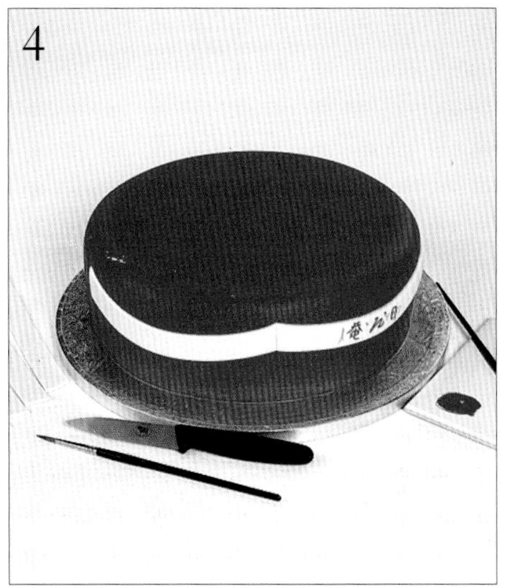
4

6 Trace the dragon pattern (see page 156) onto a continuous strip of tracing paper and transfer onto the sides of the 20cm (8in) round cake. Paint in the teeth and flames with gold dusting powder (petal dust/blossom tint) mixed with a little dipping solution to a paint consistency. It evaporates quickly so if the gold paint becomes too dry, just keep adding a little more solution.

Colour 150g (5oz) modelling paste golden yellow with autumn leaf food colouring. Thinly roll out a small amount. Place the dragon tracing with the pencil side down on the paste, then transfer the head onto the paste. Remove the tracing. Cut out the dragon's head and along the jaw lines, omitting the teeth, with a sharp knife. Moisten the side of the cake and stick the paste to the cake, matching up the shape with the outlines on the cake. Smooth the edges with your fingertips, then mark the dragon's mouth, nose and eye with a veining tool. Finally, add scales by pushing in the end of a thick drinking straw at an angle. Cut out the other sections of the dragon, matching the joins at the dotted lines. Moisten the surface of the dragon at each join, then blend with your fingertips until the joins are disguised.

7 Roll two small cones for the dragon's horns, flatten slightly and stick at the top of the dragon's head. Roll smaller cigar shapes to fit around the bases of each horn. Thinly roll out a small amount of paste and transfer the pattern for the dragon's eyes onto the surface. Cut out and stick on the dragon's face, smoothing the edges with fingertips. Indent the eye socket with the end of a paintbrush. Roll a tiny eyeball and stick in the hole.

Cut out five circles with the 15mm (5/8in) cutter and cut a hole in the centre of each with the thick straw, then two circles with the 12mm (1/2in) cutter and use the no.3 tube (tip) to cut out the centres of these. Stick three large circles onto the dragon at the first set of three fins,

6

and then two large circles followed by the smaller ones at the next set of fins. Roll long cones and stick to the cake underneath the dragon. Position them so they look curly and flowing. Allow to dry overnight. Mix some more gold dusting powder with dipping solution and paint the whole dragon, being careful not to get any on the surface of the cake.

8 Trace the design for the 15cm (6in) cake (see page 156) onto a strip of paper and transfer it to the surface of the cake, as before. Paint with the same blue colour used for the willow pattern, using a no.1 brush for outlining and a no.4 for filling in.

9 The 10cm (4in) dummy will form the pagoda. Roll 750g ($1\frac{1}{2}$lb) ivory sugarpaste to 2.5cm (1in) deep and as long as one side of the board. Cut it into four strips, each about 2.5cm (1in) wide. Wet the board and lay one strip of sugarpaste on the board, butting one edge up against the side of the dummy.

Repeat for the opposite side and then cut through the paste at a right angle at each corner of the dummy. Repeat for the other two sides, using strips that run the full length of the side of the board. Use a sharp knife to mark on the brick pattern, firstly with horizontal lines, then staggered vertical lines.

Roll out 450g (14oz) black sugarpaste 1cm ($\frac{1}{2}$in) thick. Cut into strips as above. Lay the strips on top of the ivory paste, beginning with a different side to last time. Smooth and trim as before. Mark 2.5cm (1in) squares on top of the black with a knife. Leave to dry overnight.

10 Roll out 450g (14oz) white sugarpaste into a long strip roughly 42cm (17in) long, 10cm (4in) wide and 6mm ($\frac{1}{4}$in) thick. Moisten the sides of the dummy. Cut a straight edge along one length and at each end, then roll up like a bandage and unravel around the dummy with the cut edge facing down. Start at one corner, and overlap the excess. Cut through the overlap and remove any excess sugarpaste, then smooth down.

Knead in a teaspoon of gum tragacanth or tylo powder to the remaining black sugarpaste, then roll out the paste to 1cm ($\frac{1}{2}$in) thick. Cut one 13cm (5in) square and one 8cm (3in) square, and leave to dry. Knead together the remaining black paste, roll out to 3cm ($1\frac{1}{4}$in) deep. Cut a 6cm ($2\frac{1}{2}$in) square and leave to dry. Trace the template for the side of the pagoda (page 157) and transfer to the side of the dummy. Paint the trellis and doorways with baby blue and grape violet mixed with a little superwhite and water. Try to match to the blue used for the willow pattern. Leave to dry.

Roll out 50g ($1\frac{3}{4}$oz) red sugarpaste thinly and cut eight 1cm ($\frac{1}{2}$in) strips for the pillars. Stick the strips to the sides of the dummy, using the pencil lines as a guide. Trim the pillars at the bottom in line with the lowest blue horizontal line. Round off the edges with your fingertips. Roll eight small balls of red paste into sausages and stick at the base of each pillar on the pagoda floor, easing the four corner ones into a curve. Roll eight smaller balls into sausages and stick on top of the previous

sausages to disguise the bottom edges of the pillars. Stick the 13cm (5in) square on top of the pagoda with royal icing.

11 For the lower pagoda roof, roll out 650g (1lb 5oz) ivory paste 3cm (1¼in) thick, smooth and trim. Cut out an 11cm (4½in) square. Mark lines on top of the square 15mm (⅝in) away from each edge. From this marked line cut into the paste, curving outwards towards the bottom corner. Repeat on the other three sides. Dampen the black paste and gently position the lower roof on top. Smooth once again and leave to dry overnight.

Spread a little royal icing on top of the lower pagoda roof and lay the 8cm (3in) black square on top. Spread a little royal icing on that and place the final black square on top. This will become the pagoda's upper room. Roll out 25g (¾oz) of red paste and cut into strips 6mm (¼in) wide. Stick to the sides of the upper room, as depicted in the photograph.

12 Roll 200g (6½oz) ivory sugarpaste into a smooth ball for the pagoda's domed roof. Form into a dome shape with a flat bottom. From this shape, ease the base into a square by patting with your hands at opposite sides and turning. Pick up the dome with the flat side facing upwards and using your fingers, tweak the corners into points that curve downwards slightly. Transfer the dome to the pagoda and stick in place with royal icing. Continue forming the corners and smoothing

11

the dome. Make sure the corners from the black base underneath are covered over.

Roll out 15g (½oz) autumn leaf modelling paste. Cut out a circle with the 23mm (⅞in) cutter and eight circles with the 1cm (½in) cutter. Stick the large circle on top of the dome, and the smaller circles at the top of the red pillars. Roll a small ball in the same colour and then tweak into a flat square with corners that curve upwards. Stick this on top of the circle on the dome. Roll three smaller balls of decreasing size and pile up on top of this. Make sure they are symmetrical. When dry, paint with a mixture of gold dusting powder and dipping solution.

13 To make the decorative cornicing, trace the curve (see page 156). Colour 25g (¾oz) of flower paste red. Roll balls 1cm (½in) in diameter, allowing four for the pagoda plus some spares. Cover with cling film. Take one ball in the palm of your hand and roll into a long cone shape, fat at one end and

12

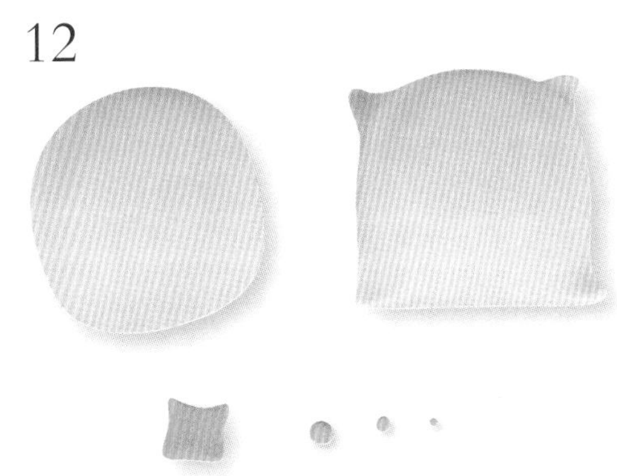

tapering towards the other. Lay it on the tracing to ensure a consistent shape. Repeat for the others and leave to dry. Colour one tablespoon royal icing with the red food colouring, matching it to the red sugarpaste. Fill a piping bag with red royal icing and, using a no.1.5 tube (tip), pipe a line along the edges of the lower pagoda roof. Stick the cornicing in place.

14 Cut an 11.5mm (½in) wooden dowel into eight sections: four pieces measuring 18cm (7in) plus the depth of the 25cm (10in) cake and four measuring 12.5cm (5in) plus the depth of the 15cm (6in) cake. To create the bamboo pillars, mark the depths of the two cakes on the corresponding dowels. Push them into some oasis (florists' staysoft). Colour 200g (6½oz) modelling paste mid-cream. Roll a small amount into a ball, and then into a sausage. Decide where the

joints will be on each pillar and paint some masking jelly around the pillar at this point. Take one sausage and wrap it around the pillar, blending it with your fingertips at each side. Repeat for the remaining pillars. Remember to have all the joints at varying heights to look more natural. Paint the pillars with a thin covering of masking jelly down to the pencil line which marks the cake depth. Roll out approximately half the paste to about 3mm (1/8in) thick, and as wide as the pillars are long. Flip the paste over, trim across the top and down one side. Working on the work surface, lay the paste over one of the pillars, only covering the part of the dowel that will be above the surface of the cake. Roll it so the paste is wrapped around the pillar. Trim to fit, leaving a small overlap. Hold the pillar at the uncovered end. Gently ease the covering paste over the joint where the sausage of paste is to expel air bubbles and make sure it is stuck. Overlap the paste where it meets the cut edge and run your finger down it so you can now see on the surface where the join is.

> **HELPFUL HINT**
>
> The oasis will hold the dowels until you are ready to use them. When you cover the dowels with sugarpaste they will need to be dried upright as resting them on a board will give them one flat side.

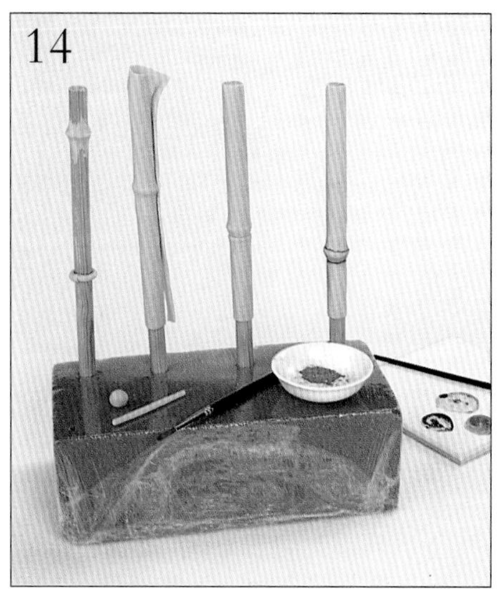
14

Cut down this line, then peel away the excess icing. Gently rub with your fingertips to smooth the join. Trim the top of the pillar by cutting against the edge, then smooth. Mark a groove around the pillar at the joint with the back of a thick-bladed knife held at an angle.

15 Repeat for the remaining long pillars, then roll out the rest of the paste for the shorter ones and cover. Leave all the pillars to dry overnight before dusting. Mix together a little brown and cream dusting powder. With a clean, dry no.4 brush, dust around the joint of each pillar and a few long 'V's from the joint above and below. Finish by painting a dark line around the joints and a few light feathery lines along the length of the bamboo with a mixture of caramel and black, and a little dipping solution.

16 Cover the boards of the 30cm (12in) and 20cm (8in) cakes with the remaining red sugarpaste. Leave to dry, then pipe a small shell around the base of both cakes using a no.1.5 tube and red royal icing.

17 Take four cake dowels and insert them into the largest

19

cake. Mark on the sides of the dowel with a sharp knife at the point where they reach the surface of the cake. Take them out one at a time and score on this line with a sharp knife, then snap the dowel with your hands. Insert back into the cake making sure they do not stand proud of the cake surface. Repeat for the 20cm (8in) cake using the remaining four dowels.

18 Use a palette knife (metal spatula) to spread royal icing on the base cake to 25cm (10in) in diameter. Ease the 25cm (10in) cake off its spare board but leave it on its thin board. Lift the cake and thin board and place on top of the largest cake, making sure that the fronts of the two cakes are in line. Push down well. Stack the 15cm (6in) on top of the 20cm (8in) cake in the same way. If any icing is squeezed out, scrape it away with a knife, and clean the area with a damp paintbrush and blot.

19 Fix a length of 7mm (¼in) wide blue ribbon around the base of the two white and blue cakes, securing at the back with royal icing.

20 Mark the position of the pillars on the two white and blue cakes (see page 157). Make a hole with a plastic dowel at each position and then push the bamboo pillars into the cake. It is important that they are vertical, so as you push down, have the cake on a turntable and turn to view it from all angles. Make sure that the joins along the length of the dowels are at the back of the cake, and that they are vertical.

21 Roll out 60g (2oz) red flower paste. Using the set of rose petal cutters, cut seven layers of petals (see below) for the flower on the 25cm (10in) cake. As this is the largest flower, cut the two outer layers twice with the two largest cutters. Each layer is made up of five petals. Cut a small 'V' out of the edge of each petal. Cut five layers of petals for the 15cm (6in) cake (the same size flower should be used on the alternative top cake, see step 23).

Vein the petals and ball the edges to give shape. Leave the smallest petals to dry folding inwards, and leave the rest to dry on shaped foam. When dry, paint with red petal cream. Dip the stamens in sugar glue and then crushed semolina mixed with lemon yellow dusting powder. Paint the stems of the stamens with red petal cream.

To assemble the flowers, place a small square of waxed paper in the flower former. Pipe a circle of red royal icing on the paper, and lay on the first layer of petals. Repeat for the other layers, using small pieces of sponge foam to support the petals. Push in the stamens while the icing is still soft. Using the leaf templates (see page 157) roll out 35g (1¼oz) spruce green flower paste quite thick, and cut out four leaves of each size. Vein, then ball the edges and leave to dry over sponge. When dry, dust with moss green and brown, then dip in a half-and-half solution of dipping solution and confectioners' varnish.

22 Fix the large leaves between the pillars on the 25cm (10in) cake and the smaller ones on the 15cm (6in) cake using white royal icing and a no.2 tube. Use red royal icing and a no.1.5 tube to stick the flowers on the leaves and gently lower them down between the pillars.

23 Finally, stick 15mm (⅝in) wide sand dune ribbon to the cake board edges. For an alternative, less elaborate top tier, cover a 10cm (4in) round cake with red sugarpaste. Add a strip of ivory paste decorated with Chinese text, and top with leaves and a red flower (see below).

21

23

Equipment and recipes

Listed below are many items of equipment that are useful to have to hand when decorating cakes. To follow are basic recipes for cakes, reflecting a growing trend to use types of cake other than fruit cake for weddings.

ESSENTIAL EQUIPMENT

For reasons of space, these tools and materials have not always been listed with the individual cakes.

ADHESIVE (MASKING OR 'MAGIC') TAPE to secure paper templates
ANGLE POISE LAMP for drying paintwork or runout work
CAKE SCRAPERS to smooth royal icing on the sides of a cake
CAKE STANDS shapes and sizes available to suit all cakes
CAKE TINS (PANS) useful to have a variety of sizes and shapes
CLEAR ALCOHOL for thinning colours and sticking sugarpaste to marzipan
CLING FILM (PLASTIC WRAP) for wrapping paste in while not in use
COCKTAIL STICKS (TOOTHPICKS) for modelling
CONFECTIONERS' VARNISH for adding a sheen to decorative pieces
CORNFLOUR (CORNSTARCH) use to dust surfaces when modelling items off the cake
DIPPING SOLUTION for thinning varnish or mixing with dusting powder
DOWELS for supporting stacked cakes
FINE MESH SIEVE useful for sieving icing sugar before use
FOAM SPONGE for supporting decorative pieces while drying
GREASEPROOF (WAX BAKING) PAPER for baking and templates
GLYCERINE added to royal icing for easy cutting
GUM TRAGACANTH a firming agent to make paste set hard very quickly; tylo powder is a cheaper alternative
HB PENCIL for tracing templates
ICING (CONFECTIONERS') SUGAR for royal icing and dusting work surfaces
KITCHEN TOWEL useful for blotting and removing excess paint from brush
LIQUID GLUCOSE to add elasticity to royal icing
PAINTBRUSHES OF VARIOUS SIZES for painting and dusting the cakes
PALETTE KNIFE (METAL SPATULA) for spreading royal icing; use a cranked palette knife for lifting runout work
PIECE OF OASIS (FLORISTS' STAYSOFT) for drying freestanding pieces, such as figures; wrap in cling film
PIPING BAGS AND VARIETY OF TUBES (TIPS) for piping royal icing
ROLLING PINS large and small; white polypropylene pins are recommended
RULER for accurate measuring
RUN-OUT FILM for creating decorative runout and pastillage pieces
SCISSORS for cutting out templates
SHARP KNIFE essential for making clean, accurate cuts in cakes and icing
SMOOTHERS to smooth marzipan and sugarpaste
SPARE CAKE BOARDS of varying sizes for decorating cakes on before stacking
STRAIGHTEDGE used to smooth the top of a royal-iced cake
SUPERWHITE POWDER makes food colourings opaque
TILTING TURNTABLE makes working on the sides of a cake much easier
TRACING PAPER for tracing templates from the back of the book
WAXED PAPER also used for creating runout shapes on
WHITE TILE OR PLATE for mixing food colours

TOOLS AND CUTTERS

Manufacturers of recommended tools are listed below. The piping tubes (tips) are made by PME Sugarcraft or Bekenel.

CA = Cake Art
C = Cel Products
CS = Confectionery Supplies
CC = Creative Cakes
CSD = Creative Sugar Designs
CV = Cynthia Venn
DI = Dried Image
FMM = FMM Products
GI = Great Impressions
HH = Hawthorne Hill
HP = Holly Products
HS = House of Sugar
J = Jem Products
MF = Mary Ford
OP = Orchard Products
PC = Patchwork Cutters
PME = PME Sugarcraft
R = Renshaws
SS = Simply Sweet
SK = Squires Kitchen
S = Sugarflair
SC = Sugar Celebrations
TKT = Tinkertech Tools
W = Wilton

✻ ✻ ✻ ✻

Equipment and recipes

RECIPES

Fruit cake

(for quantities see chart below)

90g (3oz/1/2cup) currants
60g (2oz/1/3cup) sultanas (golden raisins)
60g (2oz/1/3cup) seedless raisins
60g (2oz/1/2cup) glacé (candied) cherries, rinsed and chopped
30g (1oz/1/6cup) finely chopped mixed peel
1 tablespoon sherry (rum or brandy) for soaking fruit
60g (2oz/1/4cup) butter
60g (2oz/1/3cup) soft brown sugar
1 large egg
75g (2 1/2oz/1/2cup plus 2tbsp) plain (all-purpose) flour
Juice and rind of 1/4 lemon
(use butter and eggs at room temperature to prevent curdling)

Method

1. Line and grease the baking tin (pan) with a double layer of greaseproof (wax baking) paper.

2. Mix the fruit together and leave to soak overnight with the sherry.

3. Beat the butter and sugar together until light and fluffy. Gradually add the egg, beating thoroughly.

4. Fold in the flour, then mix in the fruit and lemon juice and rind.

5. Transfer the mixture to the cake tin and level the mixture. Bake in a preheated oven at 140°C/275°F/ Gas mark 1.

6. When the cake is baked, leave it in the tin until it is completely cold.

7. Remove the cake from the tin, leaving the greaseproof paper in place. Prick the top of the cake with a skewer and sprinkle over the soaking mixture (see right).

8. Wrap the cake in waxed paper or greaseproof paper and then foil. Leave in a cool place for at least three weeks before decorating. Extra soaking mixture can be added if required.

Making special sized cakes

If the depth of the cake required is critical to the design of the wedding cake and needs to be extra deep, it may be better to join several standard depth cakes together and then trim them to the required depth. However, if the cake only needs a little more depth, a thicker layer of marzipan may be all that is needed.

As with all special occasion cakes, it is recommended you have a 'trial run' when using a new recipe.

Soaking mixture

This is a mixture of half spirit (sherry, rum, brandy) and half glycerine. One large batch of soaking mixture can be made up and stored in a bottle with a screw top. Shake the bottle thoroughly before use. Use one tablespoon of soaking mixture for every 500g (1lb) of the finished weight of cake. For example, if the baked fruit cake weighs 2kg (4lb), then the amount of soaking mixture would be four tablespoons.

Cake quantities guide

If making several different sizes and shapes of fruit cake then use multiples of this basic fruit cake recipe. Multiply the recipe above according to the chart below. Approximate baking times for the various cakes are also shown below.

Cake sizes	30cm (12in)	25cm (10in)	20cm (8in)	15cm (6in)	10cm (4in)
Round	8 1/2	6	3	1 1/2	1
Square	10 1/2	7 1/2	4	2	1 1/2
Hexagonal	10	6 1/2	4	2	1 1/2
Petal	8 1/2	6	3	1 1/2	/
Oval	7	4 1/2	2 1/2	/	/
Approx. time	5–5 1/2hrs	4–4 1/2hrs	3 1/2–4hrs	1 3/4–2hrs	1 1/2–1 3/4hrs

Contemporary wedding cakes

CHOCOLATE CAKE RECIPE

This quantity is enough for a 20cm (8in) round cake. As an approximate guide, double this recipe for a 25cm (10in) round cake and halve this recipe for a 15cm (6in) cake.

110g (3½oz) good quality dark chocolate
3 tablespoons water
200g (6½oz/⅞cup) butter
200g (6½oz/1 generous cup) dark soft brown sugar
1 teaspoon vanilla essence (extract)
4 large eggs
200g (7oz/1¾cups) self-raising flour
Pinch of salt

METHOD

1. Line the bases of two shallow 20cm (8in) round cake tins (pans) (about 2.5–4cm [1–1½in] deep).

2. Preheat the oven to 180°C/ 350°F/Gas Mark 4.

3. Melt the chocolate in the water and allow it to cool slightly. Cream the butter and sugar together until light and fluffy. Separate the eggs and beat the yolks, vanilla essence (extract) and then add the melted chocolate to the mixture. Fold in the sieved flour and salt.

4. Whisk the egg whites to a soft peak; fold into the mixture carefully, without over-working them.

5. Divide the mixture between the tins and level the tops. Bake the cakes for 20 to 25 minutes until they are firm to the touch. Leave them to cool for one minute in the tin before turning out onto a cooling rack.

GANACHE

This recipe for ganache can be used as a delicious chocolate filling for the chocolate cake above.

150ml (5fl oz/⅔cup) whipping cream
250g (8oz) dark chocolate buttons or grated from a block

METHOD

1. Put the cream in a pan and heat gently until boiling. Remove from the heat and pour over the chocolate. Stir until the chocolate has melted and has blended with the cream. Pour into a clean bowl.

2. Allow the ganache to cool and set. It can then be kept in a refrigerator for several weeks until required.

3. If the ganache has been refrigerated, allow it to come back to room temperature. Whip the ganache with a balloon whisk or use a mixer until it becomes light, fluffy and paler.

4. Split each layer of cake into two. Spread over the ganache using a palette knife (metal spatula) and sandwich the layers together. Deeper cakes, such as the Chocolate drapes and roses cake (see pages 52–5), will need several cakes stacked together to make up the necessary height.

VICTORIA SANDWICH CAKE

250g (8oz/2cups) self-raising flour
4 large eggs at room temperature
250g (8oz/1cup) very soft butter
250g (8oz/1cup) golden caster (superfine) sugar

METHOD

1. Preheat the oven to 375°F/ 190°C/Gas Mark 5. Grease and base line two 20cm (8in) round cake tins.

2. Beat the butter and sugar together until pale and fluffy. Add the eggs, a little at a time, beating the mixture well after each addition.

3. Fold in half the flour, using a metal spoon, then fold in the rest.

4. Divide the mixture evenly between the two tins, level with a knife and bake for 25–30 minutes until firm to the touch and just beginning to shrink away from the sides of the tins.

5. Leave in the tins for a few minutes, then turn the cakes out to cool on a wire rack.

* * * *

Equipment and recipes

Buttercream filling

220g (7oz/$^{7}/_{8}$cup) butter, at room temperature
220g (7oz/2cups) icing (confectioners') sugar
few drops of vanilla essence (extract), optional

Method

1. Put the butter in a mixing bowl and beat until soft.

2. Gradually add the icing sugar and beat for about five minutes until light and fluffy. Lastly, add the vanilla essence (extract).

3. Use straight away or refrigerate until needed. The buttercream needs to be brought to room temperature and should then be beaten until smooth before use.

Buttercream variations

Add finely grated rind and juice of one orange and a tablespoon of Grand Marnier liqueur

Add grated rind and juice of one lemon; spread a thin layer of lemon curd over the sponge before sandwiching together with the buttercream

Replace the vanilla essence with three teaspoons of instant coffee blended with a little hot water

Add 3 level tablespoons of finely chopped toasted almonds or hazelnuts

Continental buttercream

This type of buttercream has a much lighter, creamier taste than the traditional buttercream.

330g (11oz/1$^{1}/_{3}$cups) granulated sugar
90ml (3$^{1}/_{4}$ fl oz/ scant $^{1}/_{2}$cup) water
135g (4$^{1}/_{2}$oz) eggs
350g (12oz/1$^{1}/_{2}$cups) butter, softened

Method

1. Add the sugar to the water in a strong pan, and bring to the boil. Wash down the sides of the pan with a clean pastry brush dipped in clean cold water.

2. Place a sugar thermometer in the liquid as it is boiling until it reaches 120°C (250°F). While boiling, whisk the eggs in a large bowl with an electric whisk until light and foamy.

3. When the sugar is ready, pour it into the eggs in a slow, steady stream keeping the whisk at high speed. Carry on whisking until the mixture is cool.

4. When the mixture reaches blood temperature gradually add the butter, at about a teaspoon at a time, continually whisking until the buttercream is smooth.

5. Use the buttercream straight away or refrigerate it until needed, then allow it to warm up to room temperature. Beat the buttercream again before use.

Sugarpaste

For large quantities, buy ready-made sugarpaste (rolled fondant).

(makes 625g [1$^{1}/_{4}$lb])

1 egg white made up from albumen powder
2 tablespoons liquid glucose
625g (1$^{1}/_{4}$lb/4$^{1}/_{2}$cups) icing (confectioners') sugar
white vegetable fat (if required)

Method

1. Put the egg white and liquid glucose in a bowl, using a warm spoon for the liquid glucose.

2. Sift the icing sugar into the bowl, adding a little at a time and stirring until the mixture thickens.

3. Turn onto a work surface dusted with icing sugar and knead the paste until soft, smooth and pliable. If the paste is dry and cracked, fold in a little vegetable fat and knead again.

4. Wrap in a polythene bag or cling film and store in an airtight container.

Flower paste

Flower (or petal) paste differs from sugarpaste mainly due to the inclusion of a powder called gum tragacanth, which enables the flower paste to dry much faster and to set a lot harder than sugarpaste. This makes it useful for modelling work. For convenience, when working with large quantities buy ready-made flower paste.

40ml (1⅓fl oz/8tsp) warm water
2 teaspoons powdered gelatine
500g (1lb/4cups) icing (confectioners') sugar
4 teaspoons gum tragacanth
2 teaspoons liquid glucose
15g (½oz) vegetable fat
35ml (1fl oz) egg white (fresh or albumen powder)

Method

1. Measure the water into a small dish and sprinkle over the gelatine. Leave to soak for one hour.

2. Sift the icing sugar and gum tragacanth into the bowl of an electric mixer and warm gently to blood heat.

3. Dissolve the gelatine mixture over a pan of hot water, add the liquid glucose and vegetable fat, and stir until dissolved.

4. Place the bowl containing the icing sugar and gum tragacanth on the electric mixer, add the gelatine mixture and the egg white and beat for approximately five minutes until white and stringy.

5. Store the flower paste in a polythene bag, inside an airtight container, in the refrigerator for 24 hours before use. When removed the paste will be hard. Knead it in lightly greased hands until the paste is soft and stretchy. This type of paste can be cut into small pieces and frozen.

Mexican paste

Mexican paste contains a large proportion of gum, which makes it set quickly, and very hard. This is useful for modelling work, as the piece will not collapse easily during the working process. It is also used for thin cut-outs, for example on the Champagne celebration cake (see pages 76–9), as it retains a shape without shrinkage. Mexican paste is not suitable for flower making, as it does not have the elasticity required.

(makes 250g [8oz])
250g (8oz/2cups) icing (confectioners') sugar
3 teaspoons gum tragacanth
1 teaspoon liquid glucose
6 teaspoons water

Method

1. Sift the icing sugar and gum tragacanth together.

2. Add liquid glucose and water, then mix by hand with a spatula to form a smooth paste. The mixture is quite dry and crumbly, and will need pressing together firmly. Add extra water a drop at a time.

3. Turn out onto a dusted board and knead until smooth, then leave for 24 hours before use. After 24 hours the paste will seem very hard. Knead it and it will soften up quickly.

Modelling paste

Modelling paste is a half-and-half mix of flower paste and sugarpaste that is useful for making paste figures.

Food safety

Remember, as always with any food work, to provide a clean working environment, ensuring that surfaces and equipment are clean and ready for use.

MARZIPAN

Most royal-iced cakes require a crisp right-angled edge, especially for runout collars. This can be created with the marzipan covering. When rolling out marzipan use icing (confectioners') sugar to prevent the marzipan sticking to the surface. Knead the marzipan to make it pliable and easier to roll.

Use a neutral flavoured and coloured jam to stick marzipan to the cake, such as apricot jam/masking jelly. (Apricot jam should be boiled, then sieved prior to use.) Apply to the cake with a pastry brush.

Marzipanning round cakes

1. Brush the cake top with apricot jam/masking jelly (see above).

2. Roll out a portion of marzipan into a neat circular shape, just larger than the cake top. Position the cake on the marzipan and press carefully. Trim away excess marzipan.

3. Knead the remaining marzipan together. Roll out in a long sausage shape, then roll flat, increasing the width to just slightly larger than the depth of the cake side.

4. Place the cake on the board. Mark

Marzipan quantities

30cm (12in)	2kg (4lb)
25cm (10in)	1.5kg (3lb)
20cm (8in)	1kg (2lb)
15cm (6in)	500g (1lb)
10cm (4in)	350g (12oz)

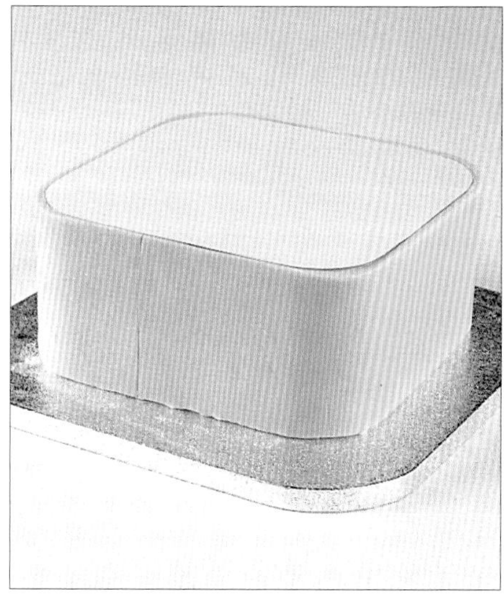

the marzipan about 15mm (½in) longer than the cake circumference to create an overlap. Trim to neaten, then roll it up, starting at the uncut shorter edge. Brush the cake side with apricot glaze.

5. Unravel the marzipan around the cake side. Where it overlaps, cut through and bond the edges together. Trim off the excess marzipan from the top edge. Press the marzipan firmly onto the cake side.

Marzipanning square cakes

1. For the top of the cake use the same method as for round cakes, but roll out the marzipan into a square shape and position the cake on top.

2. For the sides, either wrap a continuous strip of marzipan around the edges, as for a round cake, or roll out a large rectangular shape of marzipan just larger than the width of the cake side and four times the depth of the cake side. Brush the sides of the cake with apricot glaze. Hold the cake with the marzipanned top level with the cut edge of the rolled out marzipan.

3. Trim around this side, then lift the cake and rotate to the next side and repeat. Continue until each side is covered. Neaten with smoothers.

Marzipanning large square cakes

For larger cakes, roll out the marzipan and cut four rectangles the size of the cake sides. Apply the prepared pieces by lifting them onto the cake side, and smoothing into place.

Marzipanning shaped cakes

Cover the tops of shaped cakes, such as petal and hexagonal, using the method for round cakes. Use the round cake method for the sides of cakes without corners, like oval and petal; and the square cake method for cakes with corners.

Marzipanning a cake for sugarpaste

A cake that is going to be covered with sugarpaste needs smooth edges and corners. Apply the marzipan as described above, and rub the edges with the palm of your hand. It is also possible to apply the marzipan to the cake in one piece; however this may mean that the top edge will become too rounded, and you may lose some of the depth of the cake.

Cake stands

Visit your local sugarcraft shop to find out about the wide ranges of shapes and sizes of cake stands available.

Templates

The following pages contain the templates for the cakes, listed with the cake name, template description and relevant page numbers. Several of the templates have been reduced to 50 per cent of their original size to fit. Photocopy the templates for use, enlarging them as instructed.

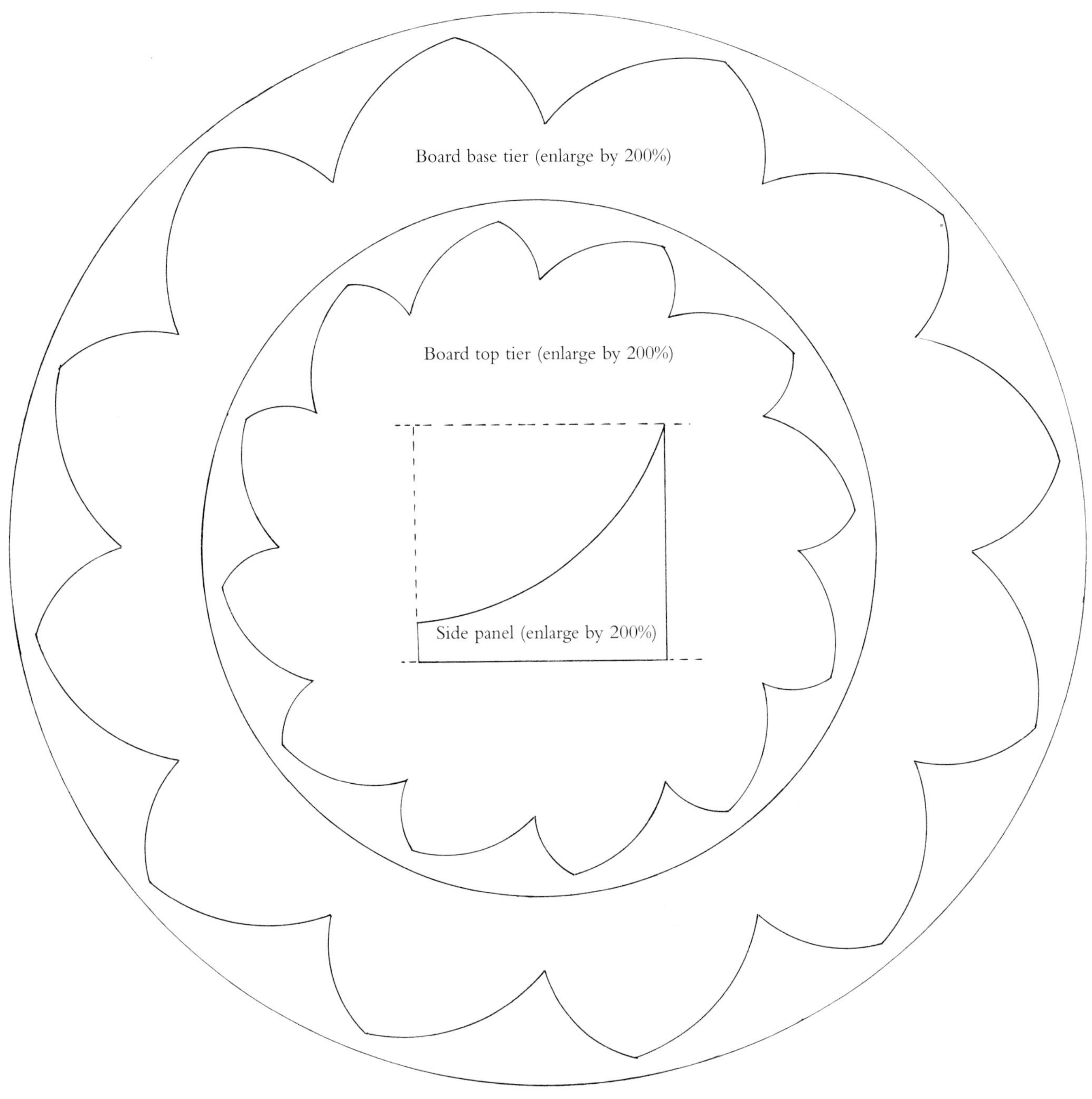

Lily celebration, pages 38–41

Lily celebration, pages 38–41

Board linework (enlarge by 200%)

Side panel (enlarge by 200%)

Side panel for base (enlarge by 200%)

Corner panel (enlarge by 200%)

Top collar for base cakes (enlarge by 200%); use at 80% of enlarged size for top tier

Collar, top tier (enlarge by 200%)

Collar, base tier (enlarge by 200%)

Embroidery blossom, pages 34–7

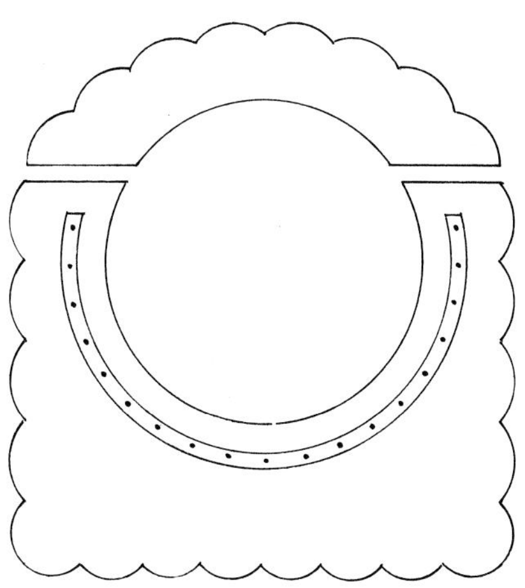

Top tier, side panel and board sections (enlarge by 200%)

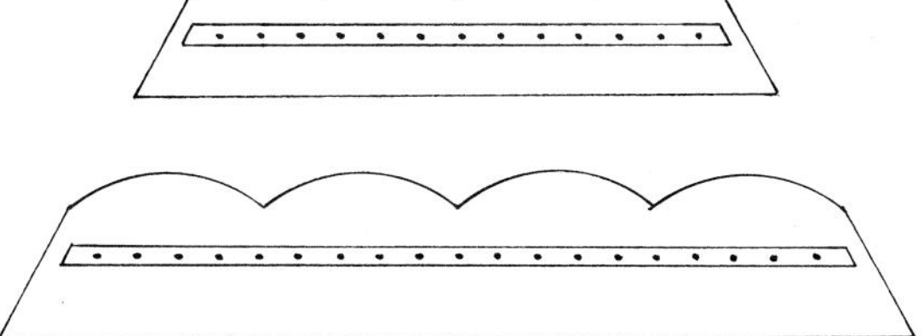

Top tier, top collar (enlarge by 200%)

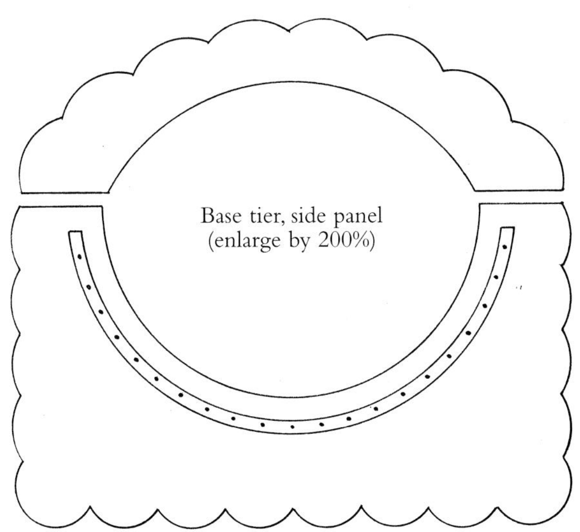

Briar rose, pages 22–5

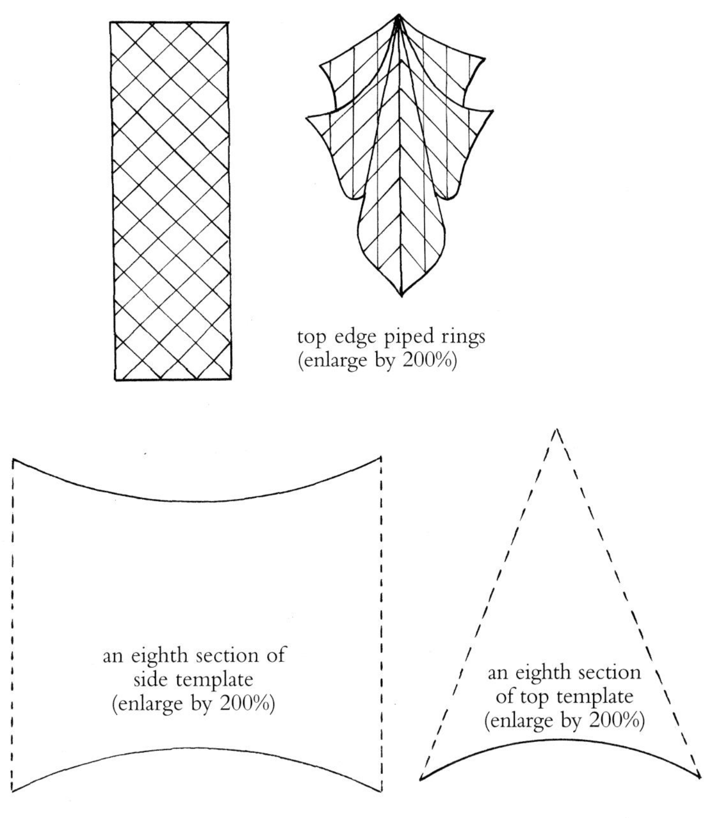

Victorian nostalgia, pages 18–21

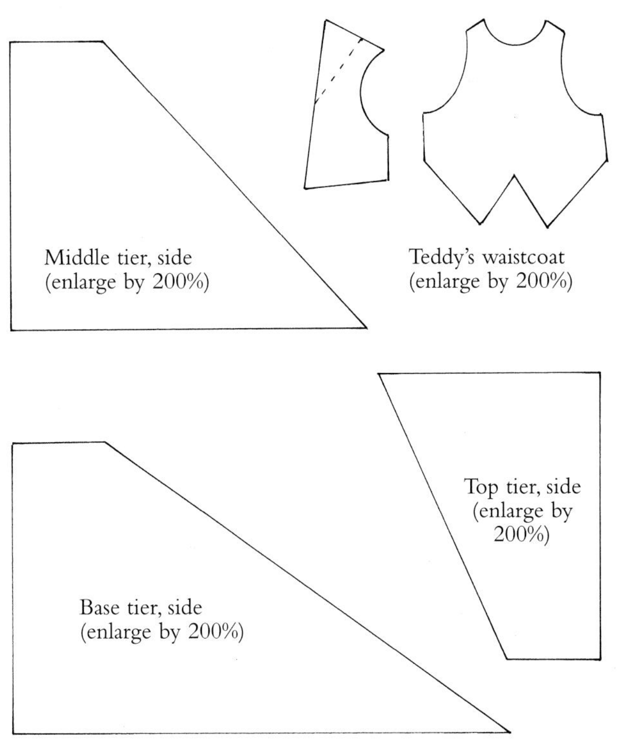

Champagne celebration, pages 76–9

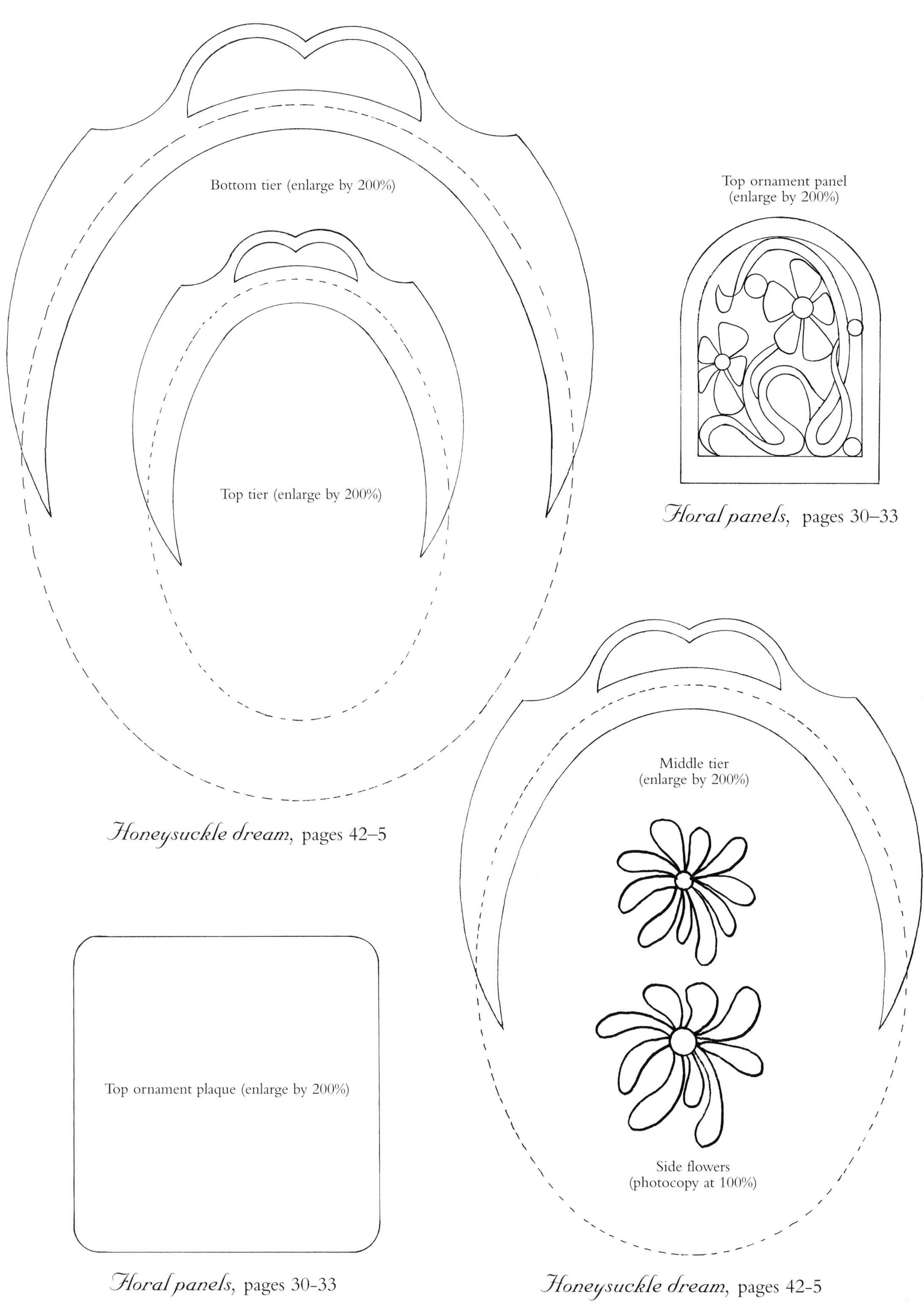

Floral panels, pages 30–33

Honeysuckle dream, pages 42–5

Floral panels, pages 30-33

Honeysuckle dream, pages 42-5

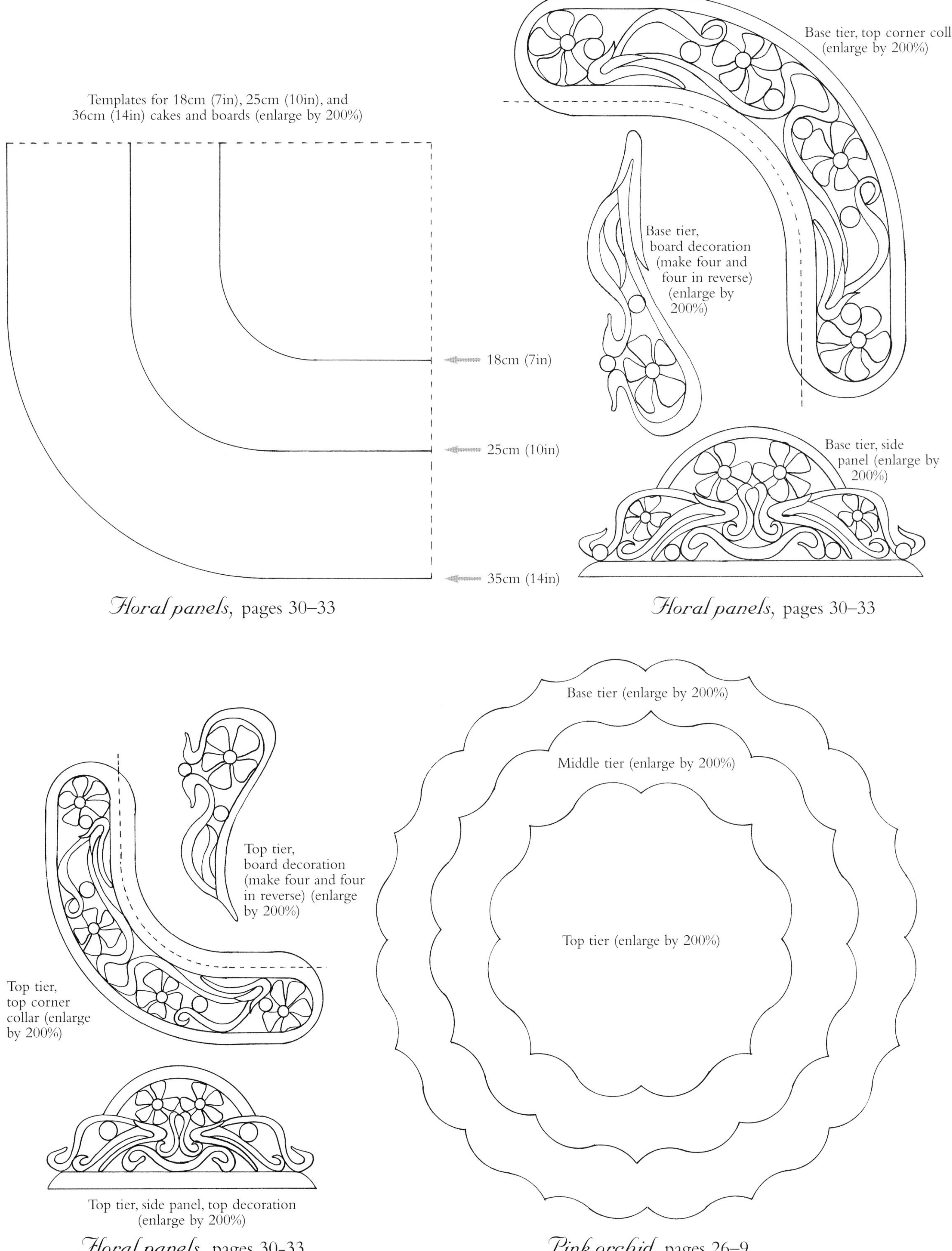

Floral panels, pages 30–33

Floral panels, pages 30–33

Floral panels, pages 30-33

Pink orchid, pages 26–9

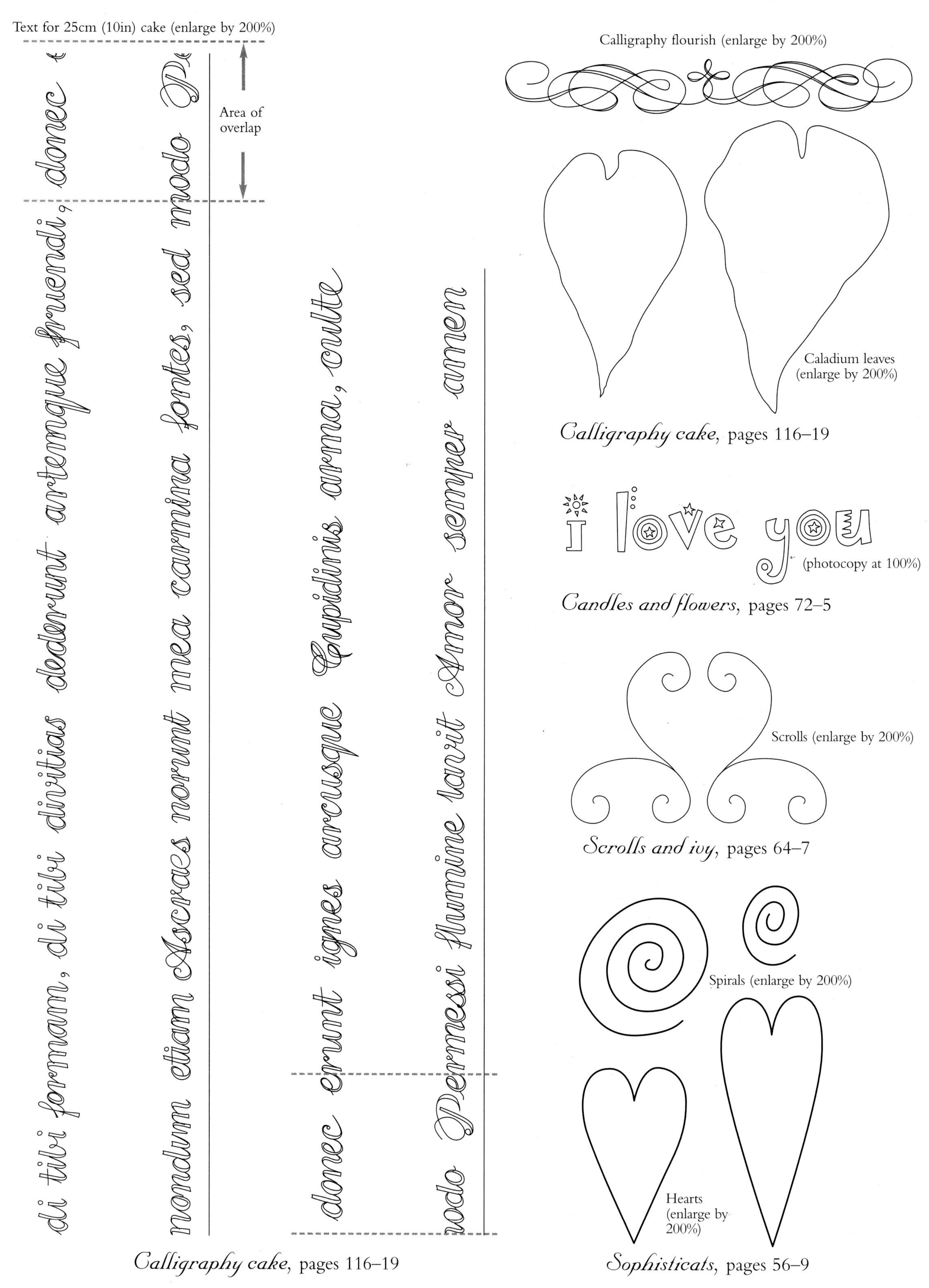

Calligraphy cake, pages 116–19

Calligraphy cake, pages 116–19

Candles and flowers, pages 72–5

Scrolls and ivy, pages 64–7

Sophisticats, pages 56–9

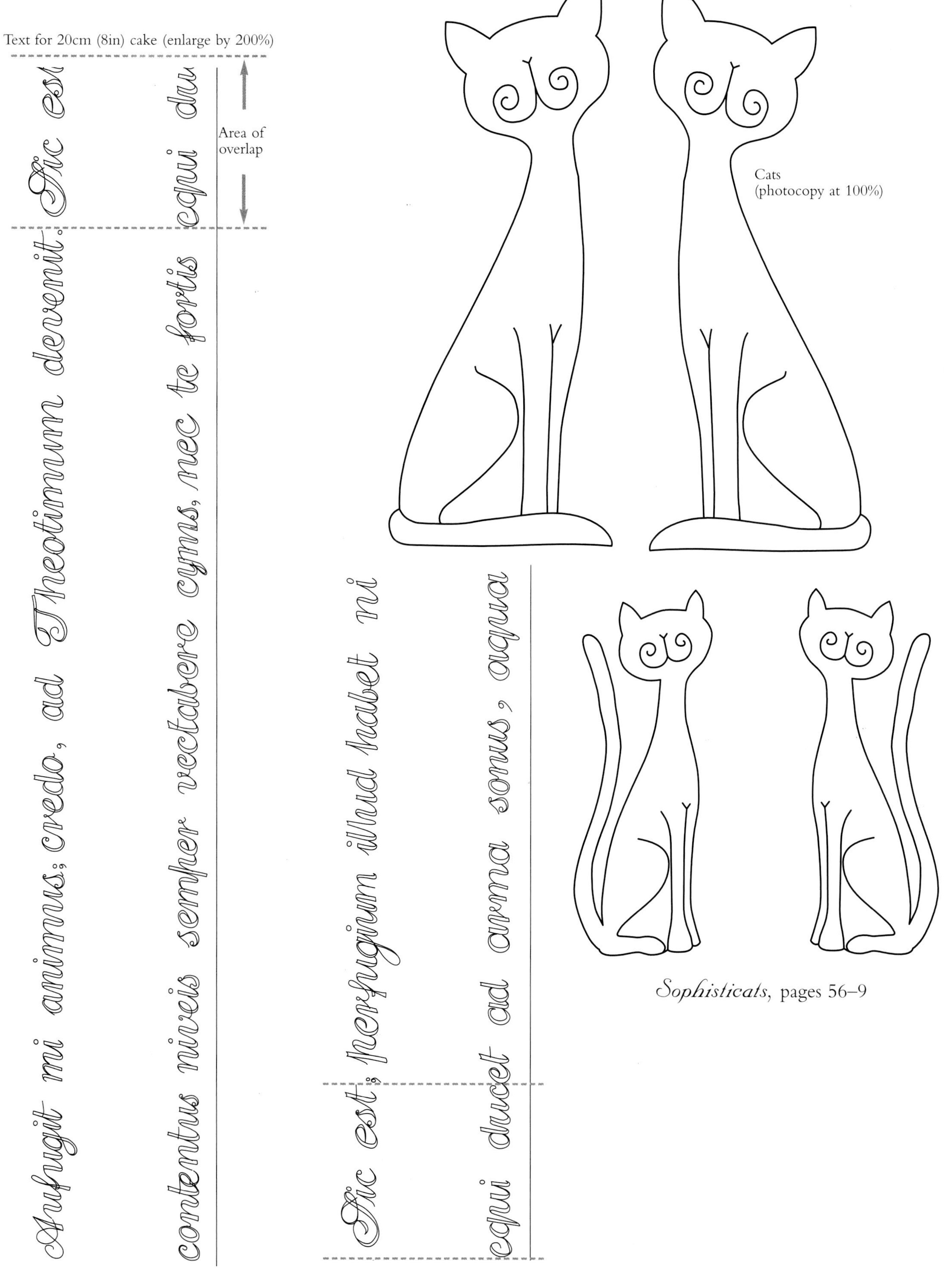

Sophisticats, pages 56–9

Calligraphy, pages 116–20

15cm (6in) cake (enlarge by 200%)

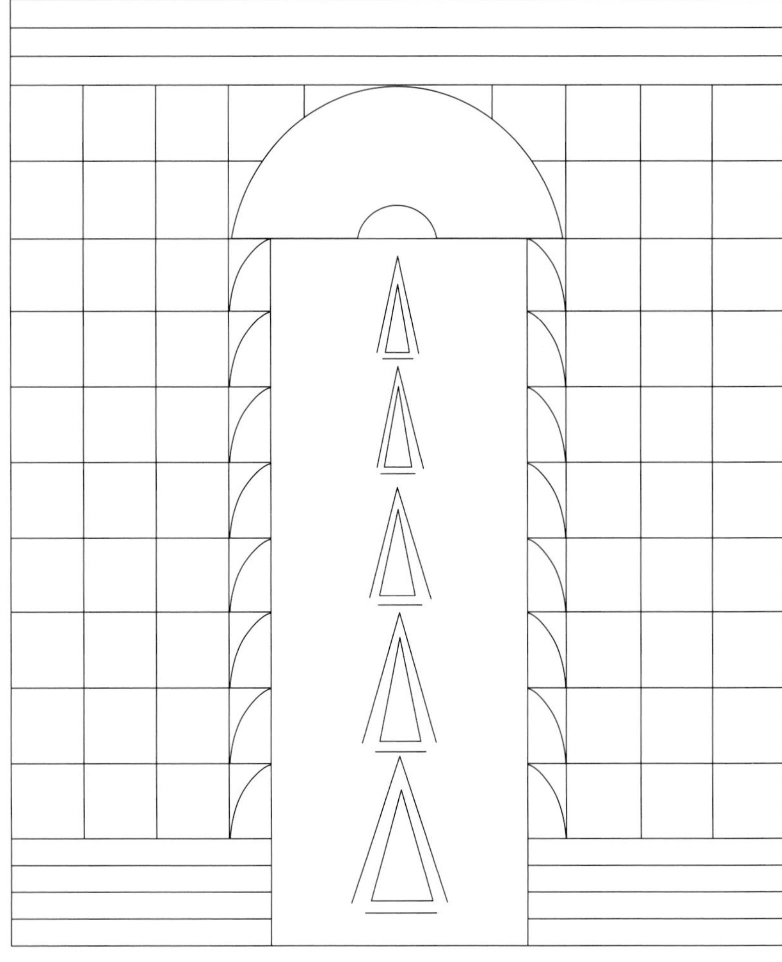

20cm (8in) cake (enlarge by 200%)

Art deco, pages 102–7

Butterfly and leaves
(enlarge by 200%)

20cm (8in) and 15cm (6in) cakes (enlarge by 200%)

30cm (12in) cake (enlarge by 200%)

Art nouveau, pages 92–6

Cascading waterfall, pages 97–101

Scallops
(enlarge by 200%)

Waterlily petals
(enlarge by 200%)

1 2 3 4 5 6 7

Waterfall pieces
(enlarge by 200%)

Scallop template (enlarge by 200%)

+

Art nouveau, pages 92–6

Large

Medium

Small

Waterlily pads (enlarge by 200%)

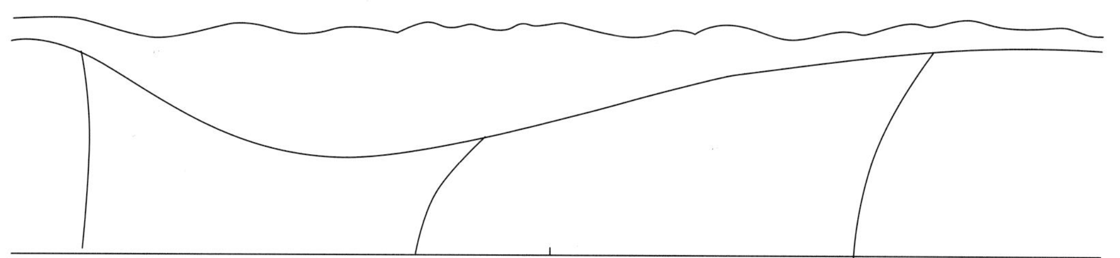

Field (enlarge by 200%)

Homestead (enlarge by 200%)

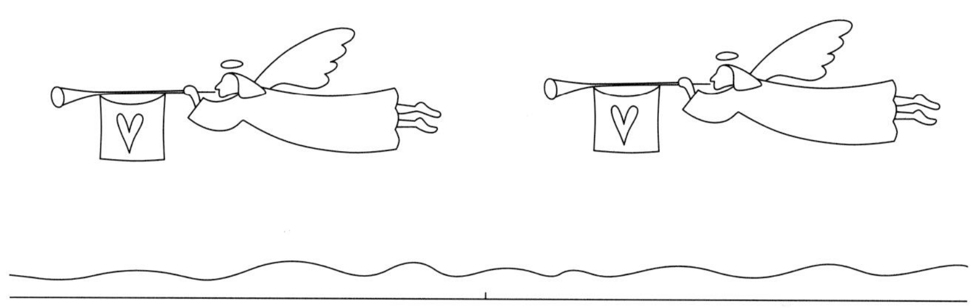

Angels (enlarge by 200%)

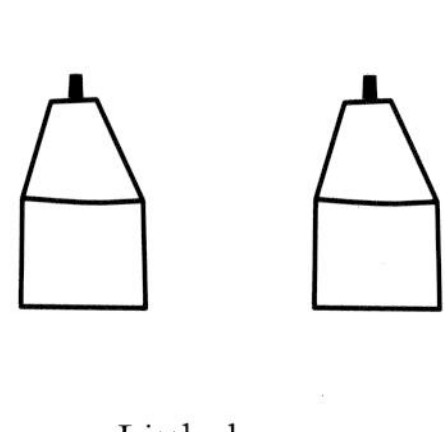

Little houses
(photocopy at 100%)

Heart
(photocopy at 100%)

Folk art, pages 110–15

Elephants for the 30cm (12in) cake (enlarge by 200%)

Elephants for the 25cm (10in) cake (enlarge by 200%)

Scrolls and heart

Indian elephants, pages 124–9

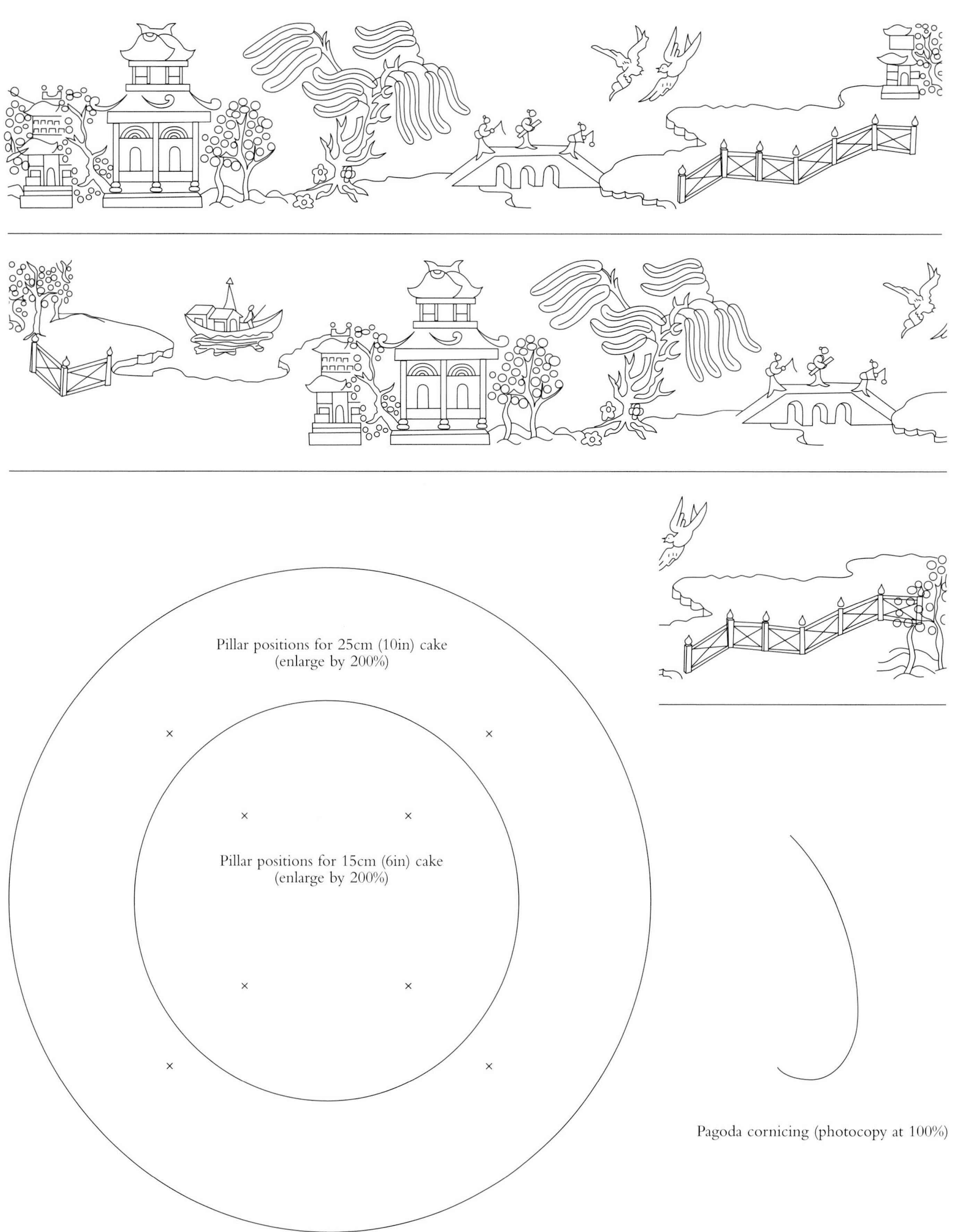

Oriental splendour, pages 131–7

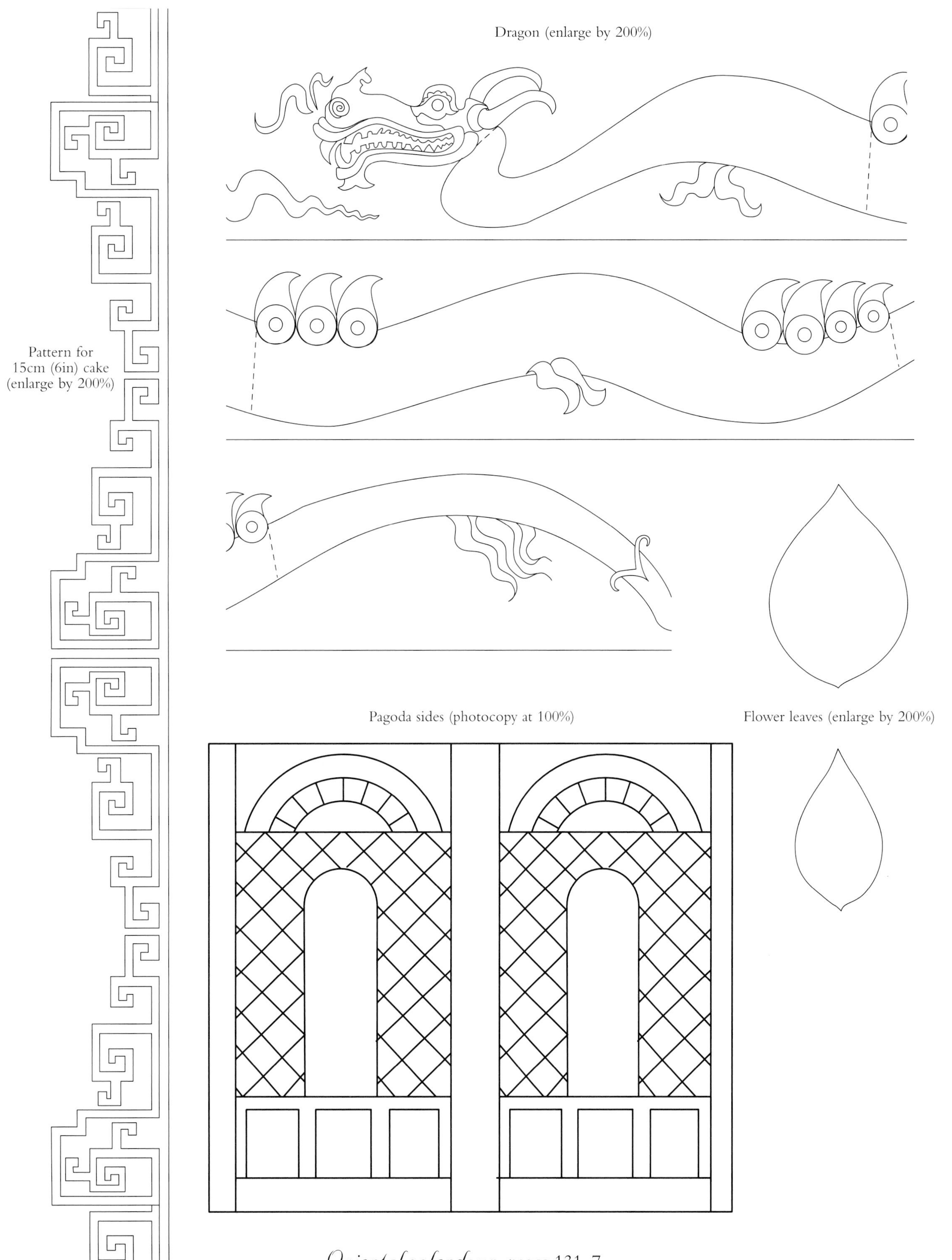

Oriental splendour, pages 131–7

✻ ✻ ✻ ✻

Acknowledgements

Nadene Hurst

My grateful thanks to my friends Clare and Margery for all their help, and especially to Kathleen, who helped make the flowers when time was running out.

Thanks to Bev at Sparkling Sugarcraft for her support and instant supplies when they were desperately needed.

A big thank you to all the cake decorating manufacturers who have provided equipment, not just for this book, but over a long period of time, to enable me to create new ideas.

I can be e-mailed at:
nadene@nadenesideasinicing.co.uk

Julie Springall

I would like to thank the following for their assistance:

Bespoke Country Collection
42 Bar Street, Scarborough,
N.Yorks, YO11 2HT
Tel: + 44 1723 378728
For the gingham ribbon and raffia used on the Folk art cake (pages 110–15).

Great Impressions International
Greenlea, 14 Studley Drive,
Swarland, Morpeth,
Northumberland, NE65 9JT
Tel: + 44 1670 787061
For the caladium leaf veiner used for the Calligraphy cake (pages 116–9).

Hawthorne Hill
Milvale Studios, Milvale Street,
Middleport, Stoke on Trent,
Stafffordshire, ST6 3NT
Tel: + 44 1782 811 877
For the butterfly cutter/mould used for the Art nouveau cake (pages 92–6).

Imaginative Icing
22 Falsgrave Road, Scarborough,
North Yorkshire, Y012 5AT
Tel: + 44 1723 378 116
Website: http://www.imaginativeicing demon.co.uk/E-mail: sugarcrafters@ imaginativeicing.demon.co.uk
For supplying cake dummies and other supplies, plus hire of cake stands used in the photos and providing the beautiful matching favours for my cakes.

Wax Lyrical Limited
3 St Helen Square, York, YO1 8NQ
Tel: + 44 1904 656 636
For the candlesticks used for the Calligraphy cake (pages 116–19).

David Wregg Engineering
'Fine Cut' Sugarcraft Products
Workshop 2, Old Stable Block,
Holme Pierrepont Hall, Holme
Pierrepont, Nottingham NG12 2LD
Tel: + 44 115 933 4349
For the elephant cutters used for the Indian elephants cake (pages124–130).

A huge thank you to my mother-in-law Janice Springall, of Imaginative Icing, for help with the recipes and charts, wedding favours, babysitting, loan of van, advice and being wonderful; to Ray Springall of McRay Press for use of his photocopying facilities; to Alice (Great Gran) Barker for lending me reference books; to my friend and colleague Brenda Flinton for making the beautiful flowers for the Calligraphy (pages 116–9), Oriental splendour (pages 131–7) and Cascading waterfall (pages 97–101) cakes; to my colleagues at Imaginative Icing: Anthony Springall, Jenny Aston, Joanne Pratt, Jane Dunwell, Karen Clark, Sylvia Ross, Caroline Morris and Madge Moon; to David Ireland for his wood turning skills in crafting the impressive pillars for the Indian elephants cake (pages 124–130); to Alan Horton, conductor of the Scarborough Concert Band for the kind loan of music used as reference for the Calligraphy cake (pages 116–9).

I can be e-mailed at:
joolee@springall.free-online.co.uk

Suppliers

AUSTRALIA

Cake and Icing Centre
651 Samford Road
Mitchelton
Queensland 4053
Tel: + 61 7 3355 3443

Cake Decorators' Supplies
Shop 1, 770 George Street
Sydney 2001
Tel: + 61 2 9212 4050

Finishing Touches Cake Decorating Centre
268 Centre Road
Bentleigh
Victoria 3204
Tel: + 61 3 9223 1719

Petersen's Cake Decorations
Rear 698 Beaufort Street
Mt Lawley
West Australia 6050
Tel: + 61 9 9271 1692

The Cake Decorating Centre
1 Adelaide Arcade
Adelaide
South Australia 5000
Tel: + 61 8 8223 1719

IRELAND

Cakes & Co.
25 Rock Hill
Blackrock Village
Co. Dublin
Tel: + 353 1 283 6544

NEW ZEALAND

Hitchon International Ltd
220 Antiqua Street
Christchurch
Tel: + 64 3 365 3843

Starline Distributors Ltd
28 Jessie Street
Wellington
Tel: + 64 4 383 7424

UNITED KINGDOM

Confectionery Supplies
27 Eign Road
Hereford, HR1 2RU
Tel: + 44 1432 271 200

Creative Stencil Designs
Flanders Moss
Station Road
Buchlyvie
Stirlingshire, FK8 3NB
Tel: + 44 1360 850 389

Culpitt Cake Art
Culpitt Ltd
Jubilee Industrial Estate
Ashington
Northumberland, NE63 8UQ
Tel: + 44 1670 814 545

Guy, Paul and Co. Ltd
Unit B4, Foundry Way
Little End Road
Eaton Socon
Cambs, PE19 3JH

Holly Products
Holly Cottage
Hassall Green
Sandbach
Cheshire, CW11 4YA
Tel: + 44 1270 761 403

House of Cakes
18 Meadow Close
Woodley
Stockport, SK6 1QZ
Tel: + 44 161 285 6299

Patchwork Cutters
3 Raines Close
Greasby
Wirral, L49 2QB
Tel: + 44 151 678 5053

P.M.E. Sugarcraft
Brember Road
South Harrow
Middlesex, HA2 8UN
Tel: + 44 20 8864 0888

Renshaw Scott Ltd
(suppliers of Renshaw's Regalice)
Crown Street
Liverpool, L8 7RF
Tel: + 44 151 706 8200

Sparkling Sugarcraft
361 Bury Old Road
Prestwich, M25 1PY
Tel: + 44 161 773 3033

Squires Kitchen
Squires House
3 Waverley Lane
Farnham
Surrey, GU9 8BB
Tel: + 44 1252 711 749

Sugar Celebrations
37 Farringdon Road
Swindon
Wiltshire, SN1 5AR
Tel: + 44 1793 513 549

USA

Beryl's Cake Decorating & Pastry Supplies
P.O. Box 1584
N. Springfield
VA22151-0584 USA
Tel: + 1 800 488 2749

❊ ❊ ❊ ❊

Index

First published 2000 by Murdoch Books UK Ltd.,
Merehurst is an imprint of Murdoch Books UK.
Ferry House, 51-57 Lacy Road, Putney,
London, SW15 1PR

First printed 2000. Reprinted 2003.

ISBN 1 85391 807 5

A catalogue record of this book is available from the British Library.

Comissioning Editor:
Barbara Croxford
Design:
Fay Singer
Project Editor:
Rowena de Clermont-Tonnerre
Editorial Assistance:
Sarah Wilde
Photographer:
Laurence Hudghton
Publishing Manager:
Fia Fornari

Chief Executive:
Juliet Rogers
Publisher:
Kay Scarlett

Colour separation by Colourscan, Singapore
Printed in Singapore